TRADEFULL MERCHANTS

The Portrayal of the Capitalist in Literature

JOHN McVEAGH

Routledge
Taylor & Francis Group
LONDON AND NEW YORK

First published in 1981 by Routledge & Kegan Paul Ltd.

This edition first published in 2026
by Routledge
4 Park Square, Milton Park, Abingdon, Oxon OX14 4RN

and by Routledge
605 Third Avenue, New York, NY 10158

Routledge is an imprint of the Taylor & Francis Group, an informa business

British Library Cataloguing in Publication Data
A catalogue record for this book is available from the British Library

ISBN: 978-1-032-97576-4 (Set)
ISBN: 978-1-041-15177-7 (Volume 38) (hbk)
ISBN: 978-1-041-15185-2 (Volume 38) (pbk)
ISBN: 978-1-003-67821-2 (Volume 38) (ebk)

DOI: 10.4324/9781003678212

Publisher's Note
The publisher has gone to great lengths to ensure the quality of this reprint but points out that some imperfections in the original copies may be apparent.

Disclaimer
The publisher has made every effort to trace copyright holders and would welcome correspondence from those they have been unable to trace.

TRADEFULL MERCHANTS

The Portrayal of the Capitalist in Literature

John McVeagh

ROUTLEDGE & KEGAN PAUL
London, Boston and Henley

First published in 1981
by Routledge & Kegan Paul Ltd
39 Store Street,
London WC1E 7DD,
9 Park Street,
Boston, Mass. 02108, USA and
Broadway House,
Newtown Road,
Henley-on-Thames,
Oxon RG9 1BN
and printed in Great Britain by
Biddles Ltd, Guildford, Surrey

British Library Cataloguing in Publication Data

McVeagh, John
Tradefull merchants.
1. English literature - History and criticism
2. Capitalists and financiers in literature
I. Title
820.9'0352'338 PR149.C/

ISBN 0-7100-0729-9

I dedicate this book to Tom Wild.
He said the right thing when it mattered.

CONTENTS

PREFACE

In the imaginative literature of sixteenth-century England the violent replacement of feudalism by a capitalist social order can first be seen revolutionizing the attitudes of men. This is a change which has gone on happening ever since, and literature has gone on recording it; but no one has yet offered to conduct a full exploration in the work of creative writers of the impact which so long-drawn-out a change has had on their conceptions of the capitalist story itself. The story is a very long one. It stretches from the first stirrings of men's awareness of capitalist experience to their adjustment to it while it was seeking, or forces were pressing it, to establish itself as the dominant social relation; and then, in the period of capitalist ascendancy during the eighteenth, nineteenth and twentieth centuries, expands to include their ever reformulated and updated critique of it, and, frequently, excitement with it, down to our own day. Obviously scholars are to be found who have studied the phenomenon of capitalism in literature in part, within the limitations of certain fixed periods, or in the specific case of an individual author, or work, and the following pages will show how much I am indebted to such previous explorations. Indeed, I could hardly have conceived my project without them. Nevertheless, as far as I am aware it is something new in literary studies for an individual to propose to tell in one short book the story of man's involvement with capitalism in English life as it is reflected in the corpus of English literature from the fifteenth or sixteenth to the twentieth centuries. I am very conscious of the great, perhaps too great ambitiousness of such a scheme of work, and of its attendant dangers.

The hugeness of the task might have frightened me off at the very start (but it might not) if I had known just how big it was going to turn out to be. For, it might be asked, how could a single reader hope to say anything both true and original about five centuries' literature? And perhaps it will be judged that I have not done so in fact. Yet the subject seemed to continue to unfold itself in an orderly way as things went on, until, without quite having seen it coming, I found myself eventually led to the recognition that the whole post-medieval literature of commerce really conducts one single unbreakable debate as to the nature of the economic organization then establishing itself everywhere, and its meaning, and its effects, and that a survey of the entire development might fill a strange gap in our awareness. I am conscious that it has taken plenty of cheek to offer to reduce to one or two sentences, as I frequently have, the results of the agony of slow discovery which is many a writer's true life. And if I had been able to find any alternative to it I would not have allowed myself such presumption. But I had no alternative if the survey was to be achieved. The purpose of the book prevented any. A country was to be mapped, not ploughed field by field.

A similar appeal to the size of the subject under discussion must explain, and I hope justify, why I decided to limit myself to English capitalism, and English literature. I have not yet read enough to attempt a summary of the modern world. Obviously the story of capitalism in the literature of continental European countries, and in American literature, to look for the present no further afield, could and should extend the story told here, if that seems to anyone worth adding to; but I am afraid that such additions must be made by other and more capable hands than mine. It is also because the subject is so large that I have felt it could only be handled satisfactorily in a short book, though much harder to write than a long one, for at all costs the writer had to remain the one in charge of the material and not the other way round; thus rigorous compression was the only method, the only way not to be swamped. I remain aware of the danger of this, and realize that I may have failed to escape it sometimes by compressing to the point of exclusion, or by not allowing myself to say what should have found a place in the discussion even if only a small one. For compression has its own intrinsic temptation; there is almost no statement which cannot be made shorter if the will to shorten it is there. What is hard is to know how to keep the statement true while reducing it, and how to compress in proportion, and when to stop compressing. As to my success there, of course, readers must judge for themselves, but it is due to the original conception of the book to say that it was meant to be one which would be capable of holding an interested reader's attention for a sitting, rather than for a lifetime, and a not too extended sitting at that. I shall be happy enough if I am felt to have had something to say and to have said it satisfactorily, and, given that, I shall not worry that it could all have been said differently, or that much more might have been added to it in this place and in that, all of which I know only too well.

I had to decide early on how much history and economic history to include, and how to include it, for obviously in such a discussion it was important that there should be some, and that the criticism of literature should constantly be kept rooted in an awareness of the actual events and real experience of its time. But this turned out a knotty problem. Shortage of space prevented anything elaborate, like an introductory essay of any length on the history of capitalist development, even if it were taken for granted that readers drawn mainly to the literature would feel inclined to read it, and that readers who were historians would not find it too simple; yet nothing very interesting or unfamiliar could be attempted in a span brief enough not to distract attention from the main discussion. Interspersed summaries of the economic and social change of each period, introducing the chapters on literature, say, or closing them, or just between them, seemed too wooden a method to adopt, as well as suggesting too much in the wrong way and too simply. Tabulated data was a still worse idea, and boring. I decided at last that since it was a critical study of literature I was writing, nothing else should be introduced obtrusively into it; instead all would be made to flow out of or lead straight into the literary discussion. Some signposting still had to be provided, and I have tried to provide it as the need arises, but have frequently left much to the reader's own awareness of the forming contexts of literary development from age to age; too much, it may be objected at times; but if my analysis seems cryptic, or unattached to a recognizable life context, it is a failure of performance rather than of intention. Always the thought was before me that to aim at exhaustive treatment in any single part was to risk sacrificing the proportion of the whole, and that in so ranging a discussion it was generally better to under-suggest than over-describe. A point at which I depart from this muffling, but not undervaluing, of the social and economic emphasis, comes near the end of the first chapter. There I thought it essential to specify the broad features of the onset of capitalist practice in England in the sixteenth and seventeenth centuries. For a few pages, then, in that place, the discussion of the literature is put on one side; but it is only for a few pages; and the description is a very broad and simple one; the chapter is an introductory survey of what leads up to the real analysis, after all. Yet even there what is said of the movement of history in Renaissance England comes after, and then is closed by, an analysis of the literature of the period, and is kept as far as may be in the background. Elsewhere, the demand made on the reader's willingness to fill in much of the economic and social context of what is discussed is higher, though I have always tried to include the essential indications. The main point is that in spite of the importance of the economic aspect priority is naturally given in what follows to the imaginative meaning of the works discussed, rather than to their social argumentation, except as that is imaginatively realized. And the reason for this is obvious. It is art's poetic spontaneity which draws us to it in the first place, and keeps enticing us back to it afterwards; and so I have tried to keep that aspect of things always in the forefront of the argument and hope that what I have written will succeed, above all, in telling us something about literature.

Naturally, we could identify a beginning to the process considerably earlier in history than the sixteenth century if we wished. But a sharp start is made to the discussion if we begin the story then, and that has an advantage in a study covering so large and complicated a topic as the present one. The late fifteenth- and early sixteenth-century discoveries opened up men's minds to the new world, and brought back to Europe masses of unexpected treasure along with the unlimited promise of more. In England the monastery lands were parcelled out after 1536, releasing huge fluid reserves of wealth. In 1571 the ban on usury was reversed. These were critical moments in the economic shake-up and expansion which, as is well known, helped to set capitalism on the move. In sixteenth-century literature we look for and find not a literal but an imaginative reflection of this convulsion of the traditional organization of life in, for example, the way in which the old-fashioned allegorical drama disintegrates and reconstitutes itself as the drama of Marlowe and Shakespeare; not that there is a simple causal relation from one to the other; both occurrences take place at the same time. During the seventeenth century the monied and propertied men pushed aside the tradition of centuries and rewrote the constitution in their own image, then during the eighteenth century enjoyed and wished to perpetuate the exercise of their power, which by then was complete, based on land no less than on money from trade, and apparently traditional. Jacobean comedy, mid-seventeenth-century poetry, and the prose and verse of the Augustan period register the realignments of these years, at first by launching hostile criticism at the men who were involved in and apparently responsible for social and economic upheaval, and who benefited from it most, later by a species of moral and imaginative accommodation to it as inevitable, and lastly by endorsement and panegyric shot through, however, and soon quite soured in its praise, by a deeper tremor of apprehension than any yet as the eighteenth century drew to its close. The eighteenth-century Whig oligarchs had aimed at making things stay just as they were, with themselves in charge, but perpetuity in such a mode was to prove elusive. In 1832 a new industrial breed of money-makers elbowed them half to the side and refashioned the social hierarchy to suit themselves, and for a generation or two ruled the roost in their turn, until, in the late nineteenth and early twentieth centuries, they were obliged to share more widely the prestige and authority they enjoyed; householders, for instance, acquired the vote in 1867, agricultural workers in 1884, women over thirty in 1918. The explosion of new poetic forms and new ideas in the Romantic period, and the exploring realism of the Victorian novel, express these successive upheavals which made up the aftermath of the Industrial Revolution. In our own time we have seen the members of an emerging proletariat refuse to remain victimized, threaten revolutionary change once their leaders recognized the way to social power, then, turning property-owners themselves, think less bloodily, and more conservatively, and shelve for the time being a revolution which, to many, events have appeared to overtake. A reflection of the story of this swing and return of the pendulum can be read in the apocalyptic and then more restrained literature written during the early and middle years of the present century. Finally, out of this last phase of an ever reconstituted order some new system, at the moment inscrutable, is doubtless forming itself before our eyes in postwar Britain and will lead a future generation no one can say where.

Nothing in this series of literary and social change is unknown, or hard to see, but out of such a survey of it a question presents itself which has given rise to the present book. In the material renewal and moral agony here summarized, the half a thousand years' gestation term of the modern world, which struggles within us into some unforeseen organization while we speculate on its origins, how did the men of creative intelligence picture to themselves the human type at the centre of it all? What does literature make of the capitalist? How does his representation keep pace with outer change? More connectedly, what continuous line runs through the portrayals in drama, poetry and prose fiction of the seventeenth-century usurer, the eighteenth-century merchant and nabob, the nineteenth- and twentieth-century banker, industrialist, tycoon and business manager, down to our own day, when the capitalist portrayal, in comparison with what has gone before, appears to be slackening? The issue is a profoundly interesting one, surely, yet no writer has so far tried to answer it in a comprehensive way. In the present book such an answer, and I hope a coherent one, will at last be found.

A last explanation must be offered as to the method of argument which the book adopts. Compression was forced on me by the unusually large subject, as I have said, but always I have so compressed as to throw emphasis on the central figure in each literary period, if I could identify any single writer as that, as far as the discussion of commerce is concerned. Usually they turned out to be the dominating figures in the literature of their time in a more general sense as well, as we might expect. So Shakespeare, Dryden, Defoe, Scott, Dickens and D. H. Lawrence centre in themselves, in what follows, the essential points in the argument about the economic condition of things in their own lifetime, and speak in large part for their age. Less central but often not less interesting writers I have tended to align in relation to them. I am not blind to the fact that this can produce a distorting effect in one way, particularly in its tendency to simplify the actual, and to misrepresent, I hope not too seriously, by the omission of a name or a book that merited some mention but could not be squeezed in, the general portrait of the age being drawn. On the other hand, nothing was to be gained by my trying to run through every work and every writer in each century and, in the interests of some abstract notion of fair mindedness, not subordinate them into a coherent argument. Or so I judged. Since no other way appeared possible of controlling an unwieldy topic, finally, it is not a matter of regret for me that this has made for a kind of incompleteness in parts. It never was my aim to exhaust every commercial theme and character in English literature, a project so enormous and pointless as to be horrifying even to think about, but to fix the analysis which imaginative writers have achieved of the decisive feature of the last 500 years of English civilization. In the following pages writers and reputations are sometimes tossed about, the limitation on space combined with the nature of the argument requiring it, but of course no needless disparagement of any work of creative intelligence, which I take to be the highest achievement man is capable of, has been my intention at any point whatever. Living writers may safely be left to defend themselves, if need be. For any seeming injustice to the dead I ask their pardon.

ACKNOWLEDGMENTS

The British Academy awarded me a research grant in 1978 which made it possible for me to explore some of the obscurer material among the literature of the eighteenth century. A similar award from the New University of Ulster in the same year enabled me to pursue research into certain aspects of sixteenth- and seventeenth-century drama. I record my thanks to both institutions for their generous help.

Mike Cotsell gave sympathizing critical help to this venture from its inception and kept me from going astray more than once. He also added lots of information. I owe him most. Tony Bareham read the chapter on the sixteenth and seventeenth centuries two separate times over and had the necessary steel to say that the first version was misconceived, for which I now thank him; and for his extra patience. Jimmy Simmons encouraged me at an even earlier stage when the project was only half formed, and had friendly advice and support to give when they were especially needed. If I single these three out for particular thanks it is because singly or together they could have killed the project before it got under way and began to stand upon its own basis. Instead they chose to be interested in it and hopeful of its chances if once my several cases of wrong-headedness could be sorted out.

John Constable discussed with me the chapters on the Romantic writers and on the moderns, and I have tried to profit from his knowledgeable comments, and Bridget O'Toole pointed out to me much I did not know about twentieth-century English literature, especially its class aspects. Alastair Thomson kept on producing more early nineteenth-century writers I knew nothing about, until, looking at them, I found them directly relevant, and Simon Gatrell read quite a lot of the middle parts of the book and argued for a more extended treatment of some writers whom I had too cursorily dismissed. Bob Owens, one of my former students, taught me plenty about the seventeenth century which I did not know, and, on the literature of the same period, but also on that of the sixteenth century, Max Golding helped generously with books and expert knowledge. Doug Killam put at my disposal some of the results of his own knowledge of nineteenth- and twentieth-century English imperialist fiction. Anne Marcovitch responded understandingly to the book's middle chapters, which are its heart, on the literature of the eighteenth century and of the Romantic and early Victorian periods. I have tried, but with imperfect success, I realize, to assimilate the many excellent sharp corrections of Victor Kiernan, which he applied to the same sections of my argument, and later to the book as a whole, and to make due use of the books and articles on the economic and historical side of the question to which he directed me, as well as to profit by his reading of the literature. Dave Johnson always knew whatever I asked him. So did John Springhall, who usually went on to add more. Alan Peacock and Bertie Ussher steered me through the, to me, unknown territories of Latin and Greek literature. Phil Tilling talked willingly on Middle English literature whenever I wanted him to; Bruce Stewart on James Joyce. Martin Corner helped with a tricky section at the beginning. To all these friendly readers and colleagues I offer grateful thanks. Nothing encouraged me more in writing this book than their willingness to listen and question and explain, and generally to share what they knew with me when I needed the information; and all of it, let it be added, without hope of gain. I have only not profited more from their suggestions because, after all, I could not find it in me to rise any higher than I have managed in the present effort above my imperfections of vision. Naturally anything inadequate in the book as finally written remains my fault.

Others have helped in other ways than that of being critical. But I am forbidden to mention them.

I owe to Stephen Brook, my editor, who agreed to commission the book from me, the insistence that a study of the merchant figure in English literature, as I at first proposed it to him, could not end with the death of Dickens, but, to be complete, must be brought right up to the present day. I now see how right he was.

I wish to thank the editor of the 'Durham University Journal' for permission to reprint in an amended form in chapter 3 material first published in June 1978 in its pages as a study of Defoe and the idea of trade.

Thanks are due to Faber and Faber for permission to quote nine and a half lines from 'Going, Going' from 'High Windows' by Philip Larkin and five lines from 'The Waste Land' from 'Collected Poems 1909-1962' by T. S. Eliot - both quotations are to be found in the closing chapter; for permission to quote the same lines from T. S. Eliot I wish to thank Harcourt Brace Jovanovich, Inc. as American publisher of Eliot's writings and owner of the copyright; and I am grateful to Farrar, Straus and Giroux, Inc. for permission to quote the same passage from 'Going, Going' from 'High Windows' by Philip Larkin mentioned above, copyright © 1974 by Philip Larkin, reprinted by permission of Farrar, Straus & Giroux, Inc.

1 THE ORIGINS OF CAPITALIST PORTRAYAL 1500-1650

This study is concerned with the establishment in literature of a recognized modern capitalist theme and its development subsequently in the literary tradition, and at the outset it is necessary to state the issue in a distinct way. At the cost of simplifying then, unavoidably, the point to begin with is that the late-fifteenth-, sixteenth- and early seventeenth-century growth of English capitalist activity, as literature reflects it, constitutes a historical movement so far-reaching in its effect as to initiate an entirely new order for mankind.(1) One can more readily concentrate on the outline of this main point, and then proceed to what happens after its initiating period is over, and on its purely literary aspect, because there are excellent accounts already available not only of the economic and social transformation itself, but of its intellectual and moral and imaginative aspects, and it would be irrelevant to try to compete with these.(2)

Mercantile portrayal, then, let the proposition be worded, in sixteenth-century English literature embarks on a markedly original course, and the discussion of the issue itself takes on a tremor and depth of seriousness which are wholly new and which are traceable directly to the stirrings of the economic national life and their social consequences for all levels and kinds of men. Perhaps two or three examples from medieval literature may be cited to make this clear. The way in which we are invited to express the difference is this: the poets of the Middle Ages, though they frequently portray the merchant and his function, and sometimes adversely, do not appear to feel obliged to discuss either the one or the other as an issue. Nor for that matter do the ancient writers: Aristotle and Xenophon among the Greeks; the satirists Juvenal and Persius and the comic dramatists Plautus and Terence among the Romans. To the way of thinking of the latter writers a merchant may seem foolish or villainous, to the former domestic and social economy may seem a serious enough matter to call for applied elucidatory analysis, but in none of them, even where their words may resemble modern judgments, do we recognize the sense of crisis so evident, say, in Jacobean comedy. Earlier English literature lacks this critical sense because, though there have always been merchants, and fraudulent ones among them, mercantile and capitalist activity of the intense and wide-reaching sort that we are concerned with is post-medieval in its real manifestation. So the commercial theme in English literature before 1500, which we encounter readily enough, and which is unquestionably serious enough, and recognized as that by each writer, nevertheless has not yet developed into a more than privately moral issue.

William Langland in 'Piers Plowman' (A text *c*. 1370; B text *c*. 1377-79; C text *c*. 1390) offers sharp criticism of men given over to money-making and neglectful of their obligation to the poor and to the community; for example, in Study's tirade against Will in part 2 of the poem, and also in the entire story of Lady Lucre, Falsehood's daughter, whose detection as a corrupter of high and low men alike forms the main story of book 3. How is this different, it may be asked, as it certainly is, from the depiction of Avarice in so many interludes of the sixteenth century, when the severance from feudal moral ties and a feudal economy was irreversibly under way? Perhaps the difference can be best suggested if we recall that, in the interludes, Avarice is made to associate with Tyranny, Cruelty and Oppression, in other words has a social and exploiting aspect. Langland's objection to Lady Lucre is that she is connected with untruth, is Falsehood's daughter; his is a moral rather than a social view. To say this is by no means to deny that there is criticism of the oppression of the poor in 'Piers Plowman', or to wish to suggest that Langland somehow lacks an idea of the importance of just social relations; the whole poem after all is an outcry against worldliness and corruption by ambition and money greed. But when the trial of Lady Lucre approaches the poet's neutrality towards commerce as such does make itself plainer to see. Misdemeanours such as bribery, extortion, usury are condemned, but not straightforward profit-making; that appears to be acceptable and natural. This important discrimination gathers to an emphasis when Conscience moves to the forefront in order to remind the king that there are two kinds of payment, earned recompense and bribery, one of them fair and the other sinful, and in this way disposes of Lady Lucre's plausible but hollow argument in her own defence, which had all but persuaded the king to agree with her way of thinking, that all persons owe it to themselves to do what they can to earn a living. Langland's mode of expression here is obviously chosen so as to include in the category of approved advantage-seeking the gainful process of ordinary commerce:(3)

> That laborers and lowe [lewede] folk taken of hir maistres
> It is no manere Mede but a mesurable hire.
> In marchaundise is no Mede, I may it wel auowe;
> It is a permutacion apertly, a penyworþ for anoþer.
>
> (1377-9)

[The money, my liege, which labourers receive from their master, is not lucre at all, but a fair wage, Nor is there any lucre in trading with goods: it is simply an exchange, one pennyworth for another (Translation by J.F. Goodridge, Penguin Classics, 1959, p. 89).]

Lady Lucre, then, is condemned by Conscience because she is fraudulent. But Conscience offers no reflection, unless they employ fraud likewise, on business men as such.

The case against Avarice later in the poem is identical. Avarice is portrayed by Langland in the traditional manner as a disgusting miser who uses false weights, stretches cloth artificially before selling it, dilutes beer, takes usury, clips coins, lends money in order to encompass the property of other men, and makes systematic use of bribery. All such charges are against dishonesty and falsification in mercantile dealings, all boil down to the charge of fraud; all are moral. Langland is not objecting to the normal operations of business enterprise, which he sees as natural outlets for money greed, but to cheating. Presumably men had to buy cloth and beer and pay for them with coined money, and a shopkeeper who sold them goods at true measure for a fair price was valued and praised.

In Chaucer's 'Canterbury Tales' (*c.* 1380–1400) the merchant is made to figure as a pompous bore, for ever talking shop and laying down the law, and boasting about his wealth; but Chaucer closes his sardonic description of him by calling him a worthy man; at no stage does he offer to portray him as a man set apart from or as the enemy of his fellows. When it comes to the haberdasher, carpenter, weaver, dyer and so on, the craftsmen and lesser tradesmen, Chaucer lists them in a group and leaves it at that. Nothing appears to strike him as worthy of special remark in those engaged in mercantile work.

In 'The Dance of Death' (*c.* 1431) merchant and usurer are called out of life and reminded of the final vanity of their valueless acquisitions and misdirected energy, and this looks as if it might be the beginnings of a deeper searching critique of their way of life than any so far. But really it is not so. Summoned likewise are pope, emperor, king, child, squire, gentlewoman and minstrel, and all men, which includes all men whatever, whose hearts have been set on the things of this world instead of on the preparation for their true end. What we have in Death's speech to the merchant, and with the usurer it is the same, is a specifying of the misdirection of aim which has been mankind's general error in the idiom of his particular function; and what we have in the merchant's answer is man's perennial lamentation, in the same key, over a mistaken life now too late to be amended:

XLII

Dethe to the Marchaunde

Ye riche marchaunt / ye mote loke hiderwarde
That passed haue / ful many dyuerse londe
On hors on fote / hauyng moste rewarde
To lucre & wynnynge / as I vndurstonde
But now to daunce / ye mote yeue me yowre honde
For all yowre laboure / ful litel a-vaileth now
A-dieu veyneglorie / bothe of fre and bonde
No[ne] more coueite / than thei that haue ynow.

	XLIII
The Marchaunte answereth	Be many an hille / and many [a] straunge vale I haue trauailed / with my marchaundise Over the see / do carye many a bale To sundri Iles / mo than I can deuyse My herte inwarde / ai frette with couetise But al for nowght / now dethe [dothe] me constreyne Be which I seie / he recorde of the wise Who al embraceth / litel shal restreyne.
	(*c.* 1431)

Nothing in the references here to wide travel, gainful appetite and anxiety of spirit sets the man of trade generically apart from other men. Nothing in the poem focuses attention specifically on him any more than Chaucer had sought to do, but rather, and in the same way as Chaucer, the poet tacitly acknowledges his integration with the other members of the social body.

What these three examples suggest is surely true of the whole of English writing in the medieval period as far as that directs itself to the commercial life. There is no need to look in such literature, we are told, for 'sharp edges of contrast' between mercantile and other types of men, 'because there were no sharp lines of social demarcation. The lesser landed gentry and the yeomanry merged, respectively, in the greater gentry and the peasantry'.(4) Literature demonstrates the truth of this judgment in its illustration of the unproblematic absorption of mercantile men into the life of the community they form part of, and in its willingness to level quite harsh criticism at mercantile malpractice without seeming to wish to raise the question of whether men of trade as such were thereby indicted as a class, or had become in some way disintegral with their fellows.

When we come to sixteenth-century literature we find no such acceptance. Instead the new note is of growing hostility to commercial men, and of distrust of the natural tendency of commercial enterprise in its own right. Along with this, at first in a minor capacity, but destined to grow in time into the predominant commitment, goes an unapologetic confidence in the notion of English commercial and imperial supremacy in a Europe at last dismantling itself from being a unified ideological and religious unit, Christendom, and re-forming under the ideology of Protestant truth as so many separate nation states seeing each other as vying in interest for the resources of the world. More than anywhere else this scepticism towards the commercial function may be seen in the drama, which from about 1500 stops being just emblematic or biblical in substance and starts to become secular. Even more eloquent of the refashioning of the economic ordering of the national life since the Middle Ages, and of thinking men's awareness of it, and also usefully analytical and direct in its utterance rather than metaphorical, is Thomas More's 'Utopia' (1516); so

'Utopia' is perhaps the work to begin with as an introduction to the modern discussion.

It is to be remembered that imaginative writers so far have shown little special concern about the encroachments of commerce because commerce has not seemed to consist of more than a neutral give and take; apart from the usury issue, that is. What is new in More is so new and also so penetratingly expressed that he curiously (to us) anticipates the basic insight of the pronouncements of Coleridge on commerce three centuries after his own lifetime, and perhaps too those of Marx and Lenin up to a century later still. More, that is to say, attacks the monopolizing and exploiting practice of men who apply to the English woollen trade of the early 1500s the logical pressures of what has come to be known as big business thinking: men who make it their purpose to press for the maximization of profits above any other consideration and refuse to be deflected from the narrow aim by the moral and social considerations which, at one time, were conceived to be capable of checking the selfish hunger of gain. More's implication in drawing attention to this new feature of social relations is that we are not any longer dealing with old-style misers, however greedy, but with something intrinsic to the new system of trade and agriculture that was observably growing into prominence in the England of the day, and in Europe also. He calls the development so oppressive as to be worse than the grievance of a standing army. Raphael describes the sheep as devouring human beings and as devastating and depopulating fields, houses and towns when he wants to characterize the trend in agriculture away from crop cultivation towards pasturage, which is proving more profitable, and to bring out its cost in human suffering, higher than any affliction known to men before. He terms the capitalists who further this trend, a category which includes gentlemen, noblemen and abbots dissatisfied with the stable profits of their ancestors, insatiable gluttons, and an 'accursed plague' of their native land.(5) Since noblemen and clergymen are involved here, and not just men of trade, it is clear that what we are reading is not simply a reconsideration of the old attitude to the figure of the merchant. Much more is at stake than that. Yet this only points up the truth that a significantly widespread redirection of social effort, a revolution in the economic base of life in general, is More's recognition. Price fixing, and the holding back of supplies to create scarcity, the typical black character marks of monopolistic commerce as we ourselves have come to understand it, are described, and after this More goes on to explain that, whereas a true commonwealth is built up by and consists of common wealth, here under an exploiting system piled-up riches have the effect of introducing invidious distinctions between men and provoking and intensifying social disharmony. This brings clearly out for the second time his antagonism to the newly emerging capitalist order on the grounds that it is humanly divisive. It works, he says, so as to separate gradually but automatically the organic community of men into deprived labourers and non-working rich (p. 239):

> What brand of justice is it that any nobleman whatsoever or goldsmith-banker or moneylender or, in fact, anyone else from among those who either do no work at all or whose work is of a kind not very essential to the commonwealth, should attain a life of luxury and grandeur on the basis of his idleness or his nonessential work? In the meantime, the common labourer, the carter, the carpenter, and the farmer perform work so hard and continuous that beasts of burden could scarcely endure it and work so essential that no commonwealth could last even one year without it. (1516)

If some medieval texts may seem not far removed from this in spirit (for instance, 'Piers Plowman' in its upholding of the poor and lowly), More's objection, we must remind ourselves, is specifically to what he judges to be a new phenomenon in his lifetime, capitalist enterprise. The language may be sounding familiar, but not the argument, or the argument but not the application he makes of it. More describes for us, and seems to recognize half prophetically the gravity of the change he is witnessing, the beginnings of a new system of refashioned relations between men; relations to be based henceforth on an assumption of individual economic antagonism, the principle of the capitalist social order, and less and less, until it finally disappears, on the old general acceptance of a double obligation of service and return, or of mutual trust, the obligation so often flouted, yet not till now directly challenged, of the medieval cast of thought.

A noteworthy feature of the sixteenth-century Tudor interlude, the stage literature of transformation from morality play to Elizabethan drama, is its growing concentration of interest on the Avarice figure, not actually named until by Marlowe in 'The Jew of Malta' (*c.* 1589), in which he appears as Barabbas, but dramatically as well as morally the centre of attention and the dominating figure in a number of plays for a long time earlier than that.(6) Here again, Avarice is the medieval representation still in use, it is to be admitted, and still in existence, as it probably is even today; but also Avarice is a more up-to-date concept reflecting the new money spirit, and methods, of contemporary society. The spirit was felt as usually, but not always, malign; though we may note a specific if rare commitment to it, in passing, in 'The Nature of the Four Elements' (1517). Here Experience recommends to Studious Desire the speedy acquisition by England of the land and trade of the newly discovered territories overseas, a surprising anticipation of the state of mind of the seventeenth century. It is notable how specific, even at this early stage, the commercial nationalism of English literature is capable of being in its acquisitive hunger and competitiveness. Experience's speech, for instance, shows that he has assimilated the results of the latest research into the economic prospects of the American continent and has sound commercial statistics to back up his sense of urgency:(7)

Copper they have, which is found
In diverse places above the ground,
Yet they dig not therefore;
For, as I said, they have none iron,
Whereby they should in the earth mine,
To search for any wore:
Great abundance of woods there be,
Most part fir and pine-apple tree,
Great riches might come thereby,
Both pitch and tar, and soap ashes,
As they make in the east lands,
By brenning thereof only.
Fish they have so great plenty,
That in havens take and slain they be,
With staves, withouten fail.
Now Frenchmen and other have found the trade,
That yearly of fish where they lade
Above a hundred sail.

(1517)

Much more of this is found; but subsequently the play loses its serious commitment and relapses into comic horseplay. The note it sounds is one we shall hear again shortly, and in greater force. For the most part dramatists in the sixteenth century, as in the seventeenth, take the opposite view of commercial exploitation, perhaps because they concentrate their attention on the scene at home where the anarchic tendency of economic ambition is most apparent, and not on overseas enterprise, whose rewards are gratifyingly there but whose cost is paid invisibly in another place and by other people. We are treated therefore to a number of moral allegories in which the pattern of just living is flimsily re-established after a violent breakdown, the latter often very convincing in its delineation and sometimes engagingly vicious. At other times there is no such side to it at all, as in the interludes 'Youth' (1520) and 'Lusty Juventus' (1550), in which pleasure and riot mislead the Christian soul for a time but are rejected after his conversion to good living, and all proceeds onwards from start to finish without a hint of avarice or of money-making in the discussion.

Right through the century such non-economic allegories continue to be found. Outstanding among those in which the dramatists do struggle to express the new awarenesses in a conventional medium is the play 'Respublica' (1553), perhaps written by Nicholas Udall, the only extant Marian piece, which far surpasses all its rivals in poetic life. 'Respublica' gives convincing embodiment to More's analysis forty years earlier, but hinting that it has become an increasingly normal condition, of the systematic exploitation of the weak by ruthless men willing to let the common good suffer neglect so long as they manage to fill their own pockets. Udall's anti-Protestant aim complicates matters, for he naturally makes his villains Protestant villains, which is not of relevance to the present theme, but this does not obscure his reflection of widespread economic violence and the social disorganization which is produced by it. Avarice, Insolence, Oppression and Adulation are shown despoiling the Church and the people of England, having changed their names to Policy, Authority, Reformation and Honesty; they vie with each other to see who can grab the most booty and keep it. Later on People complains to Respublica of the economic contraction of the times as it has affected the common poor and of the steep rise in the cost of living from which everyone suffers, and which he puts down in his simple way to the 'Ill ordring' of the state's affairs. Udall moves still further from Protestant and Catholic polemics, and nearer to the present theme, when (in III, vi) he makes Avarice list the different money-grabbing ways in which since the start of the play he has managed to fill his thirteen money bags. These include arrogated leases, interest, falsely sworn possessions, bribes, selling benefices, accepting retainers, executorships, church depredations, embezzlement of the customs, selling counterfeit merchandise, exporting forbidden commodities, unjust evictions, and the like.(8) Now we can see how what was once pure vice, like bribery and counterfeiting, has, in an economy so disorganized as to be almost a free-for-all, become mixed up with bold initiative and sharp practice, such as executorships, church depredations and even forbidden exporting, as well as much unqualifiable straight crime; and it is all very much a sixteenth-century rather than a medieval mixture.

In 'The Trial of Treasure' (1567) an access of feeling builds up out of much traditional phrasing when Just applies the age-old dicta on unrestrained avarice and egotism to the condition of his own age, corrupted and perverted by the 'canker pestilent' of ambition and by the failure of men to stand content in their due places in society (III, 285). 'New Custom' (1571) attributes men's departure from grace in latter days to the decay of the fear of God and the creeping in of hypocrisy, which cloaks avarice, and is associated with cruelty, who between them seek to bring the whole realm under their sway. This last emphasis is a case in point where the new commercial instinct is shown as a social not just a moral problem, as involving the historical rise of an exploiting class. And in a commonplace of Protestant drama the instinct is detected under its apparent opposite virtue. Perverse Doctrine recommends Cruelty and Avarice, that is nascent capitalism, in its hostile depiction, now to try to go about the country as virtues, as justified thrift, and seems to habilitate them under an acceptable nomenclature into men's inmost habits of thought (III, 40):

> - What then shall I, Cruelty, be called in your judgment?
> - Marry, Justice with Severity, a virtue most excellent.
> - What will you term Avarice, I pray you let me hear?
> - Even Frugality, for to that virtue it cometh most near.
>
> (1573)

It can hardly be reading too much into this exchange, which of course is a satire on the phenomenon, to see in it the accommodation to worldly acquisition of an otherworldly tradition of thought, its motion to assimilate a new robust economic energy. For it is a familiar note in the literature. One finds the same point made in 'Respublica', which we have glanced at already, and in 'The Conflict of Conscience' (1572); and in these places again the re-characterization of Tyranny and Avarice, or re-appraisal of their old characters, involving the updating of a traditional sin as a modern virtue, suggests the emerging climate of opinion. One does not want to claim too much for the sake of neatness on the critical page. The writers are attacking what they describe. Nothing is new in hypocrisy. Bullies, probably, would always prefer to be considered administrators. But in a savagely satirical way such dramatists portray the new money greed as religious aspiration. They satirize, but they satirize because it is there, the new tendency to sanction a longing for the attainment of material wealth as, if not praiseworthy, at least a provisional suggestion of God's approval. Here is Hypocrisy speaking in 'The Conflict of Conscience' (VI, 63):

> Now must I apply all my invention,
> That I may devise Avarice to hide.
> Thy name shall be called Careful Provision,
> And every man for his household may lawfully provide:
> Thou shalt go cloaked, and never be spied.
>
> (1572)

Naturally following on from these depictions, but a much more sophisticated play, and one leading us directly into the world of Shakespeare and Jonson, is Robert Wilson's 'The Three Ladies of London' (1581); less pointedly also, its successor 'The Three Lords and Three Ladies of London' (1588). In the first of these the three ladies, who are Love, Fame and Conscience, declare that Lucre and Usury rule all and that there is nothing men will not do, nowhere they will not go, to encompass riches. There is a plain reminiscence of Langland here which becomes plainer still when Fraud and Dissimulation, Simony and Usury, newly arrived in London, find themselves rejected scornfully by Lady Conscience but welcomed by Lady Lucre and made to feel that they are at home and have arrived in their rightful place. The traditional morality was still alive, still being applied in its old terminology, evidently, although the world had changed around it. However, Wilson's points of departure from 'Piers Plowman' and from the world view of its author are even more to the point than his affinities. Asked what he is doing in London, where for a dozen years usury had now been legally practised, incidentally, Usury explains that he has only freshly been drawn to England from Venice, having recognized in London the historical successor of that commercial capital. No hint of anything like this is to be found in Langland, of course, neither do we see there the particulars with which Lady Lucre is described and filled out in Wilson's play, and the kind of things she is made to say and do, details which are redolent of the bustling economic life of the sixteenth century. She instructs Mercatore to carry out of the land grain of all kinds, leather, bell metal and bacon, and to bring in instead of them coloured glass, toys and beads. She describes the 'infinite numbers' of people in London, Bristol, Northampton and a dozen English towns who pay extortionate rents because of the scarcity of accommodation which the recent influx of large numbers of foreigners has brought about. There is a relevant social symbolism even in Usury's play aim: to kill Hospitality. By Hospitality is meant the old generous form of housekeeping, the provision for all comers to the table, housekeeping conceived as a form of service. This is now to disappear and make way for gainful self-seeking, for what Usury represents. One economic mode is dramatized as driving out another. Wilson is still writing heavily allegorically, but the social references he makes are specific, and they come thick and fast, and every reference has bite. His stand is wholly with the old order. In 'The Three Lords and Three Ladies of London' Usury finds himself sent packing by Pomp and Policy with the declaration that London's grandeur depends not on usurious wealth but on 'well-ventured merchandise', a Shakespearean note, and on 'honest Industry' (VI, 482).

If space can be found for a glance at one more play we might note as relevant here, indeed almost summarizingly relevant, a scene in the anonymous play 'A Knack to Know a Knave' (1592) which represents symbolically all that is argued here about the reflection in pre-Shakespearean drama of an outdated moral attitude being relinquished and a new one, the capitalist attitude, being adopted in its place. A priest, a coneycatcher and a farmer explain to their bailiff father how they exploit people by fraudulent practices, and in the farmer's attempt to explain and vindicate his conduct a new moral gloss is expressly placed on the principle of selfish advantage, by which, according to the orthodoxy of centuries past, but not according to the view of the centuries to come, men incurred the penalty of damnation (VI, 518):

> Father, you know we have but a while to live,
> Then, while we live, let each man shift for one;
> For he that cannot make shift in the world,
> They say he's unworthy to live in it:
> And he that lives must still increase his store,
> For he that hath most wealth of all desireth more.
>
> (1592)

Competitive individualism, the theory of the survival of the fittest, the principle of limitless acquisition: these are the ideas hinted at.

It is surprising how accurately are anticipated in these crude sixteenth-century plays, which struggle to make sense of a world thrown out of all familiar delineation, and in a language ill adapted to the reality they seek to encompass, some of the major principles of the industrial capitalism of nineteenth- and twentieth-century English life. The social picture conveyed in the middle- and late-sixteenth-century plays of which we have here seen a selection, whose allegorical dress makes them look at first glance so like a traditional reflection of men's affairs, reveals a community subject to ruthless and egotistical appetite, torn from its secure relationships and convictions rooted in the past, and fluctuating in a wild unpredictable manner and at a rate almost out of men's power to assimilate. From static medieval condemnations of fraud and usury, static because unchallenged not because lacking in conviction, we find ourselves, after this dynamic interval, on the brink of the morally dislocated world of Shakespeare and Jonson. It is like a world, as the drama reflects it to us, in which as the spiritual connections have dissolved away between men every individual is forced to turn aggressor in self-defence. In the play last mentioned Honesty enters shortly after the farmer has completed his self-justifying speech and describes the condition of society as he has seen it all over the land. His list is of well-heeled dishonesty; of innumerable petty exploiters backed by fewer bullies, the bullies ruled and organized by aristocrats and great men of wealth; of custom frauds at the water side; of cheating in the market place on a small scale, and large-scale cozening on the Exchange. A decayed knight who regrets the passing away of the fashion of old hospitable housekeeping, such as his father made it a point of honour to follow, is advised by the farmer to avoid extravagant expenditure, leave off his great train, keep a few simply fed fighting men and no more, reduce wages all round, water the beer he hands out to his dependants, pay off his retainers and cut out the wasteful practice of giving Christmas presents except to such persons as will be likely, in return, to 'yield you some commodity' (VI, 545). Such an advocacy of cold conduct places Goneril and Regan for us in a new light; they are not cruel; they are economical. Piers Plowman then enters, and complains that the commonwealth is robbed. He measures the acuteness of the crisis of distress under which English social life is now labouring by the fact that he and his wife, never in want during fourscore years, find they have at last been driven to beg in order to maintain themselves. It is not that they cannot find work. They have work but their wages are too low to keep them alive. Thus an economic revolution is the play's inmost subject. When Piers talks of robbers, he refers not to highwaymen but to the new owners of the land.

Set beside these forceful attacks, the commercial-imperial optimism voiced by the anonymous author of 'The Nature of the Four Elements' seventy years earlier, which we noted above, may seem plaintive. But in fact by the close of the sixteenth century, by the time of Elizabeth, the commercial and bourgeois allegiance, and more widely still the spirit of adventurous travel and fortunate discovery, were established and vocal modes of feeling, and, as far as the latter sentiment was concerned, had perhaps become the characteristic outlook of the age. What this means in terms of the implications, some of them economic, of dramatic and other writing which ostensibly deals with un-economic matters, is obvious enough. 'Without the voyagers, it has been said, Marlowe is unthinkable.' (9) Some pressure of commercial aspiration, or reaction against it, some shadow or reflection cast by the new values of capitalism on the feeling of the age may be discernible in forms of writing which we have no space to go thoroughly into here; for example, the treasure imagery of so much sixteenth-century love poetry.(10)

In the dramatic writing of the age of Elizabeth the optimistic mercantile case is put by such writers as Dekker and Thomas Heywood. Crudely realized it may be, and in its time a minority view; but their outlook is that of the future. With frank confidence they celebrate mercantile aspirations and the mercantile class, and project unapologetically the hope that England will dominate the other nations of Europe, and of the world, by outstripping them all economically. And they remain undeterred by any such thing as the notion of artistic restraint from saying all this unsubtly, and in explicit representation, so that their conceptions may sound crass. But we may note that an endorsing play must always be harder to write well than a questioning one, imaginative composition being exploratory rather than positive by its very nature, and at least these writers uphold citizen morality and the prudential calculus in terms which are directly relevant: an appeal to the heart.

In Dekker's 'The Shoemaker's Holiday' (1599) Simon Eyre cannily buys up the cargo of a merchantman which no one else knows about, the gainful motivation guiding him instinctively to secure his own advantage: this makes him not a narrow but a hearty human being, not anti-social but more congenial than before. On the one hand his trading outlook is not sentimentalized; he will not employ more men that he can find work for, even when those seeking employment are needy. But out of those under his care, and within his circle, he forms and cherishes a real community. 'Peace, *Firke*, a hard world, let him passe, let him vanish, we haue iourneymen enow, peace my fine *Firke*': such is Eyre's response to the appearance of Lacy in his workshop looking for work. (11) With this it is worth comparing his speech on election as Lord Mayor (*Works*, I, 74):

> This day my felow prentises of *London* come to dine with me too, they shall haue fine cheere, gentelmanlike cheere. I promised the mad Cappidocians, when we all serued at the Conduit together, that if euer I came to be Mayor of *London*, I would feast them al, and Ile doot, Ile doot by the life of *Pharaoh*, by this beard *Sim Eire* wil be no flincher. (1599)

Of course, guild life is being idealized in such a representation, and it is obvious why: guilds are a relic from the past, and on the retreat. But in view of what was to become a major charge levelled against the mercantile class by its critics, that it destroys spontaneity and generous feeling, it is important that Dekker insists on reciprocal warmth as part of the bourgeois style, and, although he does not argue it out, convinces us of its possibility. Bolder suggestions, such as may seem implied when (V, v) the king is made to pay a visit to Eyre, not the other way round, may be made more important than they are. It was not a unique idea. We may see this from the brief but central exchange between Hobson and Queen Elizabeth in Thomas Heywood's 'If you Know Not Me, You Know Nobody: Part II' (1605) (I, 317):

Hob. God bless thy grace, Queen *Bess*.
Queen. Friend, what art thou?
Hob. Knowest thou not me, Queene? Then thou knowest nobody,
Bones-a-me, Queene, I am *Hobson*; and old *Hobson*,
By the Socks, I am sure you know me.
(1605)

Here and in Heywood generally, though Heywood, like Dekker, lays plenty of stress on the merchant's warmth, a grander significance is being invoked. In several of Heywood's bourgeois dramas, like 'The Foure Prentises of London' (1600) and 'The Fair Maid of the West' (1610), we see citizen life presented familiarly, but also spiritedly, and in a mood prepared to make audacious comparisons: Heywood sees the whole world in his citizens' small lives, heroic concerns in their ordinary undertakings, and he makes his audience aware of these implications too. 'The inevitable association of the brave deeds of Bess and Spencer with those of the gallant sea-heroes of England would thrill the hearts of the Londoners who still bore in mind the glorious days of the Armada, and of Raleigh, Frobisher and Drake.' (12) This expansion of soul is an important and sometimes underrated element in such plays, so easy to mock.

Coming back to the second part of 'If You Know Not Me, You Know Nobody', we find that its true significance lies not in the portrait of Hobson, the hearty neighbourhood merchant whom nobody can put down, important though he is as a bluff citizen type, but in that of the elder Gresham, the father of Hobson's apprentice. Gresham is drawn as a strong personality in national and international power politics. He is cast as anything but ludicrous. He represents the mercantile interest in Elizabeth's England, newly conscious of its potency, determined to be listened to and respected, but for all that heartily patriotic, and seeing its fortunes as tied in with and identical to those of the nation as a whole. In Heywood's elaborate dramatization of Gresham's first conceiving the idea of the Royal Exchange when caught in a rainstorm, then proceeding to plan the project through, win approval for it, build it, and at last have it ceremonially visited and so to speak authorized by Queen Elizabeth, we are processionally led through a formal endorsement of all that Gresham stands for. And it is stressed that he stands for something enhancing. Gresham's Exchange is a free gift to all other merchants, a recognition of their desert and excellence. Gresham himself is shown as a supermerchant who benefits his class and country by getting rich because he redistributes his riches among his fellows and to their exaltation and the discomfiture of less happy nations. One cannot dismiss the representation as absurd; Gresham had existed, and built the Royal Exchange; and there was Hobson, to keep things down to earth.

The point for us to note is that Gresham's is a distinctly mercantile power. He is to be reckoned with in the world of the play not for his intelligence, nor his political insight, nor his moral excellence, but for his extreme wealth, drawn from commerce. He is a king among merchants; such is the idealization. Hence it is appropriate that Gresham's, not Queen Elizabeth's, is the character which irradiates the action. In a memorable scene he powders then drinks a pearl too costly for any other whole nation to buy, to say nothing of any rival merchant, and he does this while wearing slippers costing each of them £30,000: all that remains of a lost venture. The very crudeness of such an attempt to be flamboyant about material loss almost makes it more impressive. Beyond mere civic pride Heywood's purpose, like Dekker's, is to express national pride, which in Gresham can point to an English merchant more successful than any foreign rival, and in Gresham College to the beneficent nature of power when placed in such hands.

Heywood and Dekker see the merchant and citizen as differing from one another not in function but in their degree of wealth. They belong to the same basic type; they share a common set of values, and a common outlook, and their differences do not add up to a separation. The difference is that the citizen inhabits a small neighbourhood but the merchant inhabits the whole world. Thus one is invited to see both Eyre and Gresham as heightened representations of the civic character, examples of what all could hope to achieve and be, not special types.(13) The emphasis was common enough, though less common than the condemning portrayal which ran alongside it and grew in volume and force during the first half of the seventeenth century. The hero of Thomas Deloney's 'Jack of Newberry' (1597) rises from poor apprentice to rich employer, and like Gresham and Eyre remains a giving employer not a taking one, made more aware by success of his connection with his fellows, and with his affection and charity deepened rather than dried up. The Dick Whittington legend made its appearance in print in 1605 and enforces the same simplified moral optimism.(14) Nevertheless it was to be just this distinction, that the merchant knew the world at large, when the citizen did not but instead suffered from a mind and an experience confined to his locality and to the drudgery of petty traffic, that made it possible for the merchant to escape from his despised shoppy limitations and assume a more general heroic status in the literature of later years. On the other hand, the shopkeeper was to remain a drudge in literature for another three centuries or more. This is a division, it is to be repeated, not present in the Elizabethan dramatic literature of civic celebration, but one finds it hard to see how such plays as Heywood's and Dekker's, with so static and unquestioning a message, could keep holding dramatic appeal, even by the crude method of zestful declamation.(15)

Elizabethan bourgeois drama dies out, a vociferous outburst running into the sands, later to be renewed in its essential emphasis but with a more profound and imaginative formulation, yet hardly more durably, in the novels and other writings of Daniel Defoe. The case of Francis Bacon, who also has weighty things to say by implication in favour of the commercial spirit, is directly contrary: unremarkable contemporary effect but an expansive and subterranean influence on the minds of men as the seventeenth century develops, an influence comparable, it has been said, to that of Marx or St Francis.(16) Commercial matters as such rarely figure in Bacon's writing and are more generally invoked as part of some grander concept, like science or learning or material progress or civilization, on which occasions it becomes plain that he approves of the spirit behind expanding commerce as encouraging and recommending the attainments he himself desires to reach. When, therefore, as in the usury question, Bacon finds he must decide between the traditional moral code and contemporary social and economic needs he sides with the practical men who wish to throw off irrelevant archaic restraints on commercial energy, as they judge them, and does so because they are practical, and opposes the traditionalists and the idealists. Bacon recommends the toleration of usury by law. He argues that prohibition is pointless when it cannot be enforced. He cuts through moral speculations and biblical semantics. Men, he writes, have been very witty against usury but 'since there must be borrowing and lending, and men are so hard of heart as they will not lend freely, usury must be permitted'.(17) What it concerns the state to guard against, Bacon says, is the eventuality that usury's bad consequences, which he specifies as its tendency to block up the fluid transference of currency, and favour the few rich against the many, might come to endanger healthy social activity; conversely, he recommends that usury's advantage as a means of advancing trade should be freed and utilized. Always to the fore is his sense that men must form their judgments from an understanding of realities, not from delusions, and that the danger incurred by ignoring the true state of things is the greatest to be faced. 'If it be objected that this doth in a sort authorize usury, which before was in some places but permissive; the answer is that it is better to mitigate usury by declaration than to suffer it to rage by connivance' (p. 477).

The coolness of Bacon's pronouncement in favour of usury is perhaps the most significant feature here. He concludes a centuries-long debate by implying half casually that the question, far from being a living issue, is little more than a matter of administrative prudence. Scholastic argumentation on the matter, so passionate as it had been, so fine drawn, so long, is simply ignored.(18) Bacon ends by recommending regulated usury, which he perceives will free commercial energy, which in turn will foster scientific enquiry and material advance. Thus for Bacon there is no drossily mechanical quality in the merchant's character, as there is for the satirical dramatists of the time; but neither is he inspired by the narrow nationalism to which Heywood yields. Instead he aims at an outlook positive and international, as well as all-embracing.

Such an outlook is well conveyed even in the unfinished 'The New Atlantis' (1626), where Bacon describes as the ultimate purpose of the foundation of Solomon's House the discovery, in the words of its governor, of the knowledge of the 'Causes, and secret motions of things; and the enlarging of the bounds of Human Empire, to the effecting of all things possible' (3, p. 156). Common knowledge already among his people are such secrets as the preparation of the water of paradise, and of baths of restoration, the ability to propagate without seeds, and to transform plants, and the use of cordials thin enough to pass through the hand.(19) These, which sound like miracles, are but the results of straightforward scientific techniques constantly refined as fresh knowledge has been transmitted back to New Atlantis by travelling investigators threading their way over the globe and picking up ceaselessly all the latest information available to men. Why is this scientific fiction of relevance to commercial discussion? Because Bacon calls these research detectives 'Merchants of Light', spiritual traders who supply the raw materials of knowledge and upon whose efforts society depends for its continued mastery of the secrets of life. It is a wholly approving image. Of all the reasons why commerce changed from a despised to an admired calling between Shakespeare and Dryden the present connection with advancing knowledge proved one of the most potent.

The two streams of thought so far sketched in, one celebrating commerce and the other condemning it, feed into and find expression jointly in Shakespeare's dramatic writing, whose cast is neither predominantly bourgeois nor predominantly anti-bourgeois, nor progressivist like Bacon's. Shakespeare assimilates and accepts all these pressures of feeling but does not give up one for the other. He responds to the imaginative side of commerce in his day, the age of merchant adventure, but explores its negative, selfish side too, and brings the new outlook and procedures of aggressive commercialism to the test of human experience, the test of life. It seems obvious from his writings that Shakespeare valued above all virtues the ability to be generous, to rise above the appetitive and the selfish; hence he remains unimpressed by the specific side, so to call it, of capitalist ambition, its materialistic bent and narrow nationalism. He writes 'Henry V' (1599), glorifying perhaps sardonically the chivalric hero, but does not introduce great contemporary figures into his work, such as Gresham, or the naval and military heroes of the time. On the other hand a play like 'The Tempest' (1611) captures the spirit of the age of discoveries almost without trying, suggesting a great deal more about new worlds of knowledge and conquest, new modes of feeling and new possibilities for life than is put into specific statement in the express dialogue of the play. In such a generalized suggestiveness is articulated the heroic aspiration, including the mercantile aspiration, of the age.

This double response of Shakespeare's to spiritual commerce and bargain-driving commerce is well evidenced in 'The Merchant of Venice' (1596), the play on which discussion must concentrate. His handling seems designed to keep spontaneity and calculation separate, neither to cancel one by its opposite nor to harmonize them, but rather to confront them with one another, separately embodied, irresolvable, and with a powerful suggestion of dramatic energy coming from the resulting clash. Antonio is negative, perhaps, because he is half the portrait of a merchant, the present-giving half, but without a real job to do. Thus he feels he belongs nowhere.(20) Shylock also is half a merchant's portrait; the other half. A similar division operates in 'Timon of Athens' (1607), in which the prodigal Timon and the generous Alcibiades are contrasted with the 'usuring' senate (III, v). A harmonized temperament would include both aspects, it is to be supposed. Shakespeare splits them and intensifies the play's energies.

Shakespeare's specific interest in 'The Merchant of Venice' seems to be to project an image of the speculative adventurer in Bassanio and then, using this as background, to analyse in Shylock and Antonio the workings of the essential money transaction itself. This is what catches his attention at the moment in history when a traditional economy and ethic were broken, and a new order embarked upon which was leading men to a future uncertain in its nature, to say the least. In this connection one cannot fail to perceive his firmly traditional moral stand. He organizes the Shylock story so as to display the humanly inadequate commercial priorities. He organizes it so. It is not like that in the sources. But in Shakespeare's manipulation the story of the bond becomes an allegory of the denial in money men of the necessary relations of life. He accepts the dramatic awkwardness of Portia's forgotten statute in the trial scene in act IV, which this leads him into; it is embarrassing, of course, and self-weakening; but as a by-product of his emphasis on making the right moral conclusion emerge from the story he had taken over it testifies to a concern more noteworthy still. It is obvious that the forced christianization later on will not touch Shylock's heart, but here too, considering it as a moral dilemma, less as a dramatic exploration, how else is Shakespeare to enforce the wrongness of the business ethic, and how redeem the materialist but by applied pressure? Spiritually, however, the play is anything but redemptive, and Shakespeare gives us plenty of evidence in his portraits of villainy in other plays that he believed only limitedly in the change of heart.

One talks so readily of Shylock because he is the money man. Antonio is the true merchant of Venice, yet Antonio is only the merchant considered in his uncommercial, or perhaps untechnical, manifestation: not the dealer but the darer. Antonio is never seen trafficking. His negotiation of the loan is utterly unbusinesslike. He refuses to be bothered with detail. He can hardly bring himself to talk to Shylock, and then only grossly insultingly. So standoffish a fellow would not last a month in the demanding and demeaning real business world. We cannot align Antonio with Gresham or Eyre, therefore, whose commercialism is the grain of their nature, but must accept his as a different kind of function; he stands for transcendent generosity. In the Italian source the Antonio figure could be generous because his merchant days were over; he was retired and rich. Shakespeare makes Antonio generous by nature while still in the middle of his business career, and irrespective of its demands. His purpose? To sharpen to the extreme the contrast he wishes us to perceive between what Antonio and Shylock stand for: between spirituality and worldliness; between appealing commerce and despicable commercialism.

Almost alone among the dramatists of the time, or of any time, Shakespeare, having engineered this so sweepingly simple yet all-inclusive contrast, then goes out of his way to strengthen the technical aspect of the story and to render especially vividly the bargain-driving, hard-hearted aspect of business practice in its specific manifestation in the Elizabethan London of his day. Thus the idealism of his delineation is rooted firmly, and so to speak validatingly, in a distinct awareness of how the commercial world is and operates. Here too a comparison with the major source brings out the justice of what is said; Shakespeare's rendering of the transaction is incomparably more real and telling. When Bassanio and Antonio arrive to negotiate the loan (I, iii) Shakespeare gives us a stark and wholly original portrayal, in Shylock's conduct towards them, of how the tenacious business mind clutches whatever stray chance of an advantage is thrown out by the expressions and interchange of the encounter, and builds them all into a destructive and overwhelming position of bargaining superiority. The Jew in the Italian story which was Shakespeare's source, who is just 'a Jew at Mestri', not even given a name, exacts the pound of flesh agreement from Ansaldo, has it drawn up and witnessed in a formal bond, counts out the ducats, hands them over, and that is that.(21) No deal could be more trouble-free, so to speak. Shylock, by contrast, after Shakespeare has finished with him, moves through the whole encounter in a laborious, slow, considering manner which is highly sinister in its calculating and sadistic intentions. He keeps going over the terms of the loan, which he already knows. He racks Bassanio with impatience. He will not undertake to say whether he will choose to advance the money or not, until he has reduced his client to a state of anxious distraction (I, iii, 1-7):

- Three thousand ducats; well.
- Ay, sir, for three months.
- For three months; well.
- For the which, as I told you, Antonio shall be bound.
- Antonio shall become bound; well.
- May you stead me? will you pleasure me? shall I know your answer?

(1596)

Antonio entering, Shylock then pretends not to be attending to the conversation because he is trying to reckon up his ready cash; and that there is not enough of it; and that to make up what Bassanio needs he will be constrained to borrow from Tubal; and that Tubal is cruel. He lengthily tells over the story of Jacob, tricking his way into the ownership of a flock of sheep. He makes a point of checking the interest rate in his little book. When Antonio, driven from his patience, presses him to decide one way or the other he complains about his ill usage over the years. Perhaps there is something pathetic in this display of power. If so, it is not allowed to serve as an exoneration. Shylock is made by Shakespeare to condemn himself by so relishing his own strong bargaining position, and his clients' weakness, and by exploiting both to get his own back for a lifetime of contemptuous usage, and by thinking only of money and revenge and nothing else in the human problem he finds himself by life's chances called upon to deal with. And in his normal business function, Shakespeare shows, in the regular process of commerce, he finds the natural weapon of revenge. Nothing could be more conclusive than such a demonstration of the antagonistic nature of the commercial relation, which lends itself so adeptly to cruel motivation and sadistic greed. Yet, we admit again, Shakespeare is not writing to a thesis, and registers other meanings at the same time. A reason why Solanio and Salerio are present in the play is to add to the documentation of the busy mercantile Venetian life which is its background, but, without subtracting from this effect, Shakespeare makes them talk of argosies, maps and sea roads instead of dockyards and cargoes, and gives commercial Venice a romantic slant rather than a physical trading realization. He does not try to accommodate with each other the gross and the spiritual manifestation of commerce, perhaps declines to see them as mutual, yet it was just such an integration that literature during the next century and a half was to aspire to bring about. Though in one sense, therefore, 'The Merchant of Venice' goes to the root of the matter, leaving nothing unsaid about the commercial spirit, plenty of additional discussion and investigation still remains to be filled in, and plenty to be still discovered.

Countering the bourgeois optimism of Heywood and Dekker, indeed swamping it in drama for a hundred years, are the Jacobean and Caroline satirists and the Restoration comic dramatists, whose portrayals of city life and business dealing are vividly hostile and uncompromising; indeed, almost unexploring in their moral antipathy to the spirit and population of the world of commercial enterprise. For Jonson, Middleton, Marston, Massinger and the rest the merchant is a fool or a knave, or both, and his hopes and values are almost programmatically cursed and laughed at. This high degree of revulsion is itself a fact to note and think over. For example, the intensity of it warns us off treating the city comedies of these authors as representative portrayals of their age, as documentary writings. They are concentrations on the bourgeoisie, at that time so opportune a target, of a general mood of moral discordance, formed of whatever elements; half their anger derives its inspiration from the satirical personality and adopted mood. We are confirmed in this recognition when we recall that, Jonson apart, and even in Jonson hardly with regard to specific men of trade, they are writers who tend not to share the imaginative stirring which romantic commerce sparks in Shakespeare; that they fail to face up to the arguments of Bacon; that they ignore the bourgeois case, but do not rebut it, and less still try to transcend it. Yet theirs was the analysis that held out and continued to dominate the mind of the age. Not until the middle years of the seventeenth century, when a revolution at home had brought the business classes into the centre of politics and a realignment of world powers had raised naval and commercial countries to dominance, and the combined effect of both these developments had forced on English writers a thorough revaluation of inherited concepts, the indignity of trading endeavour among them, did literature start to adjust itself in a major way to the new ways of looking which new experience had made necessary. Even then the drama lagged behind; it was in other forms of writing that the significant breakthroughs were made. In the Jacobean age, drama is still vital, not a decadent genre, and its antipathy to commerce, its narrow and intense focus, its repetitiveness of theme and situation are to be explained, if at all, by other factors than the dictates of a literary convention. Why, one wishes to ask, was there so pronounced a need for anger in the first decades of the seventeenth century? Why was it felt that the mercantile classes should bear so much of the brunt of it? Obviously, answers to such deep questions are not easily to be found. But it is open to suggestion that the catastrophes of the sixteenth century, the economic disturbance, the widespread privation, the shaking up of a whole world into something unknown and frightening, the irreversibility and unpredictability of it all, had all prepared the consciousness of men for some sustained explicit denunciation, some loud protest unmuffled by complexity, an object to blame, and some energetic blaming. The object was found, was ready to hand and used to the role, in the merchant; and the dramatists were prepared to supply the variants of abuse.

What is not strongly present in Shakespeare's portrayal of commerce is social documentation. By comparison, Ben Jonson's plays are grittily close to the body of the time, and seem exactly satisfying in their concentration on the specific scene. His mercantile and commercial figures, all exuding the flavour of seventeenth-century London, even when in foreign dress, cover a broad enough span to suggest to us that Jonson purposes to survey more or less all the type's significant variants and thus build up a proportionate picture of the age. But if Jonson takes over the street scene, and in the prologue to 'Every Man in His Humour' (1598) he stresses that he intends his work to impress us as authentic, he still offers a moral vision lifted from the London of his day rather than mere documentary realism for its own sake. What this vision is, on commerce, can be simply conveyed, so long as to say so does not seem to imply that it is also trite; for although it is an imaginatively realized judgment, it is not one seriously departed from anywhere in any of the plays. Jonson sees the trading outlook as reductive and self-defeating, and as disrupting established patterns of life, but worst of all as tending in its natural operation to efface the spiritual character of man and render him indistinguishable from the beast. In such a view the closer to trade and the trading spirit a man is, the more ingrained his personality has become with a commercial tincture, the more lost he is judged to be.

Consider how Volpone, who embodies certainly in himself the wealth hunger of the age, which Jonson apparently sees as its characteristic passion, nevertheless retains a marked impressiveness, because, as he boasts, he is not engaged in trade proper; he is too artistic; he has soul. He wants gain therefore, but (I,i):

I gain
No common way: I use no trade, no venture;
I wound no earth with ploughshares; fat no beasts
To feed the shambles; have no mills for iron,
Oil, corn, or men, to grind them into powder;
I blow no subtle glass; expose no ships
To threatenings of the furrow-faced sea;
I turn no moneys in the public bank,
Nor usure private -

(1607)

What this means, or rather claims to mean, is that Volpone's is clean money, got by witty invention. His dexterity and bold promptings are evidence of his possession of spirituality of a sort, though perverted. Corvino on the other hand, the merchant proper in the piece, outdoes everyone else in grasping inhumanity. Here is a kind of distinction not found nor sought in Shakespeare, who values the generous nature rather than the clever spirit; not that Volpone is 'valued' by Jonson. Address and wit similarly go some way towards rescuing from condemnation Face and Subtle in 'The Alchemist' (1610).

But no such diminution of guilt attaches to Jonson's commercial villains; rather he intensifies their depravity. He compounds avarice with lust in the cases of the knight Sir Epicure Mammon in 'The Alchemist' and the 'Money-Baud' Sir Moth Interest in 'The Magnetic Lady' (1632), whose multiplied vices underline their moral disorder. Even though the less distinctly individualized Kitely in 'Every Man in His Humour' (1598) is a figure hard to judge, because at first presented as dignified, then presented as ridiculous, and at last relinquished into the background, the play's message is unmistakable enough. Money greed is its central theme. When Knowell laments the precocious materialism of the children of the day, trained in acquisitive cupidity by their parents from the first moment at which they are capable of taking a lesson in, he speaks with almost the authority of a chorus, and one uttering the overall judgment on his age advanced in all of Jonson's dramatic and poetic writings.

Clearly these figures, and what he does with them, must be accepted from him seriously, as they are written seriously, and allowed to stand as Jonson's pronouncement on the money world of his time. But also we have to remind ourselves once again that the portrayal is concentrated and heightened, a sharp judgment passed on one aspect of the life of Jacobean England rather than a clear reflection of it. This is true of the plays of Jacobean, Caroline and Restoration comic drama generally, which offer a moral analysis of their time first and last, not an economic one, 'nor may they be rashly cited as evidence of actual conditions at the time.'(22) Why did they so exaggerate and select? The age felt it needed, hence really did need, a pungent expression of the critical view. The satiric mode invited playwrights to heighten what they saw. They were reacting against the simplifying civic dramatists, simplifying in other words in the opposite direction. They were moved by a doubtless genuine anger at modern economic tendencies.(23)

What is said of the basic hostility to commerce in Jonson's plays may be extended to those of the other satirical Jacobean playwrights, who emphasize the merchant's psychological failure in trying to come to impossible terms with himself and with life, and his socially dangerous attempt to impose the same terms upon his fellows. The emphasis is repeated by their successors in dramatic writing down to the time of Congreve and beyond and remained free of serious challenge in the theatre until Steele elevated the merchant to heroic status in 1722, a social restitution that still fails to class as a dramatic triumph. Thomas Middleton's 'Michaelmas Term' (1606) turns on the commodity swindle, one of the 'most notorious' frauds of the day,(24) and the somewhat involved operation is convincingly realized in all its stages, not just talked about. Early in the same play Quomodo the woollen draper expresses his class's philosophy, as Middleton sees it, when he bids his two attendants Falselight and Shortyard, whose other name is Blastfield (I, i, 81-2),

> Go, make my coarse commodities look sleek,
> With subtle art beguile the honest eye.
>
> (1606)

Going futher in 'A Trick to Catch the Old One' (1605), Middleton draws a picture of mercenariness on a universal scale made all the more intense by his toning down the satirical exaggerations usually applied, and avoiding aggressive moral condemnation. The resulting portrayal is as of a world which has turned into a vast market place, and in which getting and outdoing are the acknowledged business of life, 'the kind of world which might have been described or inhabited by Chaucer's Pardoner'.(25)

When Philip Massinger writes of the mercantile world, which is not often, he outlines the same kind of picture of things. For example, 'The City Madam' (1632) takes as its theme the issue of the century: exorbitant commercial energies. In Luke Frugal's rise, evil transformation, and fall, he sketches in Jonsonian fashion a fable of the corruption and punishment of the trading ethic, emphasizing like Jonson the out-of-place social ambition in the city madam and her daughters which both expresses and ridicules this new element in the national life. Massinger, it is said, hardly tries to be truly original. But he is clear, and what distinguishes him from Jonson, say, is the simpleness of his depiction. The creed of aggressive commercialism is canvassed with explicit directness, as in the exchange (V, ii) in which Lord Lacie makes a fruitless appeal to Luke Frugal because Luke insists on equating his honesty with his income, and further identifies conscience with reputation, reputation with credit and credit with commercial creditworthiness; in short, reduces doing good to doing well. This brings vividly home to us the enemy's view of the new commercial culture of England, held to be so much more pitiless and external than the old, according to which the code of virtuous conduct is seen as shrunk into the reckoning up of a man's public estimation and apparent worth in cash. One almost expects to hear from Luke a speech on the importance of respectability. Sir John Frugal is a merchant who stands in balancing contrast to the upstart Luke, old-fashioned, humane, but helpless against his energetic wily brother.

In his earlier play 'A New Way to Pay Old Debts' (1621) Massinger had also stressed that the mercantile class was not just a number of pushy merchants and their associates but a group with a developing ideology, a conscious force, a new social class aware of its distinct interest from the rest of the social body and determined to achieve it whatever the cost. Obviously Massinger does not fully lay out the driving purpose of this new class, to which he is unsympathetic; that would make him a Defoe, and a much greater artist. But he senses and feels it is there, and hears the sound of the feet marching. Despite the fragmentation of the character of Sir Giles Overreach, the relevant figure, who appears variously as spender and miser, power seeker and hedonist, which scatters the play's effect, we find in 'A New Way to Pay Old Debts' the hints of a self-conscious pressure group being formed - but not a guild - within the community as a whole, and, since it proposes for itself a separate good from that of the community, encouraging in its members' minds the idea of an essentially predatory relationship with their fellowmen (III, iii, 50-6).

We worldly men, when we have friends, and kinsmen,
Past hope suncke in their fortunes, lend no hand
To lift 'hem up, but rather set our feet
Vpon their heads, to presse 'hem to the bottom;
As I must yield, with you I practis'd it.
But now I see you in a way to rise,
I can and will assist you.

(1621)

Massinger, through Overreach, here describes a significant new attitude, the lines offering a view of the commercial ideal at its most stripped, the justification of conduct by profit, or apparent profit, alone. What happens to Overreach gives us Massinger's judgment on him. But more important than the moral is the delineation. Overreach is much more inhumane than Shylock, who at least hates Antonio, and perhaps the intensification and spread of commercial life and thought in the twenty-five years between the two plays may help to explain the harsher portrayal. What Massinger adds to the other dramatists is this hint of commercial men beginning to make up a pressure group and a closed shop. To Jonson foolish wretches, to Shakespeare romantics or devils, merchants to him are a set-up. It is no more than a hint. But it points to the future.

Such is the merchant figure as viewed by the writers of Jacobean city comedy: new, crass, but potent, laughed at but taken extremely seriously. Their intense sustained mockery and criticism, which are no more than suggested by what we have had the space to set down here,(26) of course providing good drama, otherwise the mode would have been dropped, draw attention to what they would hide, a fear of the merchant and what he stands for, and an irremovable anxiety as to what his aggressive presence portends for life in the future. Nor should we overlook what is also significant, the changing depiction during a generation and within an accepted typology of the characteristic traits and social habits and ambitions of the merchant classes themselves. Whereas Middleton satirizes a snobbery and a pretension which seem to him outrageously ignorant and ludicrous when he describes London citizens having a go at fashion, and intriguing for titles and estates, in such a play as Shirley's 'Hyde Park' (1632) we are reminded, 'the citizens are no longer tradespeople aping the manners of the nobility [but] people of leisure who enact the fashions of the day with an accurate perception of social values.'(27) The significance of this is that it registers the assimilation of successful commercial men into the aristocratic class which had once despised them, and the acceptance by mercantile men of aristocratic values they had once opposed. It is, therefore, a noteworthy shift in its way. But we are not dealing with a revolution because some mutineers have been taught manners and promoted to captains. The really significant change would be demonstrated in the writings of Defoe, and the outlook of Defoe's generation, when aristocratic attitudes were to be tested by their accommodation to mercantile ways of looking at the world, and rejected as inadequate if they were found to diverge in any way.

It is not then a matter for surprise that comparatively little effort seems to be made in these plays to describe transactions from the merchant's own viewpoint, to present the business side of things. The merchant is viewed as he encounters the man about town or the spendthrift or the witty aristocrat or the needy suitor for money; this gives a single narrowly hostile perspective on him and his world, and no more. As far as impartiality is concerned, it has to be said, the plays of civic fantasy are no better, unless we suppose that all tradesmen went about whooping and hollering like Simon Eyre and that merchants drank powdered pearls as a matter of course. Dekker and Heywood exalt the bourgeois mode unquestioningly. Marston, Middleton, Chapman, Jonson and Massinger despise the citizen and the shopkeeper and the merchant with an inclusive and hardly more questioning hatred. Both approaches make for emphatic drama, and in the anti-mercantile mode, which pushes out the mercantile mode swiftly and for the time being completely, the playwrights do not feel prompted as a rule to enter deeply into the discriminations of function and type in the commercial profession; a few defining strokes, if they fill in the accepted shape, are in the large majority of plays enough. (28) Such strict or easy typecasting soon goes imaginatively dead. It soon fails to cover the ever-changing facts. And if we look closely enough we can see here and there evidence of strain in quite a few plays between the given characterization and what the exploratory imagination wants to do with it, keen to get away from the worn path; the merchant is observed to draw apart from his predicted role, is then pulled awkwardly back into it. Shylock in 'The Merchant of Venice' is an outstanding example; a passionate growth begins to take place in him, then is cut short. The rare depiction of a working day at the Royal Exchange is to be found in William Haughton's 'Englishmen For My Money' (1598), in the course of which Haughton's merchant (he is called Pisaro!) is shown going to pieces psychologically under the pressure of insistent various demands and questions, his unreliable relationship with other men of business, and his anxiety about the losses he is incurring. It is hard to see that Haughton can mean us to feel sympathy for Pisaro since he expressly subordinates the play's mercantile theme to the romantic one, but this demonstration creates sympathy, and it is there. One supposes Haughton found himself not regarding Pisaro as quite the simple villain he at first appears after all, but instinctively humanizes the portrayal in the writing. In Middleton and Rowley's joint play 'A Fair Quarrel' (1617) Russell, the 'dignified rich merchant' of the dramatis personae, is transformed within the opening scenes into a 'bloodsucking churl', and transformed is the word: he disintegrates before our eyes. Here an opposite dismantling of character, but the same creative process, has taken place, and for the same reason: drama's revulsion from theorized conduct. Similar figures have been discussed already: Jonson's Kitely, Massinger's Overreach, Massinger's Luke Frugal. In such uncertain characterizations dramatic literature perhaps bears witness to the pressure exerted by a newly moulding imagination on the limits within which a social prejudice, or a moral assertiveness, seeks to constrain it. Wrenching the character back into place splits the portrayal, which leaves a weak spot in the dramatic product. But the weak spot is a growing point.

Anti-mercantile comedy proved longer-lasting than its counterpart, the drama of civic fantasy, which after Dekker and Heywood found its impulse channelled into non-literary forms, and continued to celebrate bourgeois and mercantile life and values in pageant, civic show and spectacle.(29) It is interesting that Middleton, the scorner of the city, should compose some of these civic congratulations, as did other satirists also.(30) There is nothing to hold our attention in the literary aspect of this kind of production, which is as searching as a vote of thanks at an alderman's dinner. For example, in Anthony Munday's 'The Triumphs of Reunited Britannia' (1605) a returning East Indies ship's master gives thanks, Britannia celebrates his safe return, and Neptune declares a general holiday. Then in the same author's 'Chryso-Thriambos' (1611) Time and the newly raised up Farringdon converse about the honour and amity of fishmongers and goldsmiths; there is in the six years' gap a certain conceptual narrowing observable here. In Munday's 'The Triumphs of the Golden Fleece' (1623), a dozen years further on, we are presented with no text at all, only spectacle. The visualizing tendency is evident. All these pieces, those by Munday and those by others, tend towards the same wordless and spectacular condition, which admits and makes a virtue of the artistic deadness of the pure civic idea.

In anti-mercantile drama as the century advances the realism of the satirical reflection of commerce slackens, thinning and receding in its suggestion of closeness to life as the assimilation of manners that we noted above becomes much more evident, or as the playwrights tend more towards intrigue, the Restoration emphasis, than social satire. Typical of this progressively nominal relation to actual men of trade are the merchants Warehouse and Seathrift in Jasper Mayne's 'The Citye Match' (1637). Warehouse is tricked by an insurance project schemed up by his nephew which he swallows at once in its entirety but which no self-respecting merchant would listen to for a moment. The story needs him to be outwitted, so he is outwitted, but not in a psychologically or professionally convincing manner. Outwitting is the point, and the technical details of its method are not. What is anticipated here is the Restoration code, the concern with style rather than with function; and in terms of style, the traditional terms, that is, a merchant is still judged to be a fool. This forceful and narrowing dramatic convention enables the successors of Jonson and Massinger to write some brilliant plays, but their kind of success exacts the high price of yielding up the central position which drama had occupied in literature so far. A reason why drama fades soon after the Restoration is that it ignores so much of what was happening in real life; it aims at being brilliant, or in tragedy sublime, but not representative. One cannot regret this since it made possible a kind of perfection otherwise not to be achieved. But since the playwrights continue to hold back after 1660 from exploring the new modes of valuation thrown out by a scientific and commercial age, other writers, poets from before the Restoration, and especially prose writers after it, do not, but rather take up the challenge and try to appraise fully and acceptingly the real nature of their society. Doing this, they necessarily assume the central significance which, by dramatic writers, curiously in some cases including themselves in a different medium, seems to be voluntarily relinquished.

The century and a half here sketched of the literary treatment of commercial men, from More's critique of the commercializing of late feudal society to the puritan revolution, was the forming period of capitalist England. Literature in this time, as we have seen, tries to reflect and make sense of the changes in life activity and expectations which were forced on all men as a result of the upheavals of the time. It describes for us the new social relationships that a revolutionized economic order compelled into being, and what they felt like, and what they seemed to mean for life in the future. It expresses too the new binding sense of national destiny, which, despite the bitter warfare between the classes, and between new interests and old, in England, served to unite the English people as a race against other peoples at a time when the traditional concept of a united Christendom transcending nationality was being shattered, and separate nation states, seeing other nation states as their enemies, or at best as temporary allies against a joint foe, were beginning to form the outlines of the modern world. This wider European development, which is the true context of what was happening in England, has to be kept before our minds the whole time. If in sixteenth-century England the literature of moral appraisal, such as the changing morality play, and the seventeenth-century literature of commerce both spring from revolutionary developments in English economic life and awareness, what is to be remembered is that such changes in English experience formed part of a larger redistribution. From the fifteenth century onwards the centre of gravity of economic life in Europe moved from continental to seaboard countries as a result of the new discoveries in the west, the south seas and the far east, and as the visible rewards of exploiting them became known.(31) This westward shift of its economic heart, so to speak, transformed among the countries of Europe first Spain, since it was Spain which received into its treasury all the early wealth, then more dramatically and durably the Low Countries and England, for they were the three nations so placed as to gain immediately and most from the exploitation of the new world. France came later into the contest. The ensuing history of Europe is the history of these western nations including Portugal racing for the acquisitions overseas which were going free to the hardiest competitor. It was a competition England ultimately won. By the end of the sixteenth century she had resisted the encroaching attempts of Spain. Portugal never turned out to be a matching threat. By the end of the seventeenth century England had extinguished any serious Dutch rivalry in world commerce. In the eighteenth century she was to beat off successfully a challenge from the French. The thorough ideological involvement of the fate of all Englishmen in these struggles at sea, their equally obvious relatedness to trade, and their reliance, for success, on the men and skills trained in commercial enterprise, so that in 1600 England's could be said to be an inescapably commercial destiny, made it inevitable that the long-lasting hostility to men of trade would not last for ever, or much longer. Indeed, what we see as a loud and bitter commercial argument in seventeenth-century literature is not so much the death agony of an old attitude as the birth of a new.

Paralleling this change in England's relation to the world at large, we recognize during the same period an internal change no less painful and all involving: the commercialization of English social institutions and authority, and in time English social attitudes themselves. The bare statistics of commerce from 1500 to 1660, let alone the complaints of imaginatvie moralists and rhetoricians in the same period, tell a story of the multiplying and the systematizing of projects of financial profit, of ever more rapidly increasing trading activity, of speculative voyages getting less speculative and more informed and precise in their determination, of new ventures and material activities of all sorts. If these developments demonstrate a single general truth about what was happening, they tell us and show us that in a very short space of time skill and information were replacing wonder, while specific material purposes and the calculation of likely advantage, admittedly still often accompanied by audacity of a rare sort, were superseding the open childlike curiosity of the early discoverers. They tell us that spirituality was giving way, worldly ambition gaining ground; ambition still heavily idealized, of course.

A single demonstration of this materialization of curiosity in the period under review may be suggested in the history of the merchant adventurers during those years. A century and a half before the founding of the Bank of England in 1694, the last solid proof and authorization of England's commercialized national character, 'the Mysterie and Company of the Merchants Adventurers for the discoverie of regions, dominions and places unknown'(32) had set off on its venture of exploration and hope. The very title chosen by the voyagers shows how uncalculating and open-minded was their enterprise; it is commerce they are spurred by, but commerce at the extreme end from calculated profit. Later enterprises followed very quickly, and just as quickly began to delimit and define their purposes with preciser exactness of description. In place of regions, dominions and places unknown, we read of companies setting out to establish themselves in Virginia in 1606, the Somers Islands in 1612, Ulster in 1610, 'Ginney and Binney' in 1618, Guiana in 1619, New England in 1620, New Scotland, or Nova Scotia in 1621, Canada in 1629, 'the Islands of Providence, Henrietta and the adjacent Islands' in 1629, Guinea in 1631, the East Indies in 1656, Africa in 1670, Hudson's Bay in 1668, Tobago in 1683, Greenland in 1692, and others. These are hard-headed if bold enterprises, investments and reachings out after advantageous profit, rather than gambles for glory and the chance of whatever fortune might fall with it; though no merchant voyager of the early time, not even the most fanciful devotee of the marvellous, would have been spurred on only by a sort of Tennysonian romanticism.(33) The companies suffered a decline during the seventeenth century because they were not flexible enough for the new needs of a rapidly changing economy; they were monopolies, and monopolies were found obstructive to trade. So they had to go. But in their initial multiplication and simultaneous concentration on specifically detailed rather than limitless schemes, and in what that means, as well as in their replacement by more up-to-date joint stock companies - in the development from Admiral Drake in 1577-80 circumnavigating the globe to Admiral Blake conducting a blockade of the United Provinces during the commercial war of 1653 - is imaged the change which had come over English commerce in that time, and over the estimation offered by Englishmen of their relation to the world at large.

Within the confines of England herself the evidence of this movement towards the commercialization of social life was even more striking. London became within a hundred years after Elizabeth the predominant fact of English life, a centre of government and business together, unlike Paris for example, and thus a central force in the national consciousness, a stronger than usual social magnet which attracted the spending gentry and the needy gentry, the legal profession, the financial profession and the riff-raff just because it was so big and busy a place, and which grew as a centre of consumption because of these additions which its own hyperactive nature had drawn within its range of influence in the first place. The omnipresent consciousness of trade, almost the obsession with it, in the literature, testifies to this rapid urbanization and commercialization; but of course much more than the specifically mercantile is to be related to such an economic transformation. It was in the early seventeenth century that the London season began. From the same time date hackney coaches, clubs, parks, and public gardens.(34) Consider what this must suggest about the overt concerns of the drama, say, even the drama of wit, in which a sympathetic merchant would be an anomaly, and which on its verbal surface appears so uninterested in saying anything about the serious or business side of life, or even admitting that there is such a thing. Set in the light of this recognition, such writings become significant in a fresh way and take on the relevance they always had, but seemed to wish to disclaim.

More than merely imaging this commercial revolution, internal and international, probing it with a distrustful concern for its human cost, and a hatred of its material valuation where that overrode other kinds too glibly, but also excited by its promise, is the literature of the English Renaissance whose more explicit documentations we have considered in the preceding pages. It would be a great mistake to leave the impression that only overt commercial writing testifies to the impact of the rise of capitalism on the minds of men. When space is short, as it must be in what is, after all, an introduction to the main analysis, we necessarily concentrate on those forms of writing in which the capitalist issue is most expressly canvassed, such as the drama, and leave relatively unemphasized the love poetry of the Renaissance, which appears less bound up with the subject of commerce, and, for the most part, the prose literature of the time, which has less comprehensiveness and less appeal. The relevance to the present theme of the urban documentations and moral questioning of the prose writings of Nashe, Greene and others is undeniable, however. Here is the literary evidence of the impact of the explosion of London social and economic life in the early capitalist period just talked about. And Renaissance poetry itself turns out to yield very interesting and instructive results, when, looking behind its terminology and avowed objects of attention, the reader isolates what kind of promptings may have led the poets to choose those precise themes, not others, and those formulations of them rather than some alternative expression, at that precise moment in history. Even in erotic verse, it appears, and even in its subtleties of rhetorical embellishment and poetic ornament, is to be found a kind of shadowing of the monetization of the life of the times from Wyatt to Shakespeare and beyond. In courtly love poetry the beloved is a mistress to be served; in Elizabethan love poetry beauty is represented as affluence. Such is the magnitude of the change of emphasis. Spenser's famous sonnet suggests the later, commercial, sensibility of love ('Amoretti', sonnet XV):

> Ye tradefull Merchants, that with weary toyle,
> do seeke most pretious things to make your gain;
> and both the Indias of their treasures spoile,
> what needeth you to seeke so farre in vaine?
> For loe my loue doth in her selfe containe
> all this worlds riches that may farre be found,
> if Saphyres, loe her eies be Saphyres plaine,
> if Rubies, loe hir lips be Rubies sound:
> If Pearles, hir teeth be pearles both pure and round;
> if Yuorie, her forhead yuory weene;
> if siluer, her faire hands are siluer sheene.
> But that which fairest is, but few behold,
> her mind adorned with vertues manifold.
>
> (1695)

Concerning such a poem's assumptions about the relation between beauty and conspicuous material treasure, rather than in its overt statement, whose closing couplet is made to gesture towards outweighing the whole of what has gone before, one finds much to ponder. There is a sense in which economic attitudes may brutalize even the way in which man apprehends his spiritual conceptions, it seems. This need not be a relevant comment if Spenser's were a unique poem in its age. But the reverse is true. It is representative. The story of the poetry of the sixteenth century is the story of 'the coronation of Lady Money'.(35)

2 COMMERCE APPROVED 1650-1700

The brand of drama fashioned and quickly accepted on the reopening of the theatres after the Commonwealth shows little inclination to explore the commercial side of the life of its time. Its overwhelming concern is with 'précieuse gallantry' and a 'thoroughly conventionalized social mode'. It perceives the comic rather than menacing aspects of those such as vulgar tradesmen, but also fops, pedants and rustics, who 'awkwardly misinterpret' the style they assume or are judged by, and relishes a different kind of comic experience in admiring the confident few of wit and grace.(1) This leaves little energy for the depiction of new experiences, and less inclination to probe the strain on given assumptions and seek to express fresh impulses of social desire. It is partly the dramatic mode itself which holds writers back here from exploring perhaps the most noteworthy area of their daily experience. This is shown by Granville's updating of Shakespeare's 'The Merchant of Venice' as 'The Jew of Venice' (1701), with the changes he considered the modern age demanded. In Granville's hands Shylock is trivialized as he is brought up to date. He cuts out Shylock's defence of usury, weakens his motivation, omits Solanio, Salerio and Tubal entirely, which has the same effect, and portrays him eating and drinking with and flattering his enemies. This renders Shylock an up-to-date embodiment of the money-making class at its least respectable, in fact a stock jobber, and at the same time a wretch of a villain too flatly unsubtle to hold any serious interest for us.(2) Obviously, the stock jobber is a serious figure by Granville's time; but the convention is refusing to allow him to be taken seriously.

An earlier example of the same actual attenuation of interest in commercial life in Restoration comedy, of the drama's running against the current of social change, is found in John Wilson's 'The Projectors' (1664), whose sharp, stingy usurer Suckdry and Exchange broker Squeeze are quite uncommercial in feature. Again the types call out for serious treatment, but do not get it. In the Shylock of Shakespeare we are shown how the money mind operates; in Wilson we see its frustration in the battle of wits. Squeeze and Suckdry, one might say, fail the etiquette test. To such a fineness of distinction has the moral analysis of Elizabethan and Jacobean drama, a drama so profound and many-sided in its involvement with the actuality of men's lives in its day, become tapered down in half a century;(3) or, perhaps it is better to say, to such a rigorous exclusion of most of life, not just of commerce, does the drama of wit naturally tend.

This narrowing of range, though often savage, need not entail the kind of misrepresentation which comes from misunderstanding or ignorance, for a convention is not to be judged by its omissions but by what it makes possible; and Restoration comedy achieves its own kind of truth, its own angle of vision. An example of this might be the output, dramatic and poetic, of Wycherley, who is radical in his hostility to the commercial man, and therefore not interested in patiently delineating his every type, but cannot be called facile because he dispenses with analysis in order to concentrate the impact of what he does see, and not out of slack conception. Yet we are very conscious of the distance between the world of Wycherley and the money world of the 1670s, the years of consolidation after the Dutch wars, and of colonization and trading expansion in America, in the Baltic and in the far east. Wycherley reacts to this now confident and powerful commercial energy by giving us Alderman Gripe in 'Love in a Wood' (1671), 'seemingly precise, but a covetous, lecherous old Usurer of the city', and James Formal in 'The Gentleman Dancing-Master' (1672), a fop, traveller pedant and 'old, rich Spanish Merchant' markedly not bearing the impress of a practical trading entrepreneur of the late seventeenth century. These distinctive and forceful portrayals convince as psychological creations; but they do not convince as commercial men, as professional city traders of the 1670s, because not filled out on that side.

Wycherley's position then is simple, strong and forthright. He despises the mercantile world for its materialism and coldness of heart; against it he upholds the generous ideal; and his merchant types fit in with and illustrate this estimate. Such as Alderman Gripe are damned because they live by calculation, or mistakenly try to do so, and calculation is damned because it is seen as the evil product of a spirit of possessiveness, with its emphasis on divided interests. All this Wycherley makes explicit in his poems. There we find him (Summers, 39) praising love for its power of

> Abolishing all Mercenariness,
> Or Fraud in Commerce, the worst Foes to Peace;
> By banishing all Int'rest or Design
> From Friendship, with those two Words, Thine and Mine.
> (1704)

The same point is made again repeatedly: in the poems 'Upon Friendship', 'The Idleness of Business', 'Upon Avarice', 'In Praise of Avarice' and others. It adequately explains what we find in the play. For Wycherley, like souls cannot commune over the worldly barriers erected by property, self-interest, business ambition, and since no relation more swiftly reduces to fraudulent antagonism than that of trade his antipathy to commercial attitudes comes through with special purity, and shows in the extremely unlikeable characters which they are given in his plays. It is interesting that the one instance in which Wycherley does come up to date in his commercial representation should be in 'The Plain Dealer' (1676), in which Manly, the captain of a merchantman's escort, declares that he has it in mind to turn merchant in his own right when he reaches the far east. But he is going to the far east because of the intolerable selfishness and acquisitiveness of life at home. We may be seeing in this detail no more than the Juvenalian pretext of withdrawal from a corrupt world, a pretext in an unexpected setting. Nothing affirmative is made out of the commercial intention. As in Juvenal withdrawal is the point, and it is no more than a starting ploy for the real discussion.(4)

Shadwell's articulation is less clear than this, because less thought out. On the one hand he appears willing to scoff at city values with a contempt which can be a match for anyone's,(5) yet perceives a mercantile culture is developing and making its presence felt outside the strict libertine code of Restoration comedy, and goes some way towards giving it literary expression. 'The Squire of Alsatia' (1688) is the play in which he comes closest to the new perception. Here the merchant Sir Edward Belfond stands as the centre and representative of positive values in the play, and it is of interest that he does so for his possession of those precise qualities which have made him commercially and socially powerful in the world of business. He is a man of trade who has achieved style. Shadwell describes him as one who 'by lucky hits had gotten a great Estate, lives single, with Ease and Pleasure, reasonably and virtuously. A Man of great Humanity and Gentleness and Compassion towards Mankind; well read in good Books, possess'd with all Gentlemanlike Qualities'. Lucky hits or not, this is evidently a new slant on things of which a great deal could be made. Sadly, Shadwell fails to provide the expected encounter between mercantile and aristocratic values, and offers instead an opposition between town and country, and the chance is thus lost to widen, or rewrite, the terms of the comic convention of Restoration drama, and perhaps confer on it a new period of life (1720 ed., IV, 10).

It is Shadwell's peculiarity to receive from older dramatists (particularly Jonson) a scorn of trade and traders, yet, himself a Whig and city poet, to recognize the new mercantile spirit of his age, to feel with it, and to half-wish to give it utterance; his failure, not to insist on following his real rather than inherited insight. He offers us a hint of what might have been explored when Sir Edward Belfond expounds the new education worked out for young Belfond. The scene is not dramatically alive; but it might have been; and it opens a door into the life of the working world which we almost never see in such plays. Belfond, we read, went first to France and there (II, i)

> did all his Manly Exercises; saw two Campaigns; studied History, Civil Laws and Laws of Commerce; the Language he spoke well ere he went. He made the Tour of *Italy*, and saw *Germany*, and the *Low-Countries*, and return'd well skill'd in Foreign Affairs, and a compleate accomplished *English* Gentleman. (1688)

Ostensibly traditional in design, the programme is intended to produce a complete 'English Gentleman'. But it is practical in spirit, for instance in its emphasis on the laws of commerce, and this concern for the requirements of the real buying and selling world puts in question the whole Restoration code and the status of traditional education along with it. If the laws of commerce have become a subject for a gentleman to learn about then a new theory of culture is in the making. But Shadwell, having suggested the notion, lets it drop, and fails to take it up again in his other plays; not even in 'The Volunteers, or the Stock-Jobbers' (1692), which would seem to offer the perfect opportunity for an inside portrait of the commercial world. We have to wait for Defoe forty years in the future to see the mercantile emphasis on a realistic and practical education fully explained and argued for, and satisfactorily understood in its wider implications.(6)

It is possible that Ravenscroft's 'The London Cuckolds' (1681) displays some degree of relaxation of animus against the city world, since, in spite of all the usual gibes, its hero Loveday is a merchant himself and a stylish merchant at that, and this is new; but Loveday's commercial side is quite undeveloped, and Ravenscroft is obviously not siding with the men of commerce in writing the piece but producing another anti-mercantile comedy with an unexpected twist. Crowne's 'City Politiques' (1683) snipes at Whigs as traders lacking in fine taste, and in the same playwright's 'Sir Courtly Nice' (1685) we are introduced to a returning East Indian, perhaps the first nabob in English drama;(7) but the character turns out to be an impostor. In both these plays general satire is what Crowne aims at, and commerce is included only incidentally and superficially.

Dryden's is an altogether more complicated response to the whole issue of capitalist growth, but, as dramatist, even Dryden ignores commercial life in his early and middle years, and in general shows a disinclination to deal patiently with it as a subject presumably because it appears hostile to him by its association with his political opponents. Yet, he could not but recognize its centrality in his lifetime. Usually it is the context in which Dryden makes a specific utterance which is its suggestive feature, not the bare statement. For example, in his late play 'Don Sebastian' (1689) two merchants who come to buy Alvarez, Sebastian's old counsellor, and Antonio, an enslaved amorous Portuguese, seem brought on for no more requirement than the old simple one of comic relief, especially when the second merchant tries to make Antonio go through his 'postures' before he will clinch the deal. But there is a strange insistence in the scene. Certainly comic relief is there. But why the elaborate commercial pantomime, the testing of the human merchandise, the scrutiny of contract? What point is being made? Dryden's perennial theme is power, the issue of the play, and the merchants' presence adds to the discussion of the nature of ownership, and brings a separate extra reminder of it into the audience's recognition. Power of a sort is conferred by conquest and by purchase, but not power over man's spirit, and Antonio dishonouring his master the Mufti, and Sebastian despising the Emperor whose property he has become, are both reiterating that they are not mere stock. When Almeyda learns that the price of saving Sebastian is to be the sale of her own freedom she leaves him to die. Dryden here represents his rejection of the mode of valuation which Coleridge over a century later was to characterize as the essential outlook of commerce: treating persons as things.(8)

For all its apparent abstraction 'Don Sebastian', like all Dryden's plays, is rooted in the real issues of its time. There is a definite point in his wishing to show commercial possession as a grotesque parody of true authority. At the time of writing William III was assuming the English throne lost by James II; he was succeeding in this aim because, unlike James, he proved able to accommodate to a Parliament and nation impatient of intrinsic authority in Dryden's sense, and instead aggressively commercial, even proprietorial, in its attitude to monarchy. The Glorious Revolution was to Dryden little more than an economic and political charter; it was unsacred; it tied down the government of England to the stipulated conditions of a written contract. On the other hand, when he had handled the Pizarro story in 'The Indian Queen' (1664) and 'The Indian Emperor' (1665), a story ready made for anti-commercial propaganda, as a later age found out,(9) Dryden had made of the issue only a personal-moral confrontation between Montezuma and Pizarro with few colonizing overtones and no commercial dimension of any force; this despite the fact that Davenant had already half shown him the way in 'The Cruelty of the Spaniards in Peru' (1658). But this time Dryden leaves the emphasis out. Attacks on commerce by him would have lacked evident point in the 1660s, a period of especial confidence in science, trade and technical advance. In 'Amboyna' (1673) Dryden features the merchant heroes Beaumont and Collins with their leader Towerson rather as Englishmen than as trading adventurers, and, since he is wishing to make a political not a commercial point, offers plenty of evidence of the cruel Dutch character. But he says nothing of the despiritualizing effect of economic greed, which is after all why Dutch and English are there in the first place; 'Amboyna' was written to urge more of the commercial endeavour it portrays, not less. Commerce in Dryden's plays, in short, tends not to be automatic in its representation, but selective and flexible. When he stands back to consider it in its own right, as in the opera 'Albion and Albanius' (1685), he warns firmly against its dangerous spirit, which, he insists, must be regulated for the maintenance of social order; but when that is done he finds he can respond with ardour to its splendour and potency. The scene opens impressively on 'a Street of Palaces, which lead to the Front of the Royal Exchange', into which Mercury steps to enlarge on glorious commerce in the first spoken words of the piece. He addresses the Exchange behind him. It is a piquant moment in the history of drama; Dryden makes Heywood polite ('Works', ed. Miner, xv, 1976, p. 20):

Thou glorious Fabrick! stand, for ever, stand:
Well Worthy Thou to entertain
The God of Traffique and of Gain!
To draw the Concourse of the Land,
And Wealth of all the Main, etc.

(1685)

Then after a political allegory has been enacted in which the city escapes from Democracy and Zeal, and Albion is restored to true authority, Dryden's concluding vision is brought before us. It is the similar evocation of a sumptuous commerce admiringly loyal to the monarch, curbed in its republican tendencies and made harmonious and providential in its social influence. When Dryden attacks commerce he does so because of its tendency to reduce all value to price and to set men at one another's throats, but otherwise, as this piece shows, he can ungrudgingly admire its practical achievement; but not sympathize with it. This places Dryden separate from the main current of feeling in his lifetime, but not limitingly apart. He could at times share in the mercantile ebullience which he also criticized in its grosser aspect, and well represents in his variations of theme and emphasis over forty years, despite his lack of enthusiasm for what it was becoming, a shifting society striking out for itself new necessary valuations all the time. Perhaps for Dryden the old ones were being let too casually slip out of respect; but he is engaged with, not withdrawn from a nation not yet settled into that commercialized, acquisitive, imperialist role which was to be its character for the ensuing two and a half centuries and more.

There is little more to be said on the merchant figure in Restoration drama. The varied and reconsidering response of Dryden to the world of commerce is unusual in a dramatic mode which, among his contemporaries, maintains a high degree of indifference to that side of life right through into the early years of the eighteenth century. Congreve, for instance, ignores the subject of money-making and business in the 1690s as cuttingly as Etherege had done in the 1660s and 1670s. When Farquhar introduces 'Smuggler, An old merchant' into 'The Constant Couple' (1699) and reveals him as a fornicating hypocrite, has him cudgelled by Sir Harry Wildair, forces him to dress in women's clothes and listen to Vizard reciting his own dispraises, while making love to him in error, he is introducing into the play in up-to-date form the standard gibes of anti-mercantile drama from the earliest establishment of the tradition. This unchanging outlook of the drama of the age is both its weakness and its strength, as has been said. It is a feature of comic and serious modes alike, in that when the wit convention, rigidifying, separates and distances the drama from a close contact with life, it is only carrying further in its specific way a built-in preference for the ideal over the actual which is to be observed in the apparently opposite drama of heroic aspiration. Still, the plays are excellent when good. It is noteworthy that although in one sense the dramatic literature of the late seventeenth century disappoints as a reflection of the real England which was staking all on winning commercial supremacy over each of its worldly rivals, when Steele in 'The Conscious Lovers' (1722) tries to restore the balance and introduce Mr Sealand into public esteem he produces only a sentimental flop. Steele wishes to throw out prejudice. But he throws out audacity too, and with it the truth of comic statement, the kind of truth, for example, achieved by Wycherley in the plays we have already looked at. Wycherley may omit or exaggerate in his rejection of the economic relationship between men but does not get things wrong through being weak-minded.

If literary prejudice prevents late seventeenth-century playwrights from a fair portrayal of commercial man, other writers, or the same writers in another medium, are less hampered;.err, perhaps, in some cases, in the opposite direction. The poetry of the age, for example, is much more exploratory and fine in its response to the changing pressures of life, and so is prose, and muddies often enough a seemingly clear statement with subtle counter-suggestions usually too elusive for drama. Even so early a poet as Massinger, firm against commerce in all his writings when he deals with it, and unflinchingly so in his plays, dashes his attack on luxurious London in the following lines with a fairly tangible sense of admiration (Massinger, 'Works', ed. Edwards and Gibson, IV, 399ff.):

> From all parts of the *World*, thou hadst Supplie
> of what was wanting to thy *Luxurie:*
> *France, Spaine*, and her *Canaries* sent thee *Wine*:
> slav'd *Cyprus, Sucketts*: stately *Florence*, fine,
> and well-wrought *Silkes* (ripp'd from the labouring wombe
> of the poore *Worme*, that should have byn her *Tombe*):
> *Barbary, Sugers: Zant, Oile: Tapistrie*
> t'adorne thy prowd *Walls*, *Brabant* made for *Thee:*
> Nor were the *Indies* slowe to feed thy *Sence*
> with *Cassia, Mirrhe* (farr fetch'd with deere expence):
> The Sea, her *Pearle:* and many a boystrous knock
> compell'd the sparkling *diomond*, from the *Rock*,
> to deck thy *Daughters:* In a word th' adst All
> that could in compasse of thy wishes fall;
> But theis great *Guiftes* (abus'd) first bredd in *Thee*
> a stupid *Sloth*, and dull *Securitie*
> the *Parent* of *Destruction*.
>
> (c. 1625)

In spite of the date of the piece, which makes it exactly contemporary with Massinger's anti-commercial plays considered earlier, there is a notably complex tone in the passage. It is not to read false suggestions into it, surely, to recognize in the affirmatives of 'sent thee *Wine*', 'made for *Thee*', 'nor were the *Indies* slowe', 'compell'd the sparkling *Diomond*' and so on an undercurrent hardly less emphatic than the lines' overt moral message. As dramatist Massinger is considerably less complicated than this. Such is the openness of poetry to new pressures of feeling. Donne's love poems provide several well known instances of the same ambivalence, and Herbert's utilization of commercial imagery as a means of talking about spiritual themes, for instance in 'Redemption', is another example of this colouration, or colonization, of one area of life by the pervading experience and spirit and discussion of the world of trade.

It is in poetry too that the influence of Bacon begins to make itself felt. But it is a process that happens obliquely. Bacon had recommended commercial enterprise, or the enterprising spirit, because he saw it as furthering practical improvement, and a similar indirectness qualifies its emergence as a fit and then fashionable subject for polite verse. The writer who could not bring himself to praise commerce as such could and did find it possible to praise patriotic merchant seamen, and speculative discoverers, and military leaders and admirals helping to win the seas for England; such were Waller, Denham, and Dryden as poet. We often feel Bacon near when he cannot be unmistakably pinned down, and sometimes the resemblance is misleading. Thus it is tempting to claim a Baconian prompting behind the disparagement of chastity in Milton's 'Comus' (1634) and its recommendation that all things exist and have been created in order to be exploited and put to use, and as a matter of fact it may well be that a nudge or tributary from Bacon's thought finds its way into the argument. But there are other and greater influences at work here, including Shakespeare, Marlowe and Spenser, and in any case Milton is not Baconian. He was so for a period in his youth, perhaps. But in its mature formation his mind is directly contrary.(10)

Even in Milton, though, we can see a remarkable separation of moral attitudes between the theological view, so to speak, of commercial and technological enterprise, which frowns on it as dubious and assigns it to the fallen angels, and the practical political view, which accepts and recommends it, and encourages its furtherance as a necessary desirable part of social life. As in other writers, the reconciling explanation for some of Milton's diverging statements is to be found in their specific contexts: he is against commerce in his Restoration writings, that is in 'Paradise Lost' (1667) and in 'Paradise Regained' (1671), for it during the interregnum. When the devils are shown mining and experimenting in 'Paradise Lost' under the obsessed leadership of Mammon, when Jesus in 'Paradise Regained' impresses on Satan the fate of civilizations which 'in height of all their flowing wealth dissolved' (II, 430), and a few lines later distinguishes between the gainful impulse and the true end of effort, the poet is censuring Restoration England's prominent feature: acquisitive materialism. Compared with such unworldliness, Milton's outlook as Commonwealth secretary twenty or thirty years before had been thoroughly committed and involved. He had written letters and communiqués and carried on extensive negotiations to push English trade and secure England's political and commercial advantage in the world, and had promoted energetically the renewal and extension of commercial and diplomatic treaties which he identified with the good of his nation.(11) Perhaps we may think of Milton as converted from mercantile commitment when his party of government fell from power and was replaced by another. Perhaps the difference lies in whether a godly or an ungodly ideal seemed to him to be the one being pursued. But the line is becoming very blurred. Commercialism may be and is frowned on; commerce certainly is not; but are the two ever really found apart?

Milton, we note, in his secretarial despatches, invokes the national good when he recommends English trade. Such patriotic praise of a once despised calling became more and more common as the century progressed. Like the idea of the advancement of learning, it is one of the formulations which helped to make commerce a respectable subject for verse. The matter may be put this way. Heywood's Gresham vision in 'If You Know Not Me, You Know Nobody' becomes restated, refined, stripped of its merely class associations, and shared and accepted widely enough to become in spite of a persistent hostile voice the general national sense. Not that the later writers consciously adopt Heywood's view; perhaps without realizing it they come to find they are sharing his viewpoint. But we discover in their work an urge not felt to be necessary by Heywood or Dekker to spiritualize the material emphasis of bourgeois, now national, boasts, and cut it out, or at least make it less gross, refining it into a pure-seeming, still worldly, but more idealistic form.

This is how Denham incorporates the idea into his poem 'Cooper's Hill' (1642), for instance, which may be called the first important poetic statement in the present period of discussion of the idea that trade works in a naturally beneficent and attractive way. It is trade Denham is talking about, we need to remind ourselves, for the fine-spun theorizing might obscure the fact otherwise, but already trade sublimated into enhancing energy.(12) He celebrates the generous River Thames, as he terms it, which unlike guilty violent rivers elsewhere cherishes the wealth it attracts, which is a wealth not found scattered in its gravel, but lining its banks. Denham's idea is that the river first draws to itself the world's produce, then returns it back again in godlike bestowal on the world at large. It is a vision of harmonious profitable interchange, commerce in both senses of the word. The Thames therefore is 'the world's exchange', a service centre, but one which 'makes both *Indies* ours' (lines 187, 183). At this point imperial ambition merges with commercial ambition, the collocation referred to earlier, and from their union, beneficial to the world besides, is produced England's new greatness. Under Denham's graceful gesturing in such lines a significant about-turn of the moral outlook of centuries is in the process of being gradually engineered: the selfish is being recast as the social impulse. Such is the meaning of the lines (184-7) describing how the visiting Thames, as the poet puts it, that is the band of gain-hungry trading adventurers who use and take over the river, and subject it to their enterprises

Finds wealth where 'tis, bestows it where it wants
Cities in deserts, woods in Cities plants.
So that to us no thing, no place is strange,
While his fair bosom is the worlds exchange.

(1642)

Technically, Denham is content to remain vague. He conveys no sense of marine insurance or sweating porters, or the sticky business details of an import or export deal. His vision is of a commerce which confers on gainer and loser alike in the English drive for territorial dominance overseas, so that there is no loser, a material increase and visible benefit. This vision or beautiful abstraction rolls commercial energy up into a single compound with growing wealth, patriotic fervour, technical advance, civilization and harmonious beauty ('Cities in deserts, woods in Cities'); and thus the economic achievement, once secured, is seen as leading outwards into an ever more perfect realization of the morally good. There is no need to have doubts about the morality of exploitation and subjection, if this is the truth of the matter. Fine culture is seen as brought within the reach of all by good trade returns, which incidentally raise England to international eminence, and no longer are drossy in this transfiguration. The marked change from Heywood's portrait of the money-jingling Gresham, who would have appeared vulgar to the polite witty readers of Denham and hence distressed them, but perhaps distresses us less, may fairly be traced to the diffused influence of Francis Bacon in a generally more refined and sophisticated era. From the Heywood tradition comes the hearty commercial statement. From Bacon comes the impartially argued case for enterprise and advantage seeking. Mingling, the two aspects issue in Denham's excited subtle apprehension of a world perfecting its material condition by the reciprocal action of trading endeavour. Such is the accommodation poetry starts to make to the facts of life in the England of the working out and implementation of the Navigation Acts.

Denham transforms a crude vision of commercial dominance, Heywood's, into a subtle one because he chooses to emphasize the generous re-bestowal of wealth in the flow of trade, of which naturally there must be some, if less than he is willing to claim. He plays down the relevance of the antagonistic element. Since nevertheless the idea is essentially a boast that England is the world's richest country, or the moral build-up to a boast that she might become so in the near future, it is an idea always tending by its nature to revert to the crude form. Cowley's ode 'To the Royal Society' (1663) keeps the discussion of Bacon's experimental and discovering mission, which he sees the royal scientists as continuing, as they did themselves, energetically on the idealistic level throughout, but it is with an effort that he succeeds in doing so. Sometimes a subterranean suggestion of robuster ambitions seems to press to the forefront of attention. For instance, here is his exhortation to the Royal Society to keep pressing further the limits of the known:(13)

> From you, great Champions, we expect to get
> These spacious Countries but discovered yet;
> Countries where yet instead of Nature, we
> Her Images and Idols worship'd see:
> These large and wealthy Regions to subdu,
> Though Learning has whole Armies at command,
> Quarter'd about in every Land,
> A better Troop she ne're together drew, etc.
>
> (1663)

A reader coming upon this in the seventeenth century might be forgiven for taking it at its apparent face value; but in fact the lines are a metaphor for scientific research. This, it may be, is the case of a piece of writing managing to be truer in its figurative than in its referential meaning.

Exactly the same cultivation of ambivalent meanings, the material one overlaying the spiritual, controls the organization of Cowley's Pindaric ode 'To Mr Hobs', in which he urges that we need to find out and exploit new territories since the lands of the ancient world have become exhausted and useless. His phrasing leaves it to be supposed that Cowley is speaking literally and lamenting that the fields of Italy have finally turned barren, and need replacing by new countries, but it is obvious that he is 'really' talking about modes of knowing and doing.

In Richard Fanshawe's 'The Lusiad' (1655), a translation from Camöens, Gama reaches the land of Calicut in canto VI and covers himself with true glory, the product of honourable and disinterested endeavour, the poet reminds his readers, not of monetary riches. This is the Chapmanesque point of view. But in canto VII, when Gama greets the Indian ruler, he brings out the primary argument and purpose behind his whole undertaking. This is: simply trade. Gama proposes to the Indians an amicable trading league free of animosities because limited to superfluities on each side. Then in the succeeding stanza he offers to extend the agreement to include armed support in case of need. To such contradictory impulses is the heroic argument driven when an old chivalrous ethic finds its terminology being stretched wider and wider, but not stretched far enough, to cover modern aggressive capitalism. Here are the revealing lines (stanzas 62, 63):

> Then if thou wilt, with *Leagues* and *mutuall Tyes*
> Of *Peace* and *Friendship* (stable and divine)
> Allow commerce of superfluities,
> Which bounteous NATURE gave his *Realms* and *Thine*,
> (For *Trade* brings *Opulence* and *Rarieties*,
> For which the *Poore* doe sweat, the *Rich* doe *Pine*)
> Of two *great* fruits, which will from thence redound,
> *His* shall the *glory; thine*, the *Gain* be found.

And (if it so fall out, that this fast knot
Of *Amitie* be knit between you two)
He will assist thee in all adverse lot
Of *Warr*, which in thy *Kingdom* may issue,
With *Soldiers, Arms* and *Shipps;* and coldly, not,
But as a *Brother* in that case would do.

(1655)

With uncommon foresight the Indian advisers recognize that any commercial agreement means a European takeover, and refuse to do business. But the poem ends on a note of impatient desire in the travellers, who have returned to Portugal, for the new lands waiting to be discovered, all different from each other, but all of them rich and all of them going free. Fanshawe has some difficulty maintaining in Gama, the commercial traveller, the heroic image of Gama the voyager, and endurer, but he tries.

A fourth instance of the same change in poetic sensibility to capitalism is in Edmund Waller's handling of commerce in his celebratory piece 'On the Death of Cromwell' (1659). Waller's aggressive political slant, compared with Denham's attitude in 'Cooper's Hill', may be due to the fact that his subject is a military and political leader, whereas Denham's is not. But only a thickening of the poetic sensibility explains how, in place of the earlier poet's conception of welcoming openness in trade, Waller decides to stress England's superiority to the countries she is annexing. It is a double kind of superiority, he explains, spelling the matter out: England's takeover of their produce, and also her freedom from the heat and sweat which have made it possible (lines 57-64):

The taste of hot Arabia's spice we know,
Free from the scorching sun that makes it grow;
Without the work, in Persian silks we shine;
And, without planting, drink of every vine.

To dig for wealth we weary not our limbs;
Gold, though the heaviest metal, hither swims;
Ours is the harvest where the Indians mow;
We plough the deep, and reap what others sow.

(1659)

Under so material an emphasis the bearings have appreciably narrowed. Yet the poem as a poem is far from crude because Waller aims at a musical witty exultation, and not at framing a brash congratulation of his native country on its profitable trade figures; the line on gold swimming to England, for example, is not conceived out of cupidity.

And in fact Waller's most persistent attitude is, like Denham's, Cowley's and Dryden's, ambivalent, and less pat than even these explicit lines might suggest. The spirit of his poem 'Of Salle', written against the Sallee pirates, is imperial rather than commercial, that is a shade more idealistic; and a more sombre note still deepens the perceptions of the poem 'Of A War With Spain, and a Fight at Sea', and suggests the littleness of material commitments when placed beside valour and greatness of soul. Here Waller sees in the conflict greed, ambition and honour all mixed up together, but further than that draws in the vanity which bounds all man's passionate desires, and takes our attention from material to spiritual considerations without rejecting them in the process. For instance, when the Spanish ships sink to the bottom with their rich lading, destroyed in the fight of which they are the prize, Waller first moralizes on the futility of men's striving desires, 'Whose rage buries as low that store/As avarice had digged for it before' (lines 69-70). When the Spanish leader and his wife accept inevitable death with 'spices and gums about them melting', a line nicely catching the panegyrical shift, the brave English, moved by a heroism they also share, forget the rich spoil to save their enemies. Thus competitive greed destroys itself; yet from its futile struggle comes honour; a struggle not futile, then. Is one to see this as a rejection of commerce? Hardly; for the honourable and the greedy men are the same, and if the desire for material wealth may seem less admirable than self-sacrifice, it demands sacrifice. A clearer instance would be hard to find of the merging of a moral and material vision, not their juxtaposition but their growth into one attitude, in the poetry of the Navigation Code.

The same reformulation may be observed in 'On St James's Park' (1661). Waller pictures law, trade, art, conquest and empire as integral aspects of civilization, fibres in the one growth, whose law of development the king ponders in his meditations in the royal park (lines 115-120):

> Here, free from court compliances, he walks,
> And with himself, his best adviser, talks;
> How peaceful olive may his temples shade,
> For mending laws, and for restoring trade;
> Or, how his brows may be with laurel charged,
> For nations conquered, and our bounds enlarged.
>
> (1661)

This approving attitude to trade and traders,(14) which groups them confidently with civilization and learning, is the new note in poetry, but one cannot readily assign a date to it. It is in Denham but not in Donne. It is not characteristic of the Elizabethans. But, particularly after Waller, so much more influential than Denham, the identification of trading business with the national interest becomes a commonplace in literature as it became a working assumption of the age. It was seen that the trader makes a profit not exclusively out of those around him, his neighbours and fellow countrymen, but out of people, if out of people at all, who are far distant, and also that all at home in their degree appear to benefit from the new wealth and opportunities the trader has outstandingly helped to provide. Can this man be attacked as a public enemy? Can his beneficial work be immoral? Rather the old theory of sin was felt to need redefining, and bringing into line with real life.

One sees how hard to resist this new ideal must have been, backed by Bacon's great and increasing moral authority among the Puritans, during the middle years of a century identified in practice with commerce and increasingly persuaded of its commercial destiny. Bacon's emphasis on empirical knowledge, only possible by research, and on the world's readiness to man's use, which demands exploitation, lies behind the growing enthusiastic celebration of science and empire in literature and its connected sympathy with commercial man. Waller helps to spread the Baconian view by offering his age the articulation it needs. In 'Of Divine Love' (pub. 1685) he says that knowledge and use are what confer final meaning on the material creation, an orthodox observation whose Baconian slant Waller heavily emphasizes by adding that knowledge requires that things be tested by proof and trial and that use means the taking of advantage. Creation, it seems, in the new application of the theory, has waited thousands of years for the men of the seventeenth century, particularly the Englishmen, to complete its destiny by mapping and cataloguing it, exploiting it, and making a profit out of it for themselves. Creation at first (ii, 122)

> a palace was without a guest,
> Till one appears that must excel the rest;
> One! like the Author, whose capacious mind
> Might, by the glorious work, the Maker find;
> Might measure heaven, and give each star a name;
> With art and courage the rough ocean tame;
> Over the globe with swelling sails might go,
> And that 'tis round by his experience know;
> Make strongest beasts obedient to his will,
> And serve his use the fertile earth to till.
>
> (1685)

Here the movement of thought is from valuing knowledge to valuing use, from contemplation to action. One might go further. Lines 5-8 above express Bacon's vision of illimitable tested certainties; in the next two, without amplification as yet, is suggested Defoe's exploiting creed. A comparison with what may look like a similar sentiment in Marlowe's 'Hero and Leander' (1598), in which Leander dissuades Hero from futile virginity, shows how the emphasis has changed in half a century.(15)

I have concentrated on Waller because he was influential, but of course the ideas he popularizes in these poems were already popular, and are to be met with generally in the literature of the late seventeenth century, prose and verse alike. A real life example of the kind of intellectual-practical and commercial allegiances Denham and Waller both project in imaginative writing is the brimming world described by John Evelyn in his fifty-year-long 'Diary' (1650-99). Evelyn's pages are packed with descriptions and experiments, improvements, discoveries, mercantile activities, commercial projects, scientific pursuits, speculative attempts on the difficult or impossible for their own sake and for the good they may produce. All these forms of endeavour are combined together as if Evelyn recognizes no basic difference between them; and this is indeed the case, for the spirit informing the personal record is purely Baconian: intellectual, practical, copious, exact. Ink capable of printing twelve pages or more at a time, exotic beasts from the East Indies, all-purpose varnish, improved shipping, versatile keels, the refining of taste, wonderful objects brought by traders from the other side of the world, the improving of husbandry, and of the dominions, Josiah Child's newly laid-out estate:(16) these are some of the projects and speculations he enters into. There are many others. Through them all runs the persistent, high-minded note of improving enterprise, evidently the temper of Evelyn's world, which a perception of vicissitude, in Evelyn's case, keeps from the brash.

When Evelyn theorizes, as opposed to just observing, he declares what his observations here all imply: the supreme need of men for technical mastery over their environment, and the alliance with this aim of commercial endeavour, in its widest interpretation. His interesting essay 'Navigation and Commerce' (1674), though primarily a political stab at the Dutch during the third Dutch war, goes out of its way to note of the world that its physically fragmented and shattered state, the result of the eroding influence of constant change, producing everywhere an infinite number of rivers, bays and trending shores inviting development and exploration, which might be thought to resemble one compound of ugly imperfections, is truly a feature proving that it 'seems, from the very Beginning, to have been dispos'd for Trafick and Commerce, and even Courts us to visit her most solitary Recesses.'(17) On a globe thus made for mercantile effort the ship, its vehicle, must be the most beautiful possible object, and the most wonderful and potent, and so Evelyn goes on to argue it is; for the ship, he says, the gain-seeker, 'undertakes to fathom the World it self; to visit strange, and distant Lands; to People, Cultivate, and Civilize un-inhabited, and Barbarous Regions, and to proclaim to the Universe, the Wonders of the Architect, the Skill of the Pilot, and, above all, the Benefits of Commerce' (p. 4). The spirit of commercial gain, which drives these purposes, is unequivocally recast as the moral life force. 'In a word, Justice, and the Right of Nations, are the Objects of Commerce: It maintains Society, disposes to Action, and Communicates the Graces, and Riches which God has Variously imparted' (pp. 14-15).

It is to be added that Evelyn's personal application of this new perception of things is religious. Commerce leads him back to God. Thus he rhapsodizes on the magnet as proof that the Almighty may please to choose the humblest object, such as even that 'dull *Pibble*', for his most astonishing effects (p. 61), and recommends that men should receive the truth of this fact as an instruction to their pride. But others, for instance Joseph Glanville, reflect the same general sense of all forms of effort being irrigated by profit hunger without forcing any special religious connections upon it or upon us. In 'Plus Ultra' (1668), whose title tells its own story, Glanville says in a single large congregation of references that, by the invention of the compass (p. 80),

> *Commerce* and *Traffique* is infinitely *improved*, the *other* half of the Globe *disclosed*, and that on this side the *great Sea better* understood. The *Religions, Laws, Customs*, and all the *Rarities* and *Varieties* of *Art* and *Nature*, which any the most distant Clime knows and enjoys, are *laid open* and made *common*; and thereby the *History* of *Nature* is wonderfully *inlarged*, and *Knowledge* is both *propagated* and *improved*. (1668)

A sad onlooker at the commercialization of English culture, Sir William Temple, throws a shaft into the vitals of this simplifying euphoria when he admits that navigation as a science is probably improved over that of ancient times, as is claimed, though ancient navigation was impressive, but points out that the increase is rather in information and material wealth than in knowledge, and argues that modern men probably make less valuable use of the information they enjoy than the despised ancients would have done in their place. Temple goes on to remind his readers that men still know only a tiny amount in comparison with what remains unknown, and widens the issue to that of culture, and true culture, in an attempt to cure his contemporaries of what he calls their 'sufficiency'.(18) Sufficiency is defined as a mixture of pride and ignorance, which too readily confuses factual information with wisdom; here is a pointer forward to the moral criticism of a commercial civilization in the writings of Swift and Pope.

Temple's, however, is now definitely the minority view. To the signs of the intellectual and moral acceptance of commerce in the writings of Evelyn, Pepys's diary adds more, and different ones; for Pepys, though less intellectual than Evelyn, is sharper in his social observation, and brings us close to the now rapidly accelerating commercialism and scientism of the time by which old haughty attitudes to men of trade were put on the defensive, and found themselves tending to be cast aside as irrelevant, and were forced to retreat before the new triumph of brashness and material confidence. Of this general yielding, Sandwich's exchange with his wife recorded by Pepys on 20 October 1660 is an example. Pepys tells us that she remarked 'that she would have a good Merchant for her daughter Jem';(19) whereupon Sandwich scoffingly preferred the prospect of his daughter destitute rather than tied to a citizen's apron. Sandwich, the Frenchified courtier, here speaks as courtier, anti-mercantile in the old fashion, while his wife's is the newer voice. Pepys likes merchants, it is obvious, because they seem to him to be affirming and practical, the coming type of man in a new exciting world, and on many occasions notes in his diary the good company and alert instructive conversation which he finds among them when he seeks their acquaintance out, or they his. At one time he learns the manner of northern collieries, at others of specific commercial techniques, of the spread of trade, of some of the varieties of risk and return which a now thriving capitalism is increasingly providing.(20) Pepys dabbles in a couple of these ventures diffidently. He wants the profit, but does not want the risk. Merchant adventure is not for him.

From Evelyn and Pepys we derive a documentation of the economic life and stirring commercial mood of Restoration London. They provide the context for some of the poetry, for instance Dryden's paean to commerce in 'Annus Mirabilis' (1667), yet for all that are only allusive; they are mere diarists. Literature, one feels, should provide an outright affirmation of the revolution here hinted at so repeatedly, but never yet quite argued through, if indeed such a revolution took place, in the way men assessed the economic function and the economic relationship in human life. If the change is so epochal, it may be demanded, where then is its adequate definition to be looked for in imaginative literature? The answer is forthcoming, but not just yet. Only when we encounter the profound apprehension of a new order that is set down extensively in Defoe's complete writings, of which the half dozen novels are allegorical affirmations, and 'Robinson Crusoe' the great definition, almost the myth of modern life, do we sense that the modern age finds its true articulation. But there are anticipations of Defoe; and more distinct than any other is the discussion of the new outlook needed by a new phase of civilization in Thomas Sprat's 'History of the Royal Society' (1667).

Intellectually, the base of Sprat's thought is Baconian science. He adds nothing to it. But he certainly testifies to its spread, and also to its coarsening, for unlike Bacon, whose mind was on higher ambitions, Sprat breathes the essential spirit of expanding commerce. He means the allusion flatteringly when he hopes that international contact between scientists will help to make the Society 'The general *Banck*, and Free-port of the World!'(21) He is more directly challenging and literal than Bacon in the importance he attaches to the specific mercantile function; for example, classing traders explicitly with the scientists and the philosophers in the progress of mind, and perhaps seeing them as all the more admirable for being advantage-seeking and practical, not theoretical. Hence merchants' language, along with that of artisans and countrymen, is preferred in the well-known phrase as truer than the language of wits and scholars (p. 113). Sprat, lacking Bacon's degree of intelligence and Defoe's imaginative capacity, that is to say lacking poetry, cannot grasp the full implication of what he is saying, and seeing, but half conceives that a transvaluation of culture is implied in the new priority he encourages so single-mindedly. He is assured that the change is a good thing, and that it is massive. All this we can fairly read into Sprat's praise of King Charles II for recommending that the shopkeeper Graunt be elected to the Royal Society in spite of opposition, and that snobbish contempt for him because he was only a shopkeeper should be silenced and ignored. Sprat writes: 'It was so farr from being a prejudice, that he was a Shop-keeper of London; that his Majesty gave this particular charge to His Society, that if they found any more such Tradesmen, they should be sure to admit them all, without any more ado' (p. 67).

This urbane pronouncement, which may be too urbane, and perhaps double-edged, tells its own story, of course, if it means just what it says; but Sprat's single-minded reception and application of it tells more. For him, all merchants are now to be merchants of light. As with previous idealists and internationalists, though, Sprat's world optimism wears a firmly English face. London is the city he settles on as the natural habitation of 'the Universal Philosophy' and 'the advancement of knowledg' when Babylon, Memphis, Carthage, Rome, Constantinople, Vienna, Amsterdam and Paris have all been enumerated and found wanting (pp. 86-7), and he has, of course, a supply of impartial reasons to advance for the convenient choice. London is 'the head of a *mighty Empire*, the greatest that ever commanded the *Ocean*'; she is 'compos'd of *Gentlemen*, as well as *Traders*'; because of her 'large intercourse with all the *Earth*' she is a city where 'all the noises and business in the World do meet' (pp. 87-8). We see without difficulty where this romantic rather than scientific progressivism leads, which less than a hundred years of actual history would turn discordantly back on itself: to the value judgment that London, which now outdoes all capitals in material supremacy, outdoes them all consequently, and by the same evidence, in spiritual culture, and is a new and better Athens. Sprat himself avoids crude materialism because of the elements of hope and excitement in his writing, and because he argues in plain faith, though claiming to be judging scientifically, when he stresses the noble inquisitiveness of British merchants and their contribution to civilization and enlightenment (pp. 155, 379-81, 125), and, comparing the 'industrious, punctual, and active *Genius* of men of *Trafick*' not unfavourably, to say the least, with the 'quiet, sedentary, and reserv'd temper of men of *learning*' (p. 129), judges that equal value is to be conceded to mercantile and intellectual effort.

Sprat's cast of mind was widely shared. By the closing decades of the century it had seeped through the thought of the age. Locke in 1688 and 1689, seeking to formulate his political and philosophical system, drew upon ideas 'which were already the commonplace of landowner and merchant':(22) the sanctity of contract, and accountability, and self-interest, and the priority of ownership. He returns to his age in the two 'Treatises on Government' (1690), a mirror-image of its capitalist convictions and further aspirations so accurate in character as to fix the assumptions of social theorists for more than a century. When Thomas Burnet in 1684 seeks to harmonize the two truths of revelation and science, and looks for a significant illustration to make his point, he finds the analogy he seeks in economic experience (preface):

> If a Prince should complain of the poorness of his Exchequer, and the scarcity of Money in his Kingdom, would he be angry with his Merchants, if they brought him home a *Cargo* of good Bullion, or a Mass of Gold out of a foreign Country? and give

> this reason only for it, *He* would have no *new Silver*; neither should any be Current in his Dominions but what had his own Stamp and Image upon it: How should this Prince or his People grow rich? (1684)

Press the analogy as it is intended and the prince is revealed as God, or perhaps the king of England, the merchants as scientists and philosophers and money as truth. By extension, to grow rich must be to achieve salvation. Here is a figure which moves beyond illustrating its argument and becomes an image of the thought of the time. That the metaphor, far from being original to Burnet, is frequent in the literature of the period, proves the prevalence of the attitude of mind under discussion.(23)

The old suspicion of trade as contamination, set against these defiant new claims now beginning to carry all before them, and to appeal to the whole world for their proof, comes after the Restoration to seem painfully out of relation with the facts. It persisted, of course. In Samuel Butler's 'Characters' (published 1759) the shopkeeper, the banker and the merchant are all crafty or downright frauds. The analysis could not be simpler. John Oldham's short, similarly uncomplicated judgment is that to be a trader is to be sordidly avaricious, that all forms of trade come down to one single form of trade, which is base, and that that is that. Perhaps some of Oldham's sweeping brevity is Juvenalian. But in spite of odd moments in 'A Satire Against Vertue' (1679) when the pull of the adventure analogy starts to work against the surface meaning, Oldham and Butler, along with the comic dramatists of the Restoration stage, are already looking old-fashioned: manning nearly deserted barricades. They are failing to respond to something in the age. So is Bunyan, one feels, though Bunyan is curious, morally so simple as to seem naive when in 'The Life and Death of Mr Badman' (1680) he stresses the commercial rule of life as being honest and dealing above board, but far from naive in his portrayal of Mr Badman, who plays the bankruptcy game in a cynical financing of his immoral life in a very contemporary fashion. Something in Bunyan, though, wants to refuse to acknowledge the actual developing new experiences of the life of the time. He is a throwback. Such writers are not to be judged deficient on the grounds that they are out of sympathy with the opinion happening to be gaining fashion during their lifetime. Opinion would swing round again a century later with double conviction. But they still look old-fashioned because in a fluid era their expression is a dry hard negative, too exclusive, too made up and too secondhand, being drawn from an older social phase, to apply directly to the real condition of the life of their time.

It is not that a writer lacks something in Restoration and Augustan England unless he falls in with the praise of commerce; Temple, Pope, and Swift all prove otherwise. But these writers confront directly the living thought of their time, and consider what can be said for it, and then deliver a judgment against it; not, consequently, a prejudice. One feels that such a writer as Oldham seems prejudiced against trade. From a suppler open poetic sensibility, for example Andrew Marvell's and supremely Dryden's, a more complex response might be looked for to the issue of commerce in the period under review, an issue so many-sided, so far-reaching, so new. Both poets do indeed assimilate the currents of experience in their time into their verse, and show a power of holding contraries in balance, which in an era of the reconstitution of sensibility is poetically a strength rather than a weakness. In Marvell's mysterious poems the public issues of the day, such as naval warfare and Dutch economic competition, mingle with the antipodes, the new world, exotic civilization, virgin lands, wondrousness, rarity and innocence. The poems thus reflect on commercial affairs continually, often without discussing them in so many words, and quite separately, it may be, and within a wider acceptation, than in the specific definition of the issue of trade in the poet's Parliamentary character. It is the pull of Marvell's imagination towards the strange that causes this kind of dislocation in his verse, of which there are many examples. In 'The First Anniversary of the Government under O.C.' (1655) Marvell enlarges on England's sea power, now capable of imprisoning other nations within the limits of their own lands, a pleasing paradox, then proceeds to speculate on whether or not the all-conquering English ships multiply by shedding leaves which then breed on the open waters, as do seafowl. This lovely image brings about a shift of perspective which loosens the poem's specificities, making them less significant. It is certainly still a poem in praise of mercantile and naval supremacy; but we have not explained it when we have desribed it as patriotic. Marvell's position on commerce is not one to be dogmatic about, given these ironies. In 'On the Victory obtained by Blake over the Spaniards' (1674, written 1657) he banishes wealth, the cause of war, to the bottom of the sea, but in 'Poem on the Death of O.C.' (1659) applauds as one of Cromwell's grand achievements that he 'stretch'd *our frontire* to the *Indian Ore*'. Thus at different moments worldly riches and empire are rejected and desired. Marvell's otherworldliness, rather than worldliness, is perhaps the stronger principle in his poetry. But his curiously tense imagination produces a sort of sensual intellection, as of the spirit hungering after the flesh, a very mysterious effect, and should hold us back from seeing him as finally uninterested in the seductions of the world: riches, power, profit. So should his political commitments, like Milton's, whose ambivalence of attitude he perhaps most nearly resembles.(24)

The supplest temperament of the age is Dryden's, and Dryden, because of his long writing period from the Restoration to the end of the century, is the poet who best reflects the changing currents of mood and the onset of material optimism in the years of commercial ascendancy in England; reflects, but does not share. In the plays, we saw, Dryden is in the final estimate wary rather than enthusiastic about trade, while responding, like Shakespeare, with unforced approval to its adventurous possibilities. So it is in the poems. In 'On the Death of Cromwell' (1659) the image of trade as parasitism is the metaphor he chooses to characterize those who fought in the Civil War for their own advantage, whereas Cromwell is imaged as a surgeon, opening the vein so as to staunch the blood. Holland, whose 'Idoll' is gain, buys peace from Cromwell later in the poem. Thus trade here is reduced to filthy materialism, a degradation of the spirit which Cromwell has transcended. This disparaging assessment is one to be met with in Dryden all through his writing life, but in 'Astraea Redux' (1660), written a year later, we are invited to look upon the expansion of commerce and power as introducing 'times whiter Series' of 'soft Centuries', that is the era of England's assumption of world dominion in commerce and in war. What has reconstituted base trade as something noble in a twelve-month period? Obviously, the changing political and poetic occasion. Can Dryden's basic attitude be gauged from these variations, it may be wondered? His tendency, when not disparaging mercantile effort, seems to be to go to the other extreme and contemplate its perfect cessation, perhaps because, actual commerce being distasteful, he finds it acceptable only in an ideal form. This suggests an instinctiveness of withdrawal.

But at the same time Dryden seems able to express the predominant feeling of his generation. This is a feeling of new hope, not necessarily Dryden's inward conviction but a sense he shares with his age sufficiently for him to provide for it a definitive expression.(25) He summarizes in 'Annus Mirabilis' (1667, stanzas 162-4) the scientific and commercial optimism of Restoration England.

> The Ebbs of Tides and their mysterious Flow,
> We, as Arts Elements shall understand,
> And as by Line upon the Ocean go,
> Whose Paths shall be familiar as the Land.
>
> Instructed ships shall sail to quick Commerce,
> By which remotest Regions are alli'd;
> Which makes one City of the Universe,
> Where some may gain, and all may be suppli'd.
>
> Then we upon our Globes last verge shall go,
> And view the Ocean leaning on the Sky:
> From thence our rolling Neighbours we shall know,
> And on the Lunar world securely pry.
>
> (1667)

This is very affirming of trade, certainly; indeed could not be more so, but notice what has happened to it. It has ceased to be trade as a known transaction, the securing of profit from another, and become profit all round. Providence has taken its place, and trade has been idealized out of existence.

In 'The Medall' (1682) Dryden once again characterizes commerce as destructive; it is 'living on the Spoyl'. Times have changed, and his expression has changed with them. Such oscillation is well exemplified in Dryden's double attitude to London, the centre of commerce, and its fullest expression, and to London's city population. If we recall his opera 'Albion and Albanius', dealt with above, and its moral, we may note here that in 'The Medall' too, written three years before, he curses and praises the capital city simultaneously, and argues that because of its double character, rich and dangerous, a double attitude is the only possible one to take to it. These discriminations are relevant because London is the centre and image of commercial endeavour. Dryden admires the prosperity and strength which expanding trade confers on king and people, but suspects the disintegrating tendency of the individualistic spirit behind commercial enterprise, and dislikes the political left wing. So the image he chooses for London is the river Nile, source of renewal and corruption, and in the same action (lines 173-4):

> the parallel will stand:
> Thy tydes of Wealth o'er flow the fattend land;
> Yet Monsters from thy large increase we find;
> Engendred on the Slime thou leav'st behind.
>
> (1682)

Dryden's ambivalent attitude is well projected here. Since the 'Annus Mirabilis' days, he has evidently been more sharply alerted to the political and religious menace lurking in the commercial spirit, and to its destructiveness of the principles of faith and loyalty which he holds as important. If a tendency can be discerned in Dryden's writing life it is the tendency to become more and more suspicious of commerce, not more sympathetic to it, and the reason seems to be that essentially, for him, the question comes down to one of attitudes to people as opposed to attitudes to property. For Dryden himself the vital relation is the human one. An appeal to interest or to profit always comes second to the claim of moral allegiance,(26) and this is the priority underlined in all his poems. Dryden thus defines for us in his optimistic verse the extravert commercial confidence of his England, but privately moves further away from it into distrust and dislike. He passes in silence by the founding of the Bank of England in 1694, an event which provoked a good deal of poor party verse on both sides of politics.(27) His mixed admiration and distrust of mercantile men, the distrust predominating, remind us of Shakespeare. What has changed, we may finally ask ourselves, in the century between? The answer is that the balance of national feeling has itself shifted round. In Shakespeare's day it was the admiration of commerce which was the minority view, whereas his suspicion of it was shared by nearly all. Dryden in his turn speaks for the minority when he attacks commercial men, and for his age at large when he looks on the optimistic and affirmative side. What has changed from the one age to the next is the truth that men take for granted. It has nearly changed completely round, but not quite; not yet.

3 THE MERCHANT AS HERO 1700-1750

In Dryden's closing years, Defoe, although approaching forty years of age, was only just beginning to involve himself in public discussion; and to consider the hand-over, so to speak, of the commercial issue from the unimpressed old poet to the enthusiastic younger journalist is to witness a kind of symbolic transference: from the spokesman of tradition to the modern apologist. From the point of view of the present theme, Defoe stands out pre-eminent among the writers of his age, because, being himself a trader, and not one of the most scrupulous, he brings authority and real personal experience to the discussion of the subject for, perhaps, the first time. Commerce is a subject which inspires him. He recognizes and insists that its commercial character is the most noteworthy feature of his age, and approves the development and wants to strengthen it. And yet, for all this, which sounds materialistic enough, Defoe's grasp of his subject is a strongly idealizing one. He looks to the moral and intellectual improvement of the human condition, not merely to its material increase, as his aim. He rarely mentions Bacon. But he is Bacon's true heir.

To read right through Defoe's 'Review' (1704-13) from beginning to end, to say nothing of its successor 'Mercator; or, Commerce Retriev'd' (1713-14), a more limited journal arguing for free trade to France, is to realize that Defoe's special authority and genius as a writer on trade stem from his uniting in himself two distinct kinds of insight: the kind of grasp of economic matters which is rarely found or looked for among imaginative or popular writers, and the human awareness, rarer still among economists, of the artist. That the latter is the predominating quality is shown by the fact that Defoe never achieves significance as an economic thinker. Always life breaks in and ruffles his theoretical demonstration, scatters the scheme he is laying down, and makes his page, at the cost of being technically unsatisfying, vitally humanized in its understanding and rendering of the subject. In the pages of the 'Review' when he talks of the balance of trade, or the treasure theory, fields of ripe corn, shut-up shops, gold dust, deserts, the condition of the bankrupt merchant, unknown lands, rival empires, the decaying English cloth trade and the latest city scandal distract him from his analysis; and these human issues hold his attention when mere theories, though his pages are full of speculation, do not. Admitting this theoretical fragmentariness, we may concentrate on what is chiefly striking to us in the present topic in Defoe's commercial writings: his strong idealizing apprehension of the beauty and function of the material world, his informedness and his vision, which are not obscured by the driest of details among some controversies which are very dry indeed.(1) Trade in the 'Review' is a hidden mystery, a dark gulf, the Rubicon, an undertaking that produces new worlds of untrod subjects, or a boundless ocean (i, 365; ii, 13; ii, 2). Such is the extraordinary imaginative urgency we are dealing with.(2)

Defoe is a visionary, but he is anything but unpractical. He recommends Harley's scheme to pay off England's war debts in 1711 by colonizing the territories of the south seas in the following unemotional way ('An Essay on the South Sea Trade', p. 39):

> This is then what we are to understand by a Trade to the *South Seas*, (viz.) that we shall, under the Protection, in the Name, and by the Power of Her Majesty, *Sieze, Take,* and *Possess*, such Port or Place, or Places, Land, Territory, Country or Dominion, *call it what you please*, as we see fit in *America*, and *Keep it for our own, Keeping* it implies Planting, Settling, Inhabiting, Spreading, and all that is usual in such Cases. (1711)

No illusions are held out here. 'All that is usual in such Cases' means slave labour, the extermination of indigenous races, which to Defoe was a measure morally unjustified but sometimes unavoidable, and all that history records, and which Defoe would certainly have known about, of the casual horrors of economic imperialism. What strikes us is his sense that men have reached a stage at which they no longer have it in them to resist the economic imperative. He admits of the Spaniards' policy of liquidation in South America, and in a different context, that ('Review', viii, 166-7):

> Speaking of *Human Policy*, abstracted from *Humanity, Justice, and Christianity*, I do not see how *Cortez* could do less than he did; *he saw* the Surprizing Wealth of the Country, *he saw* himself Environ'd with Mountains of Gold and Silver, an Immense Wealth, Fertility, and Production of all kind; Which Way should he propose to Conquer this Country for his Master? (1711)

'I do not see how *Cortez* could do less'; such are the words. When this can be written the expedient, that is the economically advantageous, has been raised as a principle of conduct above the just, and we are at a significant turn, or downturn, in morals. For Defoe is clear that the Spaniards were morally unjustified; but that that makes no practical difference. To put the matter the other way round may be more appropriate: he sees Cortez as having had no option, realistically, but does not excuse the policy followed. Similarly, he notes the growing independence of the commercial rule of conduct from moral life, the development which Dryden so regretted, as when he remarks that those are properly 'Impossibilities in Trade, which cannot be done to Advantage; People may be said not to be able to do in Trade, what they cannot do with Profit, and get by' ('Review', ii, 90). But he is not thereby advocating what he acknowledges to be the case. He is admitting it, and refusing to pretend about it. If Defoe were in favour of mere interested action, he would sound cynical, but, for all the openness of his imperialism, it is the Lockean obligation of use which he calls on, as in 'A New Voyage Round the World' (1724), to justify it and explain why it is necessary. Behind his aggressive exploiting approach to the material world lies an ardency removed from materialistic greed by its intense nature, and too passionate to resemble more than superficially the calculus of advantage of a later age.

We have seen the merchant appreciated by Waller, Dryden and Evelyn as the agent of material felicity, and equated by Sprat with the aristocratic ambassador; the summit of ambition, this last, of the rough old merchants of Dekker and Heywood, an ambition now finally realized. In the writing of Defoe we find along with all that the grander, less local estimation of the merchant as superman, as civilizing pioneer, as inheritor of the earth. In 'A Plan of the English Commerce' (1728, pp. 34-5) he writes:

> If *Greenland* and *Spitzbergen* are unsufferably cold; if Nature, not being able to support the Violence of it, leaves those Places uninhabited; the diligent Trader not being to be discouraged by Difficulties, flies directly thither; there among a Thousand Dangers, surrounded with Mountains of Ice, terrible, and Horrors enough to chill the very Soul to describe them, *Hunts* the great *Leviathan* of the Seas, and loads his Ships with the fat (BLUBBER) of a Thousand Whales.
>
> I might instance in the Severities of the torrid, as well as frigid Zone, and shew the Hardships undergone in Places scorch'd with the Violence of the Heat; and which are every Way as terrible in their Kind, as those of excessive Cold; such are the Diseases and Terrors of the long Calms, where the Sea stagnates and corrupts for Want of Motion; and by the Strength of the Scorching Sun stinks and poisons the distrest Mariners, who are rendered unactive and disabled by Scurvies, raging and mad with Calentures and Fevers, and drop into Death in such a Manner, that at last the Living are lost, for Want of the Dead, that is, for want of Hands to work the Ship.
>
> Yet nothing discourages the diligent Seaman, or the adventurous Merchant in pursuit of Trade, and pushing on Discoveries, planting Colonies, and settling Commerce, even to all Parts of the World. (1728)

The trader is a hero not only because he achieves the near impossible, going where even Nature almost dare not follow him, but because trade is intrinsically glorious and beneficial. Yet it is also universal, for everyone is a trader every day of their lives, and Defoe stresses this mixture of mystery and mundanity as something more wonderful still. Anticipating Adam Smith, but with a different purpose, he sees in the manufacture and distribution of a single pin, the smallest made article, the felicitously combined labour, needs, and recompense, of a multitude of peoples and lands ('A Brief State of the Inland or Home Trade', 1730, p. 13).

> To bring all this to the same Point: With what admirable Skill and Dexterity, do the proper Artists apply to the differing Shares or Tasks allotted to them, by the Nature of their several Employments, in forming all the beautiful Things which are produced from those differing Principles? Thro' how many Hands does every Species pass? What a Variety of Figures do they Form. In how many Shapes do they appear? From the Brass Cannon of 50 to 60 hundred Weight, to half an inch of brass wire called a *Pin*, all equally useful in their Place and Proportions?
>
> On the other Hand, how does even the least Pin contribute its nameless Proportion to the Maintenance, Profit, and Support of every Hand, and every Family concerned in those Operations, from the Copper Mine in *Africa*, to the Retailer's-Shop in the Country Village, however Remote. (1730)

As the eager tone of this suggests, Defoe is celebrating what the later and more famous economist was only to analyse. This is not to deny feeling to Smith,(3) and of course Defoe is analysing too; he wishes to bring out the interconnectedness of trading operations, hence of economic and social issues. But what impresses here is the commitment, the sense of pleasure, strange in any mere analyst, with which Defoe draws out the self-supplying mutuality of large-scale commercial enterprise, to which countless numbers of individual separate acts of bargain and sale, far from confusing and deflecting it, join to contribute, and which indeed they sustain. His warm description - 'with what admirable Skill', 'all the beautiful Things', 'all equally useful' - points to Defoe's ability to continue to feel wonder at something with which he is intimately familiar, being in his seventieth year when he wrote the lines, yet still engrossed by: something too which, conventionally, is still despised as mechanical and base. There is evidently for Defoe something magical in the operations of commerce, some strange kind of force which escapes prediction and by its secret agency overmasters his exceedingly knowing mind. His admiration, then, it is to be repeated, is not the dull astonishment of the outsider, but an expert's recognition of some incomputable dynamic behind the computable facts of trade and industry, of a mystery at the heart of things.

When Defoe speaks of trade in any general way, and his numerous minor tracts cannot delay us in the present constraining context, this sense of the grand harmony of men's energies and needs, and of the world's adaptedness to them, and of the limitlessness of its potential, is what he invokes; and it is this general aspect which is important. Interesting as Defoe's handling may be of the specific issues of his lifetime, such as the 'Asiento' treaty of 1713 and the South Sea Bubble of 1720 and others, we must concentrate on isolating his overall estimate of the relevance of the commercial issue to the life of his time, in which we are to see what he inherits, and what he adds, to the tradition of thought sketched in these pages.(4) Defoe's pressure on his countrymen to subjugate and use the world, his grief at delay and waste, his brimming excited knowledge of the high rewards and risks involved, his recognition that the chance is a short-lived one which will not return if missed: these are the impelling conceptions, whatever the latter's ostensible subjects may be, behind his greatest and best known writings.

Such is the message of 'An Historical Account of the Voyages and Adventures of Sir Walter Raleigh' (1720), written at the same time as 'Robinson Crusoe' (1719) and sharing its theme, and explanatory of its basic conception. Defoe recounts Raleigh's expedition to the Oroonoque at the age of sixty and in an address to the South Sea Company of his own time reminds them that the opportunity still lies there waiting to be taken up; or in the words of the book's title page, there the 'rich Country' waits to be 'Possess'd, Planted and Secur'd', with the consequence of 'immense Wealth and Encrease of Commerce'. 'Robinson Crusoe' (1719) and its sequel 'The Farther Adventures of Robinson Crusoe' (1719), but not 'Serious Reflections' (1720), the third part, go over the same theme, as do the other novels and adventure stories, and it is likely that this theme, the Baconian theme, the possibility of improving men's condition by the processes of discovery, agriculture and trade, was in all of them Defoe's primary reason for writing; at any rate, through them all the vision is held.

Naturally, for the kind of transformation Defoe anticipates, effort is needed, and therefore strenuous effort is another high Defoe priority: the sea is to be fished, the land cleared and tilled, the desert harvested of its ivory and gold, the animal kingdom tamed and trained. Every pamphlet and book on the subject reiterates the point. But always Defoe returns to contemplate the inexhaustibly teeming earth, mysterious, alluring, perpetual. 'What a treasure must lie upon that Desart!' he exclaims of Guinea, 'and what prodigious Numbers of Elephants must be found upon those wild abandon'd Plains.'(5) Over North America, he declares, stretches 'a boundless Extent of Woods, as well on the Hills as on the Plains, unexhausted, and indeed, unexhaustible', and as for South America, 'there is more gold every year washed down out of the Andes of Chili into the Sea, and lost there, than all the riches that go from New Spain to Europe in twenty years amount to'.(6) Curiosity, not greed, is the spring of the commercial impulse, which seeks to know 'what lies treasur'd up in the Bowels of the Earth, or in the Remote Parts of Uninhabited Climates, and Unnavigated Seas, Bays, Channels, and Retreats of the Waters'.(7) If the end result of such endeavour is to be 'immense Wealth' and 'Increase of Commerce', which Defoe positively hopes, the kind of phrasing he adopts shows us how spiritual, not material, his conceptions are; yet the material desire is an element too. Such exotic thrills, it may be said, are easily felt. But Defoe can see miracles in the commonplace no less than in the extraordinary. Here he is on the British herring:(8)

> The HERRINGS...come every Year in prodigious Shoals, with a voluntary sort of *Tender of themselves to the Net*, to the *Scots* Coast, where they present themselves to the *Scots*, as

their immediate Owners and Masters; they come to their very Doors, into every Creek, every Firth, every Bay, as if they Petitioned the People to enrich themselves; they cover the Seas with their incredible Shoals; and I have seen them in the *Firth* of *Edinburgh*, so *Thick*, that Boys have gone out in Boats, and toss'd them in with their naked Hands. Some are of Opinion, That at their first setting out their number is so prodigious, that they are equal in Bulk to the whole Island of Britain; from what Fountain they flow; where they begin their regular advance; what Hand directs their March, and appoints their Seasons; this is all unaccountable, they come exactly at the same Time, and to the same Places, as if they had Pilots with them that knew the way, or had been there before; and little varying in the Quantity, when they have waited upon us till we have glutted our Hands, that neither for Consumption at Home, or Exportation Abroad, we desire to take any more. They go on *Southward*, till having visited the whole Island of *Britain*, and that of *Ireland*, and effectually supplied us all, they disappear, as none knows whence they come, so none knows whither they go. They go to no other Countries, that we know of, but as if they should say, *our Commission is only to you, YOU the Subjects of the* British *Crown, if you have done with us, we are not to be a Prey to any body else; we have done our Business, and fare you well, we'll be gone.* (1713)

Defoe is a materialist, but a grateful one; he is not sordid; he does not deny the spirit. His attitude to natural creation first acknowledges its magnitude and wonder, and then looks to ways of drawing upon it, and thus puts man in his place and suffocates vanity before it has time to develop. But though man's littleness is underlined by the immensity of things, Defoe reminds his readers that nature is the servant and man the master if only he will bestir himself. Since this is so, man should bestir himself. Thus the herrings cover the seas with their 'incredible Shoals' and equal in bulk the 'whole Island of *Britain*', and seem to dwarf mere men; but they do not; 'Boys have gone out in Boats, and toss'd them in with their naked Hands'.

In contemplating this excitement of the imagination we draw near, surely, to the essence of Defoe's personality. His informing principle, his reason for writing, is not to explore or achieve gentility, straighten politics, or redefine the nature of religious truth, but to put in words his vision of things and men radiant with improvement and growth, and making real their potential, or instinctive, better selves. Of this refining process commercial action is the evidence, the means to hand. The formulation is characteristically Defoean, and profound. A real sense of the life of earth comes to the fore in everything he writes, as all readers have felt, compared with Bacon's abstracter perfectionism, and a less slick approach to commerce generally than in Sprat's somewhat programmatic view of mercantile culture. Defoe's is a mentality both close to the surface of things, and penetrating; and here we can see how much his achievement surpasses what it would have been had he limited himself to technical economics. The imaginative quality, which spoils him as a pure economist, because not kept under control, but itself controlling what is written, is distinctly a feature of his writing. For instance, there is none of it in the works of Martin, Child, Petty, Mun or Misselden, some of the familiar economic writers of and before Defoe's time, none of it in Locke, and there was to be none of it in this degree or form in the work of Adam Smith a half century later. One's only real parallel is with the apprehension of the marvellous found in Elizabethan travel literature, yet it is a parallel with a vital difference. Between the age of Elizabeth and that of Defoe the 'child-like wonder of the Renaissance about the world's vast and unknown spaces' (9) has been replaced by the distincter knowledge of them, the desire to possess, and the intention to exploit them. As more of the world became mapped and annexed during the sixteenth and seventeenth centuries, as commerce and its related activities expanded and multiplied in England beyond all limits, a growth paralleled in Europe generally, men's state of mind changed from the curious to the knowing, from yearning to ambition. They approved, in Pope's line, being men of sense; and left admiring to fools. Simultaneously an expedient notion of honour replaced the old chivalric code. The preceding chapter showed this transvaluation taking place, commerce in its literary portrayal turning from bad to good, the merchant finding himself promoted from fool to patriot. It is Defoe's importance to stand at the apex of the development of the idea and to speak with a distincter and broader authority than any other writer for the second phase of this cycle of moral change, and to convey its spirit and feel. His flourishing years from 1680 to 1730, or perhaps to 1750, twenty years after his death, form the period of brilliant optimism between that half-tentative or too bold hopefulness of scientific and mercantile aspiration, of which the writings of Waller and the early Dryden are representative, and the first stirrings of serious disillusionment with the commercial dream in the middle decades of the eighteenth century. Defoe for his own part avoids crassness because his capacity for wonder and his emphasis on growth succeed in keeping his writing, though dogmatic, supple and expressive, and free from deadness of feeling. But lesser writers are not so happy. There is much vitiated sentiment to be encountered in the Whig panegyric writing of the early eighteenth century, and much spurious commercial optimism.

His novels are even more vital than his tracts; 'romantic' is the word that suggests itself. In them a Whittingtonian pattern is repeated with variations, a progress not just from rags to riches, or from exile to acceptance, but from deprived isolation to harmonious adjustment, as well as to a handsome bank balance, so that their common theme may be said to be moral and material progress together. 'Roxana' (1724) is the exception to this generalization, but an obvious exception, a study in regression. 'Robinson Crusoe' (1719) is only seemingly a realistic novel, more truly an abstraction, the myth of western development cast into story form. If we ask a question about Crusoe's activities on the island we find them to be absurd; what does a single man want with forty-three goats? But they fall into place as a delineated idea; this is a fantasy of material and spiritual achievement. The same conception shapes the other novels into coherent statement. In 'Moll Flanders' (1722) and 'Captain Singleton' (1720) this is so obvious as not to need pointing out, but also in 'Colonel Jacque' (1722), perhaps the most fanciful of them all, Defoe's concern with the rewards of self-culture shows through in the fairy tale quality of the hero's rise in the world of money and transaction, with deposit accounts silently accumulating for him over the years and marvellous bargains falling into his hands.

But the fact is that Defoe's whole work is invigorated by this enthusiasm for culture and cultivation. So his 'Tour thro' the Whole Island of Great-Britain' (1724-7), praising the commercial and social felicity already won by a confident mercantile race, and encouraging further achievement on the same lines, is miscast as a guide book or an economic survey alone. To call it so is to make it charming or documentary and miss its urgent note. It is more like Defoe's manifesto of the age, except that we should reserve the term manifesto for 'The Compleat English Gentleman' (1729, unfinished; published 1890). Here will be found Defoe's most express declaration of the centrality of mercantile values in the England of his day. Written in his very last years, still unfinished, it conveys in summary form the ideas of a lifetime, and is much too important a document to have been so largely neglected for so long. What was hinted at in the plays of Shadwell, and what Sprat turned into open propaganda, is here argued for in substantial and overwhelming detail and with a sustained energy as brilliant as any to be found in Defoe's better known, but not better written, works. Defoe's emphasis is on improvement throughout; his purpose, to establish the merchant as the equal of the aristocrat in culture and in worth. But notice how he attempts this reappraisal; it is all-important. He decides not to show merchants achieving princely status and the princely style, like Gresham in Heywood's play, which would be merely imitative, or taking on the manners of the class above them as in the plays of Shirley. Rather, he draws the reverse picture: that of aristocrats following through the notions of the merchant class, and choosing to produce and work as their way of fulfilling a role in life. The complete gentleman now performs a useful and strenuous function in society rather than exists gracefully; yet it is not so much he that has changed as the whole of life around him, and consequently life's terms of value, to which he now must adapt or perish; such is Defoe's recognition. Defoe's imagery in 'The Compleat English Gentleman' is unusually dense. It reinforces the use ethic, the idea he is advancing. It emphasizes fine value conferred on material objects by their adaptedness to man's needs, and on the opposite side the futility of unused resources: tended gardens, polished diamonds, well set gems, worked gold; a silent organ, the unexploited sea.

Defoe stands out perhaps from among his contemporaries by the information he can provide on commercial matters, and by his vivid imagination, but not by his praise of merchants; in that he is typical of his age. And he died just in time to escape seeing his ideal disintegrate. During Defoe's lifetime the mercantile theme became fashionable and almost universal, then after about 1730 or 1740 gave ground, crumbling to pieces eventually before the economic and political crises after the middle of the century and being swept away in the avalanche of new experience brought in by the Industrial Revolution, only to re-emerge, in a curiously unrepentant form, in the era of Cobden and Bright. Despite some major hostile voices, such as Swift's, despite the repudiation of crass display by Pope and others, the era has a distinct tone of mercantile and patriotic ebullience both mixed up together. It is the age of Defoe but perhaps even more concisely the age of James Thomson, whose 'Rule, Britannia!' (1740), in its little-sung last two stanzas, brings out the present theme.

To thee belongs the rural reign;
  Thy cities shall with commerce shine;
All thine shall be the subject main,
  And every shore it circles thine.
  'Rule, Britannia, rule the waves;
  Britons never will be slaves.'

The Muses, still with freedom found,
  Shall to thy happy coast repair:
Blest isle! with matchless beauty crown'd,
  And manly hearts to guard the fair.
  'Rule, Britannia, rule the waves;
  Britons never will be slaves.'

(1740)

The song really does catch an aspect of the feeling of its times; the hopeful aspect. Linked with culture as well as with wealth and power, commerce here liberates and harmonizes, and will polish cities, adding a flourish to them which makes them 'shine'. One wonders where the shine is to be seen. What is it in a city that glows? Does Thomson have in mind the market place and the dock side, and are they what he sees as beautiful? Probably not; his verse is remote and abstract. And that is the important point to make about it. He emphasizes trade's endowing quality because he overlooks its antagonistic workings, whose cessation Defoe thought almost a miracle of unexpectedness - 'Commerce' is Thomson's subject, some goddess - and he overlooks its antagonism because he is content not to look very close at what he is talking about at all. We recognize that we are dealing with a wishful sentiment in such lines, an aspiration, rather than with an experienced truth; thus his optimism is shallower than Defoe's.

For all this Thomson's anthem is not just his, or Mallet's. It is national. The age believed what its poets were telling it, at least for a time. Defoe, Thomson, and their contemporaries press forward their optimistic claim for capitalist enterprise, and for the virtuous outcome of the profit motive, knowing it is a large and untried one, knowing it is dangerous, knowing it has never, or rarely, been put forward before, yet pressing it forward nevertheless. It is an unusual phenomenon and a rare moment in history, and one views with special interest a society so confident in its momentary domination of the forces of the world around it that it can reject what centuries of experience had implanted in the memory of men: a distrust of the dangerous will to gain. What made it possible so to admire commerce was its congruence with patriotic sentiment at a time when Britain achieved European mastery and world-wide power for the first time. 'Rule, Britannia!' commands this, but Dryden had finely expressed the merging of the two themes in 'Annus Mirabilis' nearly eighty years earlier, and one could say that during the first half of the eighteenth century such national enthusiasm becomes the outstanding feature of the literature of commerce. Its difference from Dryden's kind of patriotism is that it turns into a sentiment considerably more blatant; not just due pride nestling within a wider sympathy, and thus humanized, as in the Dryden lines, but a satisfied sense of material supremacy all too ready to assume that it is moral supremacy too.

A rich society can afford to build with artistry, and purchase refinements, and improve the landscape, and expand and beautify its towns and cities, whereas a poor one cannot. Perhaps because Britain in the late seventeenth and early eighteenth centuries showed herself eminently capable of producing such material evidence of superiority, it was felt that the spiritual superiority flowed from the material condition as a natural consequence. In that period too it could not be hidden, and therefore might seem something to boast about, that the flowering of a prosperous condition and the fine workmanship of art depended in the last resort on the returns of trade. Mercantile activity thus could be made to appear not just necessary, which it had always been, but commendable in patriotic and in aesthetic terms; and so we find the poets and playwrights, but especially the poets, arguing. In the process much is taken for granted, and the profundity of the best seventeenth-century verse on the subject, the hard-won issue of a laborious search into experience which seemed anything but clear cut, simply evaporates. Perhaps this is because the eighteenth-century patriot poets were all lesser writers than Dryden. But the external condition of society must also have had a lot to do with it. First the 1688 settlement established a government of the propertied and commercial interests in England, and placed the monarch effectively in second place to them; then in 1713 England secured the 'Asiento', or monopoly of the slave trade to the Spanish territories in America, with its unparalleled opportunities for expansion, and outstripped all her rivals in the race for world dominion. In spite of setbacks, such as the frustrations of the 1730s, and the ill success of the war between 1739 and 1746, her world supremacy and sense of progress were assured. Thus a writer wishing to explore the commercial theme in the age of Queen Anne and the first Georges would have seen less reason to be reticent, and have felt less doubt of the matter, than Dryden with his constant awareness of revolutionary change. After 1700 the prosperity and stability which all had longed for seemed to be being acquired. The merchant was doing the acquiring and the providing. He became his society's central figure, its type, and its ideal. The surprising thing about the South Sea Bubble in 1720 which should have shattered all the assumptions being handed around about the virtuous commercial instinct, is how little notice people in general take of it, and how little noise it makes in the literature.

King William's reign was rather one of struggle than achievement, but in its closing years the poetry of public celebration begins to sound the new prosperous note. The argument developed in Matthew Prior's 'Carmen Seculare' (1699) is an example. It will be recalled that in Dryden's 'Annus Mirabilis' it is the outgrowth and refinement of knowledge which is seen as justifying mercantile endeavour, and that Denham, still earlier, with some wishful thinking celebrates generous reciprocation as the special characteristic of the trading process. We now see these spiritual conceptions undergoing a transformation, or rather a solidification, into the more measurable worldly concepts of power and commercial advantage. Such is not Prior's meaning, but it is there in what he writes. He declares that Cato, Julius Caesar, Augustus, Charlemagne and William the Conqueror were great men with great failings, but in contrast King William has conferred peace on England and made the Muses, guardians of the ancient world and so its superior geniuses, dependent upon himself (lines 1-469). Thus encouraged, he proceeds, let Britain's voyagers penetrate to the poles, export wool more valuable than the golden fleece, annex the wealth of both Indies, compel submission from passing ships on the high seas, settle British power abroad, Europeanize savage tribes, and replace barbarism with the mild religion of King William. The uncivilized tribes listen with joy and respectful fear to this gospel of new experience (470-511).(10) Hyperbole of this sort is rarely far from ironic suggestion, as when Prior describes how the cruel traditional idols are cast out to make way for King William's personal image, but, for all the age's attunement to satirical implication, commerce and empire never invite mockery in such verse as this; they are too taken for granted.

Pope, for instance, better than any writer at subtle undercutting, is just as hyperbolical in 'Windsor Forest' (1713), and appears no less committed to what he is saying. From Pope's subtler imagination and more precise reference, it is true, we are offered the effect of a complex humane optimism and an affirmed sense of being, rather than a creed or pat confidence in empire, as in Prior and others, so that the claims being put forward may strike us as less bold than they really are; but bold, even extreme, they have to be called. The relevant lines are those which form the concluding section of the poem, added in 1713 when the Utrecht peace negotiations were in progress. They contain a forthright plug for the Tory policy of free trade, which Defoe also wrote for, and from which the Whigs wanted to exclude France. Partly for this reason Pope describes how Father Thames rises to declare his superiority to the Tiber, Hermus, Nile, Volga, Rhine, Ganges and other great rivers of the world because his is to be a reign of peace, which will encourage world-wide commercial expansion, which will encourage civilization. 'Ascending Villas' and 'glitt'ring spires' testify to the beauty of the peaceful era to come, during which imperial and diplomatic arbitration will be sought from Queen Anne by suing kings and suppliant states. Reminiscent of Waller, this stately glorification then leads to the more familiar forecasts: of British power extended to the far east and to the south seas, of the earth's treasures earmarked for British possession and British use, of commerce linking all nations in equal advantage, of conquest ceasing because perfectly achieved and overtaken by its own peace of which the present peace is a foreshadowing, of slavery lapsing from the earth. More than just mercantile endeavour is under scrutiny in such lines as these but there is no mistaking their thoroughly affirming attitude to trade, no suspicion that it is something to be excused or vindicated or apologized for or ironic about. If trade once was an unpoetic subject, it is so no longer. Pope achieves this endorsement by drawing into the texture of his verse echoes from other poets - Denham, Waller, Dryden are among the ones more conspicuously suggested - and by stressing the ideas of completeness and activity; in his argument trade is not a taking from life but an adding to it. Thus trees from Windsor Forest rush into the floods to become ships, so that they may tempt the polar seas. The balm bleeds, the coral glows to enrich Britain. The world's minerals are ripened to gold. The oceans, once barriers, have become roads, and instead of obstructing movement, facilitate and increase it. The revaluation has become complete, that is to say.

When Pope in later poems criticizes the false gods of a materialistic and commercial age, display, vain consumption and expense, he is not to be seen as retracting the commercial optimism here expressed; always remembering that it is not mere commerce he is talking about. The third and fourth of the 'Moral Essays' (1731-5), 'To Lord Bathurst' and 'To the Earl of Burlington', both on the subject of the use of riches, draw extensively for illustration on the social habits and trends of the day, but they are theoretical essays as well as documents of the age and really are concerned with the vices of avarice, greed, excessive indulgence and miserliness, and in general with the moral perplexity of man's divided nature. One cannot see them as utter condemnations of Pope's society simply because of the portraits of John Ward and Francis Chartres in 'To Lord Bathurst', even though in his notes Pope drives home the full impact of what he objects to in the money men of the time and their valuation,(11) because, balancing those portraits, are the lines on Harley and the Man of Ross. Admittedly we feel Pope's intense dislike of city fraud and deceit and self-deceit, even of the city style, and perhaps it would be just to lay a good deal of emphasis on this aversion from the spirit of the trading world; it certainly goes deep. Yet Pope in my feeling never quite washes his hands of his age, though always wringing them. A similar tempering of the satiric denunciation in 'To the Earl of Burlington' is to be admitted, when Pope sets Stowe against Timon's villa and introduces a sudden dislocation of animus when he avows that all the prodigal folly he has inveighed against gives sustenance to the lower orders (lines 169-72); finally he urges Burlington to build new harbours, contain floods, construct canals. Avoiding waste thus does not mean, for Pope, holding back from investment and improving expenditure, and, though avarice is condemned, prosperity, even riches, are not. The same point can be made of other passages in Pope's satires on the misvaluing and misuse of wealth, for instance those in the 'Fifth Epistle of the First Book of Horace', and the 'First Epistle of the First Book', apart from the fact that the subject is not always quite the same as commerce; namely, that there is plenty of sharp personal attack whose effect is to some extent offset by a moderate public advocacy. This is surely the general case with the satire of Pope. 'The Dunciad' is extremely condemning; but it is anything but subversive.

Returning to 'Windsor Forest', one sees that in it Pope does not actually recommend trade as such, but rather celebrates commercial expansion, newly built villas, venturing seamen merchants and the joining of old and new worlds as manifestations of a general increase in rewarding effort, and that the stress is on busy activity rather than on business. Materialism is kept at a distance by the subtlety and breadth of this conception and by the judgment that vital effort, widening the range of human experience, is beneficial. One difference between Dryden and Pope is the latter's evident delight in consolidation and materiality. Dryden could only find it in him to praise commerce by spiritualizing it.

'Windsor Forest' brings us to panegyric; a remote mode. When Augustan writers choose commerce for their subject, they stand perhaps as far from the sensibility of twentieth-century man as any English poets ever have done, or could have done; and for them too the subject must have appeared novel, and the question of its correct treatment not a little problematic. They will have found few helpful suggestions in traditional literature about how to incorporate the counting-house into heroic celebration, in the first place. Worse still, they will not have been helped by a general unfamiliarity, all too common among literary men then and since, with the technical detail of what it was that they were praising. We can identify this last condition as a writer's marked difficulty when a blandness comes into his phrasing, a tentative generality delicately conscious of the thin ice underneath. For example, in the poem 'On Queen Anne's Peace, 1713', written to celebrate the end of the War of Spanish Succession, Thomas Parnell

Declares: 'Let Oxford's schemes the path to plenty show, /And thro' the realm increasing plenty go'.(12) This tones down Harley's South Seas project into an acceptable sort of general flourish, and keeps the heroic style unembarrassed by the idiom of the stock exchange. A later effort in the same poem is less satisfactory:

> Let Traffic, cherish'd by the senate's care,
> On all the seas employ the wasting air!
> And Industry, with circulating wing,
> Thro' all the land the goods of Traffic bring.
>
> (1713)

'Let there be more and more trade,' we register, reading the lines once; but what, a second reading prompts us to ask, can be meant by the two last lines? What is industry's circulating wing? Freight transport by helicopter can hardly be the intended meaning in spite of its being 1713, and a very confident year, so Parnell must be thinking of what he calls 'Industry', that is business energy, distributing to everyone in Britain with speedy efficiency, or as he puts it bringing everywhere with 'circulating wing', the products of trade. Maybe adding to the circulation idea is Parnell's notion of the interchange of supply and demand which makes up the economic cycle; but maybe not. It seems a convoluted couplet. It is not their density of meaning which tangles lines like this, but vagueness.

The vagueness is typical. Perhaps it belongs to the panegyrical cast of mind not to look too closely at what is being praised. When, in addition, the praise of trade has turned into a fashionable theme, and even a political party issue, one may expect to encounter plenty of commendatory writing on the merchant's character and on the commercial idea which conveys little sense of the counter and the quay. One can see this ulterior pressure, stemming from the demands of politics, being brought to bear on Steele's praise of the merchant's calling in 'The Englishman' (1713). When Steele defines the merchant as 'the greatest Benefactor of the *English* Nation' and 'the Child of *Britain* who enriches his whole Family', and in another issue of the same periodical assures his readers that English merchants abroad stand like 'so many Centinels placed in all the Nations of the World to watch over and defend her trade',(13) he is putting the general Whig case that trade, rather than land, as Swift and other Tories in 'The Examiner' were arguing at the same time, was the true source of national wealth, and that the commercial, not the landed, classes were the most important section of the community; more immediately, he is attempting to influence the London Parliamentary election, unavailingly as it happened,(14) by drumming up support for Whig candidates.

But Steele is not restricted to the political party line. He aims at a larger view in declaring that the outcome of a life devoted to commercial enterprise is a more comprehensive mind, and that commerce renders men more inquisitive and less 'ductile' to tyrannical aggressors (ii, number 17); and when, putting always the optimistic gloss on what may even resemble disadvantages, and certainly would be so to a later generation, he praises the merchant as a man tied to no locality, unrestricted by a single calling, inhibited by no limitation to a single process or craft, unlike the mere trader, and, says Steele, because of this freedom from specific relations, endowed with the capacity to take a larger than usual view of life. In the second half of the eighteenth century Goldsmith and Cowper were to stigmatize precisely this freedom from, or rather lack of, personal ties in the commercial man as morally disabling, and Coleridge was to press the point even further. So it is interesting to note how extremely optimistic Steele feels it possible to be. He idealizes, as a matter of fact, as committedly as anyone. He projects far beyond Whig policy. He extols the merchant as the most deserving member of the community, as its apotheosis, as a sort of miracle-worker and modern true alchemist, who from geographical want and non-commodity extracts golden profits (i, number 4).

> This is he who turns all the Disadvantages of our Situation into our Profit and Honour. His Care and Industry ties his Country to the Continent, and the whole Globe pays his Nation a voluntary Tribute due to her from his Merit. His Hand-writing has the Weight of Coin, and his good Character is Riches to the rest of his Countrymen. (1713)

Steele is too unpretentious a writer to set the teeth on edge, but for all that one cannot but feel that there is something facile in this flattering commendation. It is certainly engaged, and well informed, but a little too polished.

Of such condescending urbanity, of course, it is Addison who is the master. And in his well-known discourse on the great centrality in his England of trade and trading, one sees how thoroughly Addison catches the tone of his era, and adds to it his own polite gloss; how smooth, but not yet quite smug, yet tending that way, is his satisfaction with a universe so evidently created in order to maintain the prosperous English trading classes in their new-found happy power:(15)

> Our Ships are laden with the Harvest of every Climate; Our Tables are stored with Spices, and Oils, and Wines: our Rooms are filled with Pyramids of *China*, and adorned with the Workmanship of *Japan*: Our Morning's-Draught comes to us from the remotest Corners of the Earth: We repair our Bodies by the Drugs of *America*, and repose our selves under Indian Canopies. My Friend, Sir ANDREW calls the Vineyards of *France* our Gardens; the Spice-Islands our Hot-Beds; the *Persians* our Silk-Weavers, and the *Chinese* our Potters. Nature indeed furnishes us with the bare Necessaries of Life, but Traffick gives us a great Variety of what is Useful, and at the same time supplies us with every thing that is Convenient and Ornamental. (1711)

More evidence of the merchant's assimilation into polite society is supplied by the drama, which attempts to sustain the Restoration formula on the one hand while softening all its asperities on the other. The mixture is not happy. Susannah Centlivre converts the merchant Freeman in 'A Bold Stroke for a Wife' (1718), who may owe something to Freeport, into the equal in wit and radiance of Colonel Fainall, the central male figure. This would have been all but unthinkable in Restoration comedy, but Mrs Centlivre keeps the mercantile jokes all there by including too a stock jobber Tradelove; on to Tradelove, along with the virtuoso, the Quaker and the beau, all the satire is channelled. What results is unilluminating. Tradelove is grimly technical. There is no significant delineation in Freeman of the commercial process or the commercial character. What one can say about him is that he shows how decorous it had become to be at least a big merchant. Steele too in his much reworked play 'The Conscious Lovers' (1722) brings before us the merchant Sealand, who claims to be 'a Man exercis'd, and experienc'd in Chances, and Disasters' beyond other men (II, ii), and to be a new kind of gentry equalling the old. This is to repeat with formal seriousness a recantation of the traditional view of commerce already put forward by Steele in his periodical writing, and hinted at in a number of plays by other writers. The trouble with it is that its intention is good; but not its dramatic representation. The character just does not convince. So the case lacks force. Mr Sealand, like Mrs Centlivre's Freeman, and Sir Andrew Freeport of 'The Spectator', is a notional merchant, an approved portrayal, a mercantile projection stripped however of Exchange crudeness but retaining the dress and language of commerce to back up his businesslike assertiveness of manner. He is the merchant seen sympathetically from the standpoint of polite literature.

Such urbane delineations are a world away from Defoe's acquisitive planters, gross with productive toil, and are made possible, and made in this mould, because it is national enthusiasm and party feeling, as well as a certain moral fair-mindedness, but not a spontaneous and genuine curiosity about the men and operations of trade, which form the impulse behind their creation. They come to us as panegyrical generalizations. For this reason they seem distanced from actuality. For this reason too they last for quite a long time in a literature which was to some extent content to recreate achievements in an accepted convention; but not as long as the hostile portrait of the merchant which they replace, of course. It is not until the middle of the century that new politcal factors, and the resumption of the novel form by major writers, combine to render them finally irrelevant, for bland optimism about traders, or any men, could not survive the attention of writers of genius in a fresh literary form. Bland optimism about trade ceased to be possible from the 1740s onwards. From approximately that time, therefore, the panegyrists cease lauding tradesmen, and have to find other objects.

Not every panegyrical utterance calls for separate discussion here. There were many, and they were similar. Pope's 'Windsor Forest' is the best of them, Prior's 'Carmen Seculare' is typical, and what is said of those poems above may be taken to refer in its general bearings to the whole genre, and leave us to notice those which add something interesting to the mere praise.(16) A later reworking of the idea of enhancing commerce which closes Pope's 'Windsor Forest', and typical of the best of the optimistic pieces, is found in John Gay's eighth fable, entitled 'The Man, the Cat, the Dog, and the Fly' (1738) and addressed 'To My Native Country'. Gay praises the spreading commerce of Britain, advises her to hold fast to trade and trade alone, and avoid other ambitious designs, and recommends to all individuals to pull their weight in the national endeavour:(17)

> On trade alone thy glory stands.
> That benefit is unconfin'd,
> Diffusing good among mankind:
> That first gave lustre to thy reigns,
> And scatter'd plenty o'er thy plains:
> 'Tis that alone thy wealth supplies,
> And draws all Europe's envious eyes.
> Be commerce then thy sole design;
> Keep that, and all the world is thine.

A gentlemanly fly thinking to live off the fruits of others' labour is crushed by the man. The cat and the dog are welcomed, doing useful tasks. Gay expresses the optimism of the early eighteenth century, with a tremor of concern for the possible loss of the benefits so newly won, and urges the course of action, a sole dedication to matters of trade, which in the event England declined to follow, especially in India.

Also fired by more than a eulogistic purpose, and so standing out from the mass of panegyrical writing, is the poetry of Richard Savage. Certainly Savage is patriotic, like so many others. Sections of 'The Wanderer' (1729), 'Religion and Liberty' (1732), 'The Volunteer Laureate, No. 3' (1734) and 'The Volunteer Laureate, No. 4' (1735) are typical panegyrical pieces, for the most part neither much better nor much worse than plenty of similar verse of the time. But he is also interested for its own sake in the abundant world about him, and in his better writing discovers beyond the patriotic argument a profounder theme, a Defoean perception of the mysterious and incalculable resources of the earth. Trade's value, riches apart, he claims in 'Of Public Spirit in Regard to Public Works' (1736), is that it loosens the locked-up mystery of things, disimprisoning the secrets of rumoured lands and seas, and actualizing possibility. This goes beyond the Pope of 'Windsor Forest' to recall Dryden's systems of new knowledge in 'Annus Mirabilis', but Savage gives the theme a different turn, stressing practical improvement as well as discovery and perhaps harking back to Bacon's scientific and technical aspiration. Trade, he says, does more than reveal the hidden truth of nature. In some cases, for instance that of a canal cut through a mountain, it adds value, and rather renders things adaptable to the needs of man than just exploits what is there. This more than passive reception of God's gifts, this subordination of nature, Savage praises highly, certainly in commercial terms and with his eyes fixed on economic prosperity, as if material improvement is the primary end of earthly effort, yet for all that with an idealism looking further than the mere piling up of more and more wealth: (18)

From peasant Hands, Imperial Works arise;
And *British* hence with *Roman* Grandeur vies.
Roads, yet unknown, through Rocks, shall winding tend,
And the safe Causeway, o'er the Clays, ascend.
From Reservoirs, the nether Pipe here owns
New, ductile Streams, to visit distant Towns.
There vanish Fens; whence Vapours rise no more;
Whose aguish Influence tainted Heav'n before.
Where Waters deep'ning glide, and wide extend,
From Road to Road, the Bridge her Arch shall bend.
Where Ports were choak'd; where Mounts, in vain, arose;
There Harbours open, and there Breaches close.
Rivers are taught a new commercive Flow;
And young Plantations, future Navies, grow;
(Navies, which to invasive Foes explain,
Heav'n throws not round us Rocks and Seas in vain.)
The Sail of Commerce, in each Sky, aspires;
And Property assures what Toil acquires.

(1736)

If commerce liberalizes, as here, the argument is that it does so not by accumulating mere wealth but by subduing the unimproved to use, and therefore to beauty, the grace of proper function. The spirit of Defoe and of Bacon could hardly be closer. In a later revision of the poem Savage strengthens this emphasis. He asks how much longer quarries teeming with the yet unused stuff of conquest and art are to lie unrescued from waste, and derives something of a moral imperative from the sense of urgency with which he presses the point home. Not to engage in the extractive industries of fishing and mining, it seems, or in building, or in agriculture, or in commerce itself, commerce proper, in which every separate other enterprise meets and joins to ensure the general improvement of man, can be seen as not very different from actual robbery (p. 231):

'Blush, blush, O *Sun* (she cries) here vainly found,
'To rise, to set, to roll the Seasons round.
'Shall Heav'n distill in Dews, descend in Rain,
'From Earth gush Fountains, Rivers flow in vain?
'There shall the *watry Lives* in Myriads stray,
'And be, to be alone each other's Prey?

'Unsought shall here the teeming Quarries own
'The various Species of mechanic Stone?
'From Structure This, from Sculpture That confine?
'Shall Rocks forbid the latent Gem to shine?
'Shall Mines, obedient, aid no Artist's Care,
'Nor give the martial Sword and peaceful Share?
'Ah! shall they never precious Ore unfold,
'To smile in Silver, or to flame in Gold?
'Shall here the vegetable World alone,
'For Joys, for various Virtues rest unknown?
'While Food and Physick, Plants, and Herbs supply,
'Here must they shoot alone to bloom and die?
'Shall Fruits, which none, but brutal Eyes, survey,
'Untouch'd grow ripe, untasted drop away?

(1737)

The thought echoes but goes beyond the closing lines of Pope's 'To Burlington', the third of his 'Moral Epistles' - 'Bid Harbours open, public Ways extend', and the rest - which define worthy expense after a long catalogue of the improper use of riches. Savage plainly has some similar moral aim in mind. But a technological enthusiasm, not the recommendation of virtuously temperate living, is what we are also seeing here. Savage's imagination is possessed by the idea of the productive potential of the earth, and impatient that such potential should be realized; and he seems to see no end to the exploiting process. It is a different and more frenetic sentiment from Pope's, for whom moderation and a sense of human need would act so as to restrain the indulged appetite for commercial and material expansion; but not less moving, in its way.

Though the optimistic attitude here described was the predominant one during the first third of the eighteenth century, it was not by any means unopposed. The traditional hostile voice is still heard. And even the affirming outlook we have been considering itself undergoes a change as the years pass, sounding more doubtful and apprehensive in the 1730s and 1740s. Yet it remains the characteristic voice of the age, as well as the Whig party line. Swift offers some corrective to its complacency, protesting against the effect on native Irish trade of exploiting and oppressive English commercial regulations, and in doing so calling in question the entire priority of commercial imperialism, or warfare by economic means, which he rightly detects to be the governing spirit of English life and policy. In consequence of this policy Irish ports and havens, he writes, of which nature has been liberal, are 'of no more Use to us, than a beautiful Prospect to a Man shut up in a Dungeon'.(19) He complains that Irish wealth and advantages are stifled by a foreign commercial tyranny and drawn off in the form of rents and profits by foreign landlords; who then insult their victims by declaring, because 'there may be a Dozen Families in this Town, able to entertain their English Friends in a generous Manner at their Tables', that 'we wallow in Riches and

Luxury' when they return to their homes in England.(20) Though Swift's general position is one of profound hostility to the commercial aspect of society in his time, to its commercial character and increasingly commercial cast of mind and system of values, he was not opposed to necessary trade and manufacture, the proper enjoyment of the advantages of a people's natural position, and wrote much to support their extension in Ireland.

Being Irish, Swift drew on a special awareness of the inglorious aspect of economic exploitation, as did Burke later in the century; it made the latter, perhaps, the outstanding defender of India, along with Sheridan, also of Irish descent. But even among English writers, especially those in opposition to Walpole, a dislike of the commercial nature of English life, especially public life, which the Whig panegyrists equate with liberty, and the Tories with corruption, begins to make itself felt in literature from the late 1720s onwards. The disenchantment is well caught in the implications of John Gay's 'The Beggar's Opera' (1728), not so much in the specific charges 'levelled' in the play against Walpole and his kind, but rather in its portrayal of a whole world ruled by money values, in which judgment, motive and feeling narrow down to mere market price. Polly stands out against the mode and Macheath rises above it, but is also trapped by it, yet notwithstanding these allowances Gay suggests a truth about the character of his age, which, for all the public advocacy of the panegyrical writers, had sombre implications: its commercialism, its universal pursuit of profit, its closeness to moral dissolution. Eight years had passed since the South Sea Bubble had burst. In Gay's reflection of life in London nothing has changed.

The chain of connected propositions was recognized and admitted at the time, that commerce produced wealth, and wealth power, and wealth and power a condition of unstrenuous indulgence which was called luxury, and luxury, it was apprehended, could destroy the whole of society if unchecked by temperate virtue and restraint. Thus commerce ended up in the last manifestation of its influence, paradoxically, as the bane of culture as well as its parent; the perception humanizes much otherwise crudely boastful verse. It must have seemed specially unfair that after her struggles towards world power during a whole century Britain should be forced to acknowledge that she was facing destruction from success itself and at the very moment when she had finally achieved it. Yet so it was, or seemed, and in the literature from the 1730s onwards, expressing and growing out of the increasing political and economic complications of those years, we begin to sense the new uncertainty with mercantile gains and mercantile priorities, the premonition of cultural collapse, the anxious probing into ancient civilizations and into the dynamic of imperial decay, which, in a more systematic and philosophical form, was to issue in Gibbon's 'Decline and Fall of the Roman Empire' (1776-88): the grand exposition of a century's obsession. Since it was not accidental that eighteenth-century England saw herself as the Rome of the modern world, not the Athens, the practical rather than intellectual centre of excellence, it followed that she should read her possible fate in the extinction of her model. The sure boasts of eighteenth-century writers are much less assured, therefore, than they look. At any rate, the spectre which haunts the English Augustan establishment is its perception of the transience of power and the fragility of earthly culture; of the sting in the tail of commerce; of the downward slide of civilization. No wonder it was the fashion to be melancholy.

Both streams, the panegyrical and the premonitory, merge in Edward Young's extraordinary production 'Imperium Pelagi, A Naval Lyric' (1729), a poem which we can see as the high point, if that is the proper term, of panegyrical writing on commerce. Young sub-titles his poem 'The Merchant', and perhaps intends it to read like the last word on the subject of beneficial trade. For instance one could hardly add anything to the following lines, with their virtual recasting of God as a business manager:(21)

> Merchants o'er proudest heroes reign;
> Those trade in blessing, these in pain,
> At slaughter swell, and shout while nations groan.
> With purple monarchs merchants vie;
> If great to spend, what to supply?
> Priests pray for blessings; merchants pour them down.
>
> Kings, merchants are in league and love;
> Earth's odours pay soft airs above,
> That o'er the teeming field prolific range.
> Planets are merchants; take, return,
> Lustre and heat; by traffic burn;
> The whole creation is one vast Exchange.
>
> Is 'merchant' an inglorious name?
> What say the sons of letter'd fame,
> Proud of their volumes, swelling in their cells?
> In open life, in change of scene,
> 'Mid various manners, throngs of men,
> Experience, Arts, and solid Wisdom dwells.
>
> (1729)

In itself, beyond noting it as a characteristic of those times, this excessive eulogy need not detain us, though it lasts for nearly forty pages,(22) but what is of interest is to see how Young has counter-balanced the flattering strain with a note of fearful anxiety, suggesting that his praise of his age, though crass, is anything but complacent. He warns against corruption, produced by too much wealth, and too much wealth enjoyment, though it does not appear to be the wealth seeking which he wishes to curb, and thus against the occupational threat to a commercial nation. He derives from the fate of Tyre a historical warning of what may happen to prosperous Britain. Tyre, like Britain, he says, was once a 'merchant land, as Eden fair', She was the 'Ancient of empires', 'The pride of isles', 'Mother of crafts', 'Pilot of kingdoms' and (ii, 348)

> Great mart of nations! - But she fell:
> Her pamper'd sons revolt, rebel;
> Against his favourite isle loud roars the main;
> The tempest howls: her sculptured dome,
> Soon the wolf's refuge, dragon's home;
> The land one altar, - a whole people slain!
>
> (1729)

If in the past commercial wealth turned a hardy race effeminate, it can do so in the present and the future. Young hammers the lesson home for two dozen stanzas or more.

Such disastrous prophecies are not present in the eulogies of Prior, Philips, Parnell, Addison and Steele, nor in the work of Defoe, but they appear and multiply in literature from about 1730 onwards; some foreshadowings may be found a little earlier, as perhaps in the writings of Temple. The sombre insight initiates a second phase in the period of optimism, and makes for a more complex and probing kind of verse. It remains preponderantly the poetry of an extravert and confident period, but a recognition of contrasts enriches it, and the apocalyptic note is never far from the cultural argument. Deeper than the specific satire of Pope's 'Dunciad', for example, written between 1728 and 1742, and particularly evident in the fourth book written in the late 1730s and 1740s, works the grim lesson Pope discerns in history of the sporadic brief flowering of learning in isolated spots of a dark earth, of its transference from centre to centre in a linear development which is no true enlargement, and of the permanent condition of impermanence in which man works, which suggests to him the extinction of culture and the last closure of intelligent existence.

In James Thomson's other poetry the enthusiasm of 'Rule, Britannia!' is ever present, but is also matched by a similar fear. In 'The Seasons' (1726-30) generally he is endorsing and positive in spite of the odd criticism, not followed through, of the slave trade, for example asking who will teach us to fish the herring, praising Peter the Great's effort to civilize the uncivilizable Russians, and describing how 'generous Commerce binds/The round of nations in a golden chain' ('Summer', 138-9).(23) But when in 'Liberty' (1734-6) he traces the rise, predominance and fall of admired civilizations - Egypt, Persia, Greece, Rome, Venice - Thomson underlines the double role of commerce which first supplied and sustained their strength, and then sapped it. When the goddess Liberty comes to Britain in Part IV of the poem she praises the growth of British mercantile achievement, no longer a mere 'peddling Commerce' plying 'between near joining lands' but star-directed adventure over the pathless ocean (lines 422-32), and commends its enhancing nature. Thomson then draws a picture of Britain's prosperous and expanding economy, with thriving cities, towns and villages, rich ports, swarming rivers, mineral treasures housed underground and a world tamed and subjected to her exact needs. Finally in the closing section of the poem he warns against degeneration and a sapping of public virtue, the cause of the decline of empire.

'The Castle of Indolence' (1748) is more explicit still on the same point; Sir Industry refines into culture a barbarous and unexploited world, and more particularly Britain, then urges the familiar warning against luxurious decadence. All Thomson's warnings against moral softness are alike. Here is how it is expressed in 'Liberty' (Part V, 200-8).

> Britons! be firm; nor let corruption sly
> Twine round your heart indissoluble chains.
> The steel of Brutus burst the grosser bonds
> By Caesar cast o'er Rome; but still remained
> The soft enchanting fetters of the mind,
> And other Caesars rose. Determined, hold
> Your independence; for, that once destroyed,
> Unfounded, freedom is a morning dream
> That flits aerial from the spreading eye.
>
> (1734-6)

The picture is of a community of neo-Roman patriots under threat from the dissolving action of too much wealth, of sturdy independence spreading into self-indulgence and silently rotting the body politic from within. Not only is it the founding concern of Gibbon's great work that we see in these verse writers' meditations in the Augustan age, though Gibbon's analysis of the decline of Rome was to be more pragmatic, but that of Goldsmith's writings, and perhaps of Burke's outlook too.

It would be wrong to judge such catastrophic fears as yet the main point. They are, however, the postscript to a stronger enthusiasm, threatening to undercut its grounds of conviction. Standing as it were on the sidelines, except that the capturing of world trade was sensed rather as a battle than a game, the poets of Whig eulogy encourage their countrymen with praise and confident cheers, but warn them to preserve the determination of their first endeavour, and not soften. Such stern counselling remains an endorsement of commercial values, but the fact that it is felt to be needed shows that we have come some distance from 'Windsor Forest'. To see luxury, the cream of commerce, as productive of ruinous ease, like Young, Thomson and the rest, and material prosperity as something dangerous, is to waken from the commercial dream of the early eighteenth century and recognize that it may be turning out a nightmare.

Naturally, though a more truly radical analysis of the commercial ethic was not to be attempted until the age of Blake and Coleridge, such a process of illumination, or disillusionment, could not simply end there. It was an attitude of mind ready made for scepticism. And scepticism tends to deepen, not go away. Economic distress and uncertainty in the 1730s and 1740s acted on it as a further irritant and so did Walpole's priorities of peace and low taxes, a policy on which the opposition journal 'The Craftsman'

(1726-36) kept up a constant fire. And in some of these political essays 'The Craftsman' goes further than party politics. In his dedication to the 1731 edition, for instance, Caleb D'Anvers, as the editor calls himself, reminds his readers that his attitude to British trade has been to defend it not only against foreign encroachments by the Spanish and the French but also against 'the Restraints of some home-bred Monopolies' and 'the clandestine Practices of *exclusive Corporations*' (Dedication; unpaged), which, he says, 'we think almost as bad'. Even allowing for the journal's political bias it is interesting to find a writer noting that the common good and the private advantage of a section of the commercial interest are beginning to diverge. Later essays and letters specify the objects of these general castigations: the South Sea trade, the monopolistic East India Company, and trade to Africa. A monopolist is as bad as a public enemy, we are told, who 'robs his Brethren of the Sunshine' (iii, 113).

Lest we over-react to this anticipation of future capitalist discussion, a later essay repeats consideringly Steele's praise of the merchant as benefactor to his compatriots, and draws a distinction between merchant and stock jobber, merchant and parasite, Cicero's mercator and negotiator, which explains and fills in why it is that 'The Craftsman' is against monopolizing companies. It sees them as made up of the latter kind of commercial man interested in private profit at all costs including the robbing of their fellow men. And this reaches out into the general hints of criticism, which are sometimes more than hints and become charges of the government of England having degenerated into little less than a tyranny safeguarded by bribes, of monopolistic corruption, and of a general base indulgence in inglorious ease. In the verse of the political opposition to Walpole, it becomes normal to equate non-involvement with cowardice and degeneracy of fighting spirit, as Johnson does in 'London' (1738), and Pope in 'One Thousand Seven Hundred and Thirty-eight' (1738), and, at a time of growing privation, to recast the rich commercial class, evidently undistressed while all others were suffering visibly severely from want, no longer as society's pioneer and provider but rather as its parasite. Henry Fielding declares in 'The Champion' (14 February 1739/40) that luxury 'hath insinuated itself among all ranks of people and introduced her daughter corruption along with her'. He describes the suffering it has caused in general, but notes that, though the tenant is 'racked' and the landlord made to 'languish' by economic hardship, tradesmen and merchants in some peculiar way seem to continue to find it possible to live 'as much beyond their gains as the gentleman beyond his estate'.(24) This, it may be, is to keep up their business credit with one another; still, their extravagance means others are starving. Moving on to the subject of trade in general, Fielding depicts the growing concern about its fluctuations, and its moral unclearness, and he expresses the discomfited realization then growing general that commerce has failed to live up to its promise. Two generations had passed since the commercial drive had appeared to men capable of pacifying and enriching the earthly condition of all. Why had it not done so? What had gone wrong? Who was to blame? What was the truth about trade? What was to be done? Pestered by these questions, having no answers, sick of the whole muddy business, or affecting to be, Fielding desires his readers (XV, 202) to

> trouble me with no more of their letters concerning trade, nor any of the following questions, viz., what will become of the customs when we have no trade? How will that branch of the revenue be supplied? How shall we breed our sailors for the future without trade? How shall we keep the dominions of the seas without sailors? Will not these sailors, who cannot find employment at home, seek it elsewhere? Will trade, if once turned out of our channel, be easily brought back? Is it not to trade that we owed the figure which we have supported in Europe? Our affluence at home? The provision for great part of our people? How will we provide for them without it? Is not this declined? Why is it declined? Is it recoverable? Why not recovered? What will become of us if it is not recovered? With many more others of this kind: to all which I answer, I cannot tell. (1739-40)

As our examination of the verse writing of these years has suggested, the mood of frustration here enunciated, ripe for a profounder disenchantment, was becoming more or less national. But it is also an outlook specially and personally characteristic of Fielding himself, who as novelist appears congenitally suspicious of the mercantile outlook, and reminiscent of Swift, Dryden and Wycherley when he recommends birth and gentlemanly culture and the affections of the heart above the pragmatic self-seeking of the bourgeois worldling. To Fielding the acquisitive instinct works in a way hostile to life, hardening the heart, dividing man from man. 'I assure you there is not anything worth our regard besides money,' says Leonora's aunt to her niece in the interpolated story of the frustrated coquette in 'Joseph Andrews' (1742).(25) Leonora, it will be recalled, is self-defeated by calculating on men's feelings too precisely, as if a love affair were a transaction, and her function within the larger story of Joseph and Fanny is to highlight their relation of generous loving trust. What makes Leonora the way she is? If we ask the question, Fielding shows us her father, a money-maker loving nothing else in the world but money, passing among his fellows for a good parent but empty of feeling.

Fielding's view of the world of merchant enterprise is adequately suggested in this inserted sketch of the lust for gain, a vice not by any means limited to merchants; but likely to predominate in the merchant world. In old Mr Nightingale in 'Tom Jones' (1749) he goes into the matter in greater, though still, it may be admitted, not very extended, detail. But the detail is carefully chosen, and informs us of the real operations of Fielding's time. We read in chapter 8 of book 14 that Nightingale, once a man bred to trade but now risen above his small origins, acts as a pure financier, and he thus invites our attention as Fielding's considered representation of the successful mercantile type of his day who has moved on from commodity dealing to the manipulation of money in its own right. In other words, Nightingale is a businessman rising into greater success in his office while moving further away from genuine human contact, and in this progress showing the author's exact observation of what was happening in English society then. (26) This progress suggests what we are to think of him. He almost believes, Fielding says, that nothing but money really exists in the world. When Tom Jones, whom he has never seen before, enters the room to speak on his son's behalf, Nightingale refuses to hear a word until he has denied responsibility for all his son's debts, whatever they may be, and announced that he will not pay one of them. It does not seem to him possible that anyone could have any other than a money motive in coming to see him. Such is the pungently sketched essential man of commerce, in Fielding's portrayal. What are we meant to make of him? The answer requires us to anticipate. He is presented as Dombeyan; but he is worse than Mr Dombey. The latter learns to transcend his monetized outlook, whereas all that Nightingale ever recognizes as linking man to man is, if another anticipation may be allowed, the cash nexus. Thus when providing his son with a wife he takes great pains over the financial arrangements, does not want to know of beauty, gentility, good temper, education or artistic sensibility while making up his 'Bargain', but is satisfied to have them thrown in free, and declares: 'I have discharged my Duty, in taking Care of the main Article'. This is settled avarice, but it is commercial avarice, the greed of a merchant financier, not of a miser. Nightingale is an aggressive money-maker, not a secret hoarder, the Shylock of the eighteenth century. Yet Fielding does not strive for particularity in his description, so that we are left unclear about each of Nightingale's transactions, and even about the nature of his first line of trade. Yet the judgment offered by the story is final: such is the man of money, it demonstrates, such Fielding's rejection of the type. The point of Allworthy's visit to Nightingale in the third chapter of the eighteenth book, when he first learns of the stolen five hundred pounds, is to equate Nightingale, the banker, and Black George, the highway robber; it is the banker who is judged to be the greater villain.

Stressing the general nature of the portrayal of Nightingale, like this, is not to imply criticism of Fielding the novelist, as if more specification were looked for and commercial and currency jargon would have helped the Nightingale scenes and made them sound more authentic in their effect. The effect is authentic already. Constantly surprising, in fact, given his assumption of moral omniscience, is how fresh Fielding's insight into the heart can really be, how unexpected his strokes. Old Nightingale's brother will be recalled, for instance. This is a man also bred to trade, also successful at it, but acting in a free and loving way when he is first introduced to us, and in the interview scene with Tom Jones, thus offering a notable but simple contrast with his avaricious brother, especially when the uncle does his best to soften the merchant father's attitude to his son. All this one good, one bad brother business seems as predictable as allegory, which of course has its own strength, but Fielding has more than that in mind. Hearing suddenly that the young people under discussion are not yet married, as he had supposed, the uncle instantly drops his appeal to love and urges that his nephew should abandon Nancy and thank his good fortune for a lucky escape from poverty. This is unexpected, yet an instantly convincing and dramatic stroke; Fielding has seemed to relax his insistence on the corrupting effect of a dedication to the values inculcated by the life of trade, only to tighten it the more.

Fielding's moral bearings are traditional, if his rendering is up to date, yet this does not make him seem less relevant. In fact his kind of emphasis on the banker's emotional sterility, a commonplace of older literature taking on new apparent truth, begins to be echoed throughout the imaginative literature of the time as a fresh suspicion makes itself felt that mercantile ambition demoralizes where it touches. 'Commerce,' says Thomas Gray in a note to his unfinished poem 'The Alliance of Education and Government' (c. 1748-55), 'changes intirely the fate and genius of nations, by communicating arts and opinions, circulating money, and introducing the materials of luxury; she first opens and polishes the mind, then corrupts and enervates both that and the body.'(27) John Dyer's 'The Fleece' (1757) reminds its readers that 'gainful commerce' needs to be joined to a 'just humanity of heart' if social and moral disruption is to be avoided;(28) though Dyer has no doubt of the blessings commerce has bestowed on man. A year before Dyer's poem John Cooper had protested in 'The Genius of Britain' (1756) against Hessian mercenaries being hired to defend England, and had pointed out the paradox of a wealthy country which could no longer defend itself.(29) The sinister progression from commercial prosperity to effeminacy to ruin is also discernible running through Mark Akenside's 'A British Philippic', written as early as 1738. Akenside identifies luxury with the gainful appetite rather than judges one to be the eventual product of the other, which is sharply telescoping of him, and sees the two of them, which for him are one, as responsible for national degeneracy.(30)

We must accept these fears as serious expectations of what might happen, as far as they go, but, abstracted from their sentimental-moral context, and measured by the yardstick of the science of economics, even eighteenth-century economics, they can look sadly misguided. David Hume scornfully attacks the sort of thinking which is responsible for them in his moral and social essays of 1741 and 1742, and argues that 'a spirit of avarice and industry, art and luxury' is requisite and beneficial to modern states and only disadvantageous when pursued 'at the expense of some virtue, as liberality or charity'.(31) Hume dispels the Roman analogy beloved of poets by arguing that Rome fell because of 'an ill-modelled government, and the unlimited power of conquests', and not from Asiatic luxury, as moralists have assumed (p.282). Gibbon forty years later was to reach a similarly undramatic conclusion.(32) Luxury, says Hume, pressing his unexpected point with some glee, 'is in general preferable to sloth and idleness, which would commonly succeed in its place, and are more hurtful both to private persons and to the public' (pp. 287-8). In the same vein he pleads for, not against, the establishment of successful commerce among other nations, who give us skills, he reminds his reader, take our commodities, and spur us to emulation. Hence, he concludes, 'not only as a man, but as a British subject, I pray for the flourishing commerce of Germany, Spain, Italy, and even France herself' (p. 338). Since a world war was in progress when Hume wrote these words, their effect on his readers would have been gratifyingly sharp.

In these commercial essays Hume not only annihilates moral-sentimental misconceptions but also does his best to dispel mercantilist theory and the protectionist legislation it encouraged; he argues for the beneficent action of free trade, of enlightened self-interest. Thus he helps to lay the foundation for Adam Smith, through whose 'The Wealth of Nations' (1776) runs the conviction that it is to the free pursuit of self-advantage by each member of the community that the well-being and prosperity of all can be traced; that private selfishness is public advantage; and, more specifically, that a commercially active and expanding society is thereby freer and healthier.(33) These avowals, so contrary to the morality of the poets, are of a different nature from paradox. They are advanced as decisive judgments, as principles. Hume and Smith argue their scientific case, as they conceive it, keenly, measuring the force of what they say, and meaning their conclusions to be carried through with their full weight. A contrast with the well-known arguments of Mandeville, who at the beginning of the century had asserted the beneficial economic effect of vice and luxury in 'The Grumbling Hive' (1705), enlarged later to 'The Fable of the Bees', brings this out clearly enough. Mandeville is very funny, and he makes the reader think. But nobody would call his paradoxes new formulations of economic science, or significant extensions to or reappraisals of what is taken to be its truth. Hume and Smith, on the other hand, do set before themselves as they write the aim of changing the way men have learned to think about a now rampantly capitalist economy. They wish to clear the latter of hampering restraints to its yet fuller expansion, constraints which are the outdated effect of outdated concepts, and bring men up to date in their recognition of what sort of commercial world it is that they have produced for themselves, and what their attitude to it should really be. They make short work of mercantilism, and, in their terms, of the familiar moral arguments against commercial indulgence.

There is no need to go into the technical arguments of the refutation in this place. Hume's essay 'Of Commerce', insinuating that public virtue in Rome or Sparta may have spurred men to industry, but will not do so in modern countries which are so much larger, so much fuller of manufactures and less easily assessed and recognized kinds of wealth and power, so that men now need spurring on to endure hardship by the 'animation' of a spirit of avarice, puts the plausible and half-flattering Roman comparison out of the discussion with delightfully subtle and forceful reasoning, for instance in the surprising recolouration of the term 'avarice', and in a very complete way. 'Of Money' inters the last remains of the treasure theory, and so does 'Of the Balance of Trade', both stressing in place of the provision of large stocks of useless money in a community its need to supply plenty of lucrative work for its diligent and active population keen to increase and circulate their commodities and the profits which accrue from them. Smith offers the definitive account of a capitalist economy judged according to these sympathetic criteria. Their magisterial analysis ought to settle the matter, as, by their tone, they appear to suppose that it does. Yet in truth it certainly does not. Moral unease at commerce seemed a kind of mental state which merely technical arguments could not dispel; and during the second half of the eighteenth century and the first half of the nineteenth the moral disapprobation of economic man, to choose a term which covers the merchant in his widest acceptation, grows more eloquent, widespread and fundamental than it had ever done before, even in the time of Shakespeare. The fact is that the political economist, who looked at the workings of capitalism as a scientist analysing a process, and the imaginative writer, who saw in them the destroying forces of multitudes of ordinary men and women, were beginning to find that they were speaking a different language from each other, and even looking at a different world.

For example, what the novelist Fielding reveals about Nightingale, the banker, is what an economist, as economist, could not or would not allow himself to consider. From the objectively economic view, Nightingale is a man who makes profits legally, whose business is on the increase, whose plentiful money is the oil of the commercial vitality of the community, and who helps to feed and strengthen the state. The imagery is Hume's. Subjectively, not objectively like this, literature gives us a different kind of revelation. We have seen Fielding's, and can recognize the same thing in Richardson, if we look for it. What moves Clarissa Harlowe's near relations to press her to marry the odious Solmes in Richardson's novel are their, as they will have seemed then, natural and understandable property and social ambitions. Solmes's estate and theirs lie contiguous, and will benefit from being joined. A marriage between Solmes and Clarissa will ensure that her personal estate, which unlike the jointures of the rest of the family is under her private control, and will go out of the Harlowe reach if she marries away from the neighbourhood, will in fact stay attached to the central acreage, and augment the influence and prestige of a rising name in the county; so the marriage project makes economic sense; it is a sound investment. What Richardson shows us are the human consequences of this desirable material investment, its sacrifice of lives to profits in the hands of the greedy and the unscrupulous.(34) We are in fact standing at that divergence of outlook between the political economist and the artist which in the nineteenth century was to be so critical an issue, driving Carlyle to denounce the inhumanity of the 'dismal science' on the one hand, and John Stuart Mill on the other to dismiss Coleridge as an 'arrant driveller' on economic matters.

Nevertheless more than just a different approach, the expression of different disciplines, is in question here. By the middle of the eighteenth century the nature of mercantile enterprise was leading people to question the commercial spirit more seriously than it had been questioned before, and here the split between moral thought and economic thought is less evident. Adam Smith shares in the concern at mercantile, or rather unmercantile, excesses, for example, and reserves for the East India Company some of his most searching criticism; he decides that the Company betrayed its trust and acted unjustly when it ceased to act commercially, and went to the bad by assuming a sovereignty not rightfully its own as a trading concern. This, which theoretically keeps commerce free from the corrupting taint, we note, was to form part of Burke's charge against Warren Hastings, except that Burke was to reach to still deeper fundamentals. The distinction between sovereign and commercial roles appealed to the minds of the eighteenth century because it looks explanatory, yet, refusing to term that commerce which, for example, was practised in India by the servants of the East India Company, keeps alive the notion of commercial endeavour as something intrinsically beneficent.

But how did the beneficent condition degenerate into the malign? What was its disordering principle? Commerce or not commerce, did not the unrestricted pursuit of gain have a part to play in the disruption and antagonism which all admitted as an increasingly significant feature in social life? Even by the men and women of the 1750s some of these anxious connections, to their children and grandchildren plain historical truths, to us commonplaces of knowledge, were beginning to be made.

4 DISILLUSIONMENT 1750-1790

All centuries in recent history have registered in art their overturnings of one form of inherited sentiment or another, but few such moral reappraisals of the material relations of life can have been so unforeseeable, sudden and apparently complete as the reconsidered commercial assumption in the years between the death of Dryden and the birth of Dickens; that is, as the change in attitude is reflected in formal literature. By the end of the eighteenth century imaginative writers seemed more or less universally convinced that the proposition of Steele and Defoe that the good of commerce and the good of the community could be equated with one another, a proposition then examined doubtfully and heavily modified before being allowed to pass by Fielding and the anxious Young, Thomson and others in the century's middle years, could no longer be judged to hold true. The first stage of that steady estrangement from trade, and of withdrawal of sympathy from the mode and doctrine of the commercial world, among the men of creative literature, that growth of antagonism between business pursuits and humane studies, is our story in the present chapter.

It is only the first stage that we are concerned with here. By the end of the present phase of discussion we shall see that a firm wedge has been driven, in men's conception, between the world of business ambition and that of moral pursuits, a development unthinkable to Sprat or Defoe, but not to Shakespeare, yet even so they form two aspects of the one life still; not two opposed and exclusive worlds of experience with no real common ground acknowledged to exist between them. In other words, though it is a growth in hostile suspicion we are to record here, the degree of hostility to capitalist action is by no means at its most intense by the year 1800. Indeed the attitude of late Augustan writers on commerce, even when severely critical (for instance, Edmund Burke's), was to seem tolerant and forgiving by comparison with the charges afterwards levelled against economic man in the denunciations of Coleridge, or, more intensely still, in the Marxist critique of the nineteenth century; not that the latter makes very much real impact in English literature until the twentieth.

Nevertheless, for people living at the time, the revision of ideas constituted a major reconsideration of inherited assumptions. External changes as well as the explorations of moral debate forced through this overhaul of settled opinions. Returning East Indian nabobs, ostentatious, corrupt, as people judged, and casting by their huge sudden wealth a sinister light on how the East India

Company's servants had carried out their employer's business in Asia, and what that business was, and whether all other business was of the same nature, provided a major cause of the growing disaffection with commerce at large. As early as 1726 Caleb D'Anvers's anti-Walpolean journal 'The Craftsman' had complained that nabobs were becoming socially insufferable because they seemed to think they could act with the same 'governing *Spirit* here, which they exercis'd abroad';(1) and nabobs seemed to increase in number and power, consequently in odium, as the century progressed. Other causes included the slave trade and traders; the war-time profiteers of the years from 1756 to 1763; the disruptive industrial revolution, now beginning to get into its full swing. Of the last feature we may bear in mind that no one at the time saw what we have since come to identify as industrial activity as anything new, since 'industrial' in our sense was not a word in use among writers. 'Industrialism', more to the point, did not exist in English until Carlyle coined the word in 1833-4 in 'Sartor Resartus':(2) a moment of historical illumination. The awareness we enjoy, looking backwards, which enables us to explain eighteenth-century commercial acceleration by the nineteenth-century development it led up to, and thus make sense of it, has to be put on one side if we wish to appreciate the state of mind in which writers at the time tried to make sense of what they saw happening in the poetry and drama and fiction they wrote, and readers tried to take the new characterizations in. They had no more idea than we have ourselves that they were the period of introduction to something else, but rather believed that things culminated in them, and continued, until taught otherwise, to consider the issues in the old terminology. Thus, what people thought they saw, hence did see, when they looked around them, was just more and more and more commerce; and the atmosphere darkened.

This distinct but at first subtle change in mood can be seen in the reflection of the commercial aspect of society offered in the writings of Smollett compared with that which we have seen in Fielding. The two novelists were commonly matched during their lives, and afterwards; but a difference is that Smollett, while more inclusive and uncondemning than Fielding in many of his portrayals of mercantile endeavour, even when the merchandise is slaves, yet offers a finally more damaging estimate of the nature and effect of commerce in the England of the third quarter of the eighteenth century. Perhaps this is because his fiction is rather more documentary in its nature than that of Fielding, so that we see the social message drawn with a firmer line, or because of Smollett's waspishness, or because the times have changed, or all three.

Examples of Smollett's receptive, unjudging inclusion of men of trade may be cited in numbers, and little is to be made of them. The prostitute Miss Williams in 'Roderick Random' (1748) is the daughter of a failed wine merchant; Roderick's friend Thomson gets hired on a merchant slaver bound for Guinea; Roderick thinks of turning merchant with Strap's three hundred pounds, then himself takes an engagement as ship's surgeon only to find it is a slave ship he has joined. No special importance attaches to these mercantile adventures; they are part of a roving experience, and of eighteenth-century life as Smollett records it; they are paralleled in the other novels.

But a more combative note comes through in 'Peregrine Pickle' (1751). Gamaliel Pickle, Peregrine's father, is a strongly hostile portrait of the negative side of the mercantile type, a creature of the trading world dried out by commerce and rendered unfit to compete in it; he lives in a passionless inert way on the fortune amassed by his energetic father, of whom Peregrine's Oxford companions declare he 'was in his life-time more noted for his cunning than his candour in trade' (chapter 25). Between the impulsive Peregrine and his cold-hearted parents, and generally the calculating world of trade around him, a mutual antipathy develops which Smollett draws in emphatically by making Peregrine's parents cast him off and systematically try to damage his fortunes through life. From this point Smollett, widening his range, draws in a whole society of commercial fraudulence and overreaching. Peregrine attempts to live economically and seeks advice on saving and making money, but suffers disastrously worse things yet at the hands of his commercial advisers; when Smollett goes into details on one of the schemes mentioned here, it turns out to be all but criminal exaction.(3) Yet is this, it might be objected, anything so special after all? We already know that eighteenth-century businessmen could be ruthless and fraudulent, like businessmen in all ages; what else does Fielding tell us? But Smollett portrays his age as mercantile, a view more far-reaching than any to be found in Fielding. Needing money, Peregrine joins a 'College of Authors' (chapter 101), organized hack writers paid to turn out saleable reading matter of every description at so much a sheet, so much a volume. Roderick Random had also heard of the existence of such a prostitute literary establishment, a writing syndicate ruled in its standards of conduct by the market value of works of imaginative composition and organized like a mercantile institution (ii, 250), just as he had encountered a mercenary and interest-governed theatre (ii, 267ff.). So there is a telling difference.

In Smollett, but not in Fielding, literature itself is seen as being commercialized, like everything else. It is what Smollett thought he saw happening in the society he was writing for; and he was right.(4) In those sections of 'Humphry Clinker' (1771) which deal with Bath and London, Smollett through Matthew Bramble, that is to say through a sensibility peculiarly organized to detect and pick out such ominous features, perceives all the signs of a society commercially over-developed, hence unstable. In Bramble's assessment of the new way of the world only the possession of money seems to matter, money however come by, and people are approved or rejected by society because of their ability or inability to pay. Bramble's essential complaint is that the monetization of English values has thrust society as a whole on to a course of thoroughly destructive self-indulgence. Here is an example of what Smollett adds to Fielding: the documentary touch. Bramble's is the pen writing the letter (letter of 23 April):

> Every upstart of fortune, harnessed in the trappings of the mode, presents himself at Bath, as in the very focus of observation - Clerks and factors from the East Indies, loaded with the spoil of plundered provinces; planters, negro-drivers, and hucksters, from our American plantations, enriched they know not how; agents, commissaries, and contractors, who have fattened, in two successive wars, on the blood of the nation; usurers, brokers, and jobbers of every kind; men of low birth, and no breeding, have found themselves suddenly translated into a state of affluence, unknown to former ages; and no wonder that their brains should be intoxicated with pride, vanity, and presumption. Knowing no other criterion of greatness, but the ostentation of wealth, they discharge their affluence without taste or conduct, through every channel of the most absurd extravagance; and all of them hurry to Bath, because here, without any further qualification, they can mingle with the princes and nobles of the land. Even the wives and daughters of low tradesmen, who, like shovel-nosed sharks, prey upon the blubber of those uncouth whales of fortune, are infected with the same rage of displaying their importance. (1771)

The words are Bramble's, not Smollett's, as the image in the concluding sentence reminds us. A traditionalist, Bramble may be expected to dislike the mixing of classes and the money emphasis of capitalist culture in its extremest manifestation, but the case for admitting Bramble as a reliable witness is that his nature is essentially receptive, though irritable, and he is not disqualified by cynicism from judging things in a just light. He is hypersensitive; he rises at insolence, weeps at generosity; Jery describes him as lacking a skin.

What is detailed here is the particularly outraged summary of the encroachment by a mercantile class in eighteenth-century England on genteel preserves, of their apparently morally indefensible sources of wealth, of their new recognition as a hostile vested interest opposed to the good of the community as a whole, and intent only on their own aggrandizement. Above all we note that in the phrasing Smollett gives to Bramble, such as 'upstart... the mode...suddenly translated...unknown to former ages', the sense is conveyed of these as distinctly modern developments. Regarding London, the same judgment is offered, that subversive luxury has made its appearance there during the last twenty-five years, and the extra point is especially emphasized that these new people make up a very powerful new class. Traders and opulent citizens, it is said, now spend conspicuously more than ever before; they keep more retainers, they run more houses, they attend more entertainments. As in the previous novels, art is no less contaminated by this spreading commercialism than every other activity, and evidently Smollett sees things getting worse year by year. Jery describes Tim Cropdale, one of a whole society of authors similarly engaged, who 'had made shift to live many years by writing novels, at the rate of five pounds a volume' (letter of 10 June). The feeling is that things have got out of hand and gone careering past the point at which they might have been stopped; that corruption must now run its course. Bramble puts the depopulation of the country down to it, as Goldsmith was also suggesting, and Lismahago holds forth on the theme that commerce, ruled by its own dynamic rather than subject to man's control, must be left to develop until it reaches a point at which it 'could not be fixed or perpetuated, but having flowed to a certain height, would immediately begin to ebb' (letter of 15 July), and then dry up; and he adds that commercial prosperity, perhaps like certain other human afflictions, would not and could not come twice to the same people.

This last idea is Smollett's progress interpretation of commercial civilization, introduced also into the fifth book of his 'History of England' (1785), and perhaps owing something to the thought of David Hume.(5) Behind the momentary alarm at English over-commercialization we thus sense in Smollett, again distinguishing him from Fielding, a profounder and almost deterministic apprehension of decline. It is a sense frequently encountered in the work of the poets, and is in fact the common historical outlook of the age of optimism. Such is the unsentimental context in which we must place Bramble's later praise of developing Glasgow and Manchester, and the coastal areas of Scotland; passages in which Smollett's characters are allowed to publish his own opinions, as we can see by glancing at the second volume of his economic geography of the world, 'The Present State of All Nations' (1768-9).(6) Such areas as these, in terms of economic development, are a long way behind the luxurious decadence of southern England, so he can applaud their gradual civilization and enrichment with a free mind. It is not productive growth that Smollett objects to, but what he sees as luxury: needless costly folly. So Scotland is urged forward along a prosperous road. Even so, Lismahago appears on the scene once again, proving that Sparta and Rome, when great, were poor, and forbidding anyone to wish an increase of commerce on Scotland, which in his view would bring on her a glut of evils ending in civil anarchy.

Smollett's disapprobation of men of trade and of trading values, it is apparent, is ever present and quite hard-hitting. Still, it does not rise much above contemptuous social impatience into true moral indignation, which is hardly a characteristic feature in his work. In that of Goldsmith, however, it is, and consequently the latter poet's often similar utterances add up to an immensely weightier pronouncement on pre-industrial England than that contained in the novels of Smollett. Another way of framing it is that Goldsmith is the first man among the writers of the eighteenth century to voice the fear that commerce, if it continues under its present impetus, will destroy life; he reminds us of Burke in his passionate and compassionate sympathy for the victims of capitalist oppression and commercialism gone wrong, which Smollett, for all his anti-mercantile fervour, rarely or never does. Goldsmith finally organizes his dislike of the mercantile world into a substantial all-out attack in his incisive poem 'The Deserted Village' (1770), but he rehearses the main points a number of times in his earlier writings. For example in 'The Bee', no. 5 (1759) he urges that proper and true education should instruct us in sober living instead of tempting us towards luxurious indulgence, and that many retrenchments and savings might be made in arts and commerce without endangering freedom. 'Commerce has therefore its bounds'.(7) Such a conclusion reminds us of Smollett, as its basic assumption, the advocacy of moderate living, recalls Pope, or Jonson, or Horace, but Goldsmith's more specific alertness to the overshadowing menace of commercialism in his time shows through in his 'History of England in a Series of Letters', published in the year 1764. It is here that he insinuates the arresting truth, for his time, that the merchant class in the last century and a quarter has assumed in importance the role previously held by king and conqueror. He then proceeds to urge on all his readers the importance of knowing about England's recent history (letter ii), since she is a nation now predominantly mercantile,(8) and at the same time imperial, and therefore at risk. In 'The Citizen of the World' (1760) he had declared that when a trading nation begins to act the conqueror 'it is then perfectly undone' (letter xv); such is his own country's plight, he warns, and strives to set up another criterion of welfare than material prosperity. He warns his reader against the tyranny of a few big men made powerful by wealth, a kind of tyranny which he notes is on the increase, and is what the national life is tending to; and in an essay of 1762 he laments the expropriation of the land of simple villagers by a 'Merchant of immense fortune in London' (iii, 196), and says that the phenomenon is a common one; wherever the traveller turns, indeed, he insists, while some of the inhabitants of the country are growing enormously rich, he sees others miserably poor, and 'the happy equality of condition now entirely removed' (iii, 197).

Here is a significant and pessimistic reversal of the moral lesson drawn by Defoe from the same sort of pattern of social change in his 'A Tour thro' the Whole Island of Great-Britain'. In that work, in the 1720s, Defoe had seen wealthy merchants buying old country estates as they merged with the established landed gentry, and building new ones as they sought to extend and rise into it, a gentry mercantilizing its own outlook at the same time, as a sure sign of national improvement. For Goldsmith in the 1760s the same concentration of power and fortune signalizes odious privilege, and the extension of a network of malign influence over a once independent populace. Which has changed, we might ask ourselves, the standpoint, or the object viewed? Both, it is evident, have travelled far in half a century; but perhaps a degree of nostalgic sentiment in Goldsmith, from which Defoe is singularly free, strengthens his impression of a culture degenerating from its once ideal condition.

These insights are brought together in 'The Traveller' (1764). Wealth and free action, Goldsmith argues there, which once were the distinguishing marks of English life, have between them destroyed contentment and then worked so as to strengthen the 'bonds' of wealth and law; obviously there is a certain amount of paradox in the idea. Out of this secondary state of things, though, of unofficial tyrannizing over the poor, the love of gain and the love of power have subverted freedom; 'and honour sinks where commerce long prevails' (line 92). Whatever the subtleties of the stages of its development might be, Goldsmith sees the vastly increasing liberty of the rich few as entailing enslavement for the ordinary people. He sees the language of political debate as now a mere debased sham, that is to say he judges that the rhetoric of a previous century, when the terminology of an idea may have carried authentic meaning, and words signified what they claimed and were supposed to signify, now is drained of all its original expressiveness and merely films over gross economic appetite.

Always these perceptions are cast in a human, sometimes in a humorous, light, it is important to add. Dr Primrose in 'The Vicar of Wakefield' (1766) is depicted arguing for true liberty and the king, against a rich man who in liberty's name rails against the present government and would have the monarch act only as he is allowed to act; and noticeably during this exchange the character of modest unworldly Primrose gives way to that of an authoritative political theorist and debater (chapter xix). This is very like Goldsmith giving us his own view. But so as to ensure that we do not get too carried away by the serious argumentation, and forget that we are reading a comedy, he has the rich man turn out to be the rich man's butler putting on airs in his master's absence. The real owner, when he comes in, shows himself a decent man, hospitable, moderate, and polite. The irony here is a necessary ingredient; pomposity and sermonizing are the special dangers of such writing.

In these political disquisitions Goldsmith's central conviction has remained. He has attacked the selfishness of gain, leading to monopoly trade, leading to power concentration, leading to oppression; and he has stressed how, by fixing on the exclusive goal of mercantile success and abandoning all other endeavours for that single aim, his society has lost its true bearings. The same theme is at the core of 'The Deserted Village' (1770), which sweeps up all previous separate complaints into a resonant denunciation of the effect actual commerce has had on the known experience of living communities of people; leaves theory on one side, for real facts. Goldsmith's simple aim is to recreate in verse a picture of the damaged lives of the victims of economic development, not to argue; or rather, for he does argue vehemently against commerce, to emphasize the real individual suffering which economic theory might overlook. As we have seen, a mass of historical and political analysis lies behind the judgment offered, simple though it seems. And the justification for his emphasis on actual life, Goldsmith implies, is that people are the real test of the acceptability of a system of economic relations. Hence, summaries of the poem's argument fail to do it justice; it must be read and felt. Hence too, it loses little force as a criticism of commerce if, in the end, depopulation is proved to have been less prevalent throughout English life than Goldsmith says it was, as his opponents claimed, for if only one such case were found to have existed, and no more, it would be enough. Goldsmith's charge after all is that commerce ignores men, and tries to judge and compare the value of human lives, which are not to be computed.

What 'The Deserted Village' does is raise the debate on the condition of England on to a new plane. The poet explicitly refuses to consider welfare in some economic or generalized definition, but only in terms of the lives of real people, often of no economic importance; and in these terms, he declares, what has happened and is happening over the country at large is no less than a cultural disaster. The village of Auburn is singled out as a typical case. It is deserted because a single rich man has bought it and cleared out of it at a stroke every other living individual. His power to do this, his power over human lives, comes from the laws which protect that which is now 'his' property, after a single bargain; and his power to buy this kind of property has come from wealth acquired in commerce. So he is ejecting from his land, with full legal justification, those who were born and brought up there, and have known no other home; and what he is doing to Auburn, others are doing elsewhere. Goldsmith sees the rise of these new men, the 'unfeeling train' of trade (line 63), as little less than a robbery of the people of England, whom he terms 'dispossessed', and their land 'usurped' (line 64); and he regrets the destruction and casting out of once vital graces, and once loved modes of existence which are rich in human significance, but poor in material reward or in science, and which economic theory, approving the increased efficiency made possible by such clearances of haphazard village communities, is not equipped to recognize. Here is a glimpse of the kind of humane, not monetary, value which Goldsmith would like to see rehabilitated: the happy commerce of the village pub (lines 225-50):

> Imagination fondly stoops to trace
> The parlour splendours of that festive place;
> The white-wash'd wall, the nicely sanded floor,
> The varnish'd clock that click'd behind the door;
> The chest contriv'd a double debt to pay,
> A bed by night, a chest of drawers by day;
> The pictures plac'd for ornament and use,
> The twelve good rules, the royal game of goose,
> The hearth, except when winter chill'd the day,
> With aspen boughs, and flowers, and fennel gay;
> While broken tea-cups, wisely kept for show,
> Rang'd o'er the chimney, glisten'd in a row.

Vain transitory splendours! could not all
Reprieve the tottering mansion from its fall!
Obscure it sinks, nor shall it more impart
An hour's importance to the poor man's heart;
Thither no more the peasant shall repair
To sweet oblivion of his daily care;
No more the farmer's news, the barber's tale,
No more the wood-man's ballad shall prevail;
No more the smith his dusky brows shall clear,
Relax his ponderous strength, and lean to hear;
The host himself no longer shall be found
Careful to see the mantling bliss go round;
Nor the coy maid, half willing to be press'd,
Shall kiss the cup to pass it to the rest.

(1770)

Things happen, we observe, in this evocation of the life of a departed culture; the song prevails, the brow clears, the drink is kissed and shared. Goldsmith could have made his description static and argumentative, but prefers to recreate the play of life. All the emphasis therefore is on human, not monetary, valuations. The broken tea cups are wisely kept, or were, and the chest paid for itself twice over in usefulness. Drawing thus a stark contrast between economic value and human service, Goldsmith proceeds to demonstrate in the remainder of the poem, where we need not follow him in detail, how these two forces, life and commercial life, are fixed in mutual opposition. The villagers cast out from their home, we read some lines later on, perish, or make their way abroad, as lost to England as if they had perished, or escape to the growing towns to perish there; sacrifices all to the monster which unhoused them in the first place.

Adam Smith burst out in 'The Wealth of Nations' (1776) that everyone knew England was better off than she had ever been in spite of all the prophecies of ruin and depopulation.(9) Nevertheless, such distrust of the mercantile valuation as Goldsmith expresses was widely shared and grew more tendentious during the final quarter of the century. It is a different kind of sentiment from the traditional hostility to commerce, Fielding's, say, or Wycherley's, who place their emphasis on the arid spiritual condition of the merchant himself and are never quite free from contemptuous amusement, as at somebody foolishly wrong about obvious priorities. Now, in the late eighteenth century, writers feel compelled to look at the issue afresh and examine it more closely and more seriously, and appear to sense that in a way not encountered before human existence is somehow directly placed under threat. Although we still meet with the older attitude of assumed superiority, for instance in the satirical poems of Charles Churchill,(10) such new anxieties are in fact the beginnings of the expression of a developing public conscience. It is from 1770 onwards that sustained objection starts to be raised against the wrongs committed for profit on the inhabitants of India, on the negro, later on the poor at home. And from the same period too the disturbing possibility starts to be canvassed that the whole nation of the English is implicated in the wrongs in question; that not a handful of bad or misguided men, but everyone of any significance in society must accept a proportion of the responsibility for slavery, depopulation and extortion.

It will not seem exaggerated to the reader of Burke's India speeches (1784-95) to say that in the implications Burke draws from the British presence in the Indian sub-continent he asks his listeners to pass judgment on their own actions, carried out by their own representatives, according to or in defiance of their own values; that is, asks his countrymen to define where they stand on commercial depravity. What distinguished England still from all other nations, Englishmen had always told themselves, was her mercantile supremacy. Now the signs were that she was beginning to degenerate. Was not the commercial spirit itself a part of this moral regression, perhaps its cause? An inevitable reassessment of the merchant dream is one reason for this growing scepticism; inevitable, because when Goldsmith wrote in 1770 the dream had had time to materialize but had failed to do so. Certainly, commerce had made England rich; but only part of England had benefited from those riches. And this was only a small item in the programme. All the rest remained unperformed, and placed further from reach. Commerce had not liberated. It had not enhanced men's lives. It had not dissolved the separate antagonistic nations into a human family. Commerce was turning out a failed spell. That was one cause of disillusion. Another was the changing role of the merchant himself during the same years. A tendency described in the economic history of the middle decades of the eighteenth century is for commercial companies to grow larger, and, as we saw reflected in the novels of Fielding, for merchants themselves to become figures more and more remote from daily experience and from shop or office contact, their business interests increasing in diversity and abstractness, in the sense that credit and investment took over as their stuff of trade from commodity sale and purchase. At the same time, and in consequence of these new developments, their rivalries and animosities became intenser, and operated on a larger scale. In short, capitalism intensifying threw men more and more off course from their expected goal. Dryden in 1667 had promised commerce would 'make one City of the Universe' but a hundred years later all knew it would not and could not. All knew it had sharpened divisions instead of allaying them. Uncommercial men found the workings of trade baffling, and were repelled by its people, who, they saw, whatever else was hidden from them, did not approximate to Defoe's or Steele's ideal merchant, and whose methods of getting money were not made easier to forgive by their even more antagonizing ways of spending it.

Especially was this felt to be true of the servants of the East India Company, who supplied the last generation of eighteenth-century Englishmen with its bête noire in the form of the arrogant nabob loaded with vulgar wealth and criminality; and whose indictment in the person of Warren Hastings, at least as Burke wished to persuade men to interpret that case, was the indictment of a whole civilization gone to the bad, a smaller Nuremberg trial of its era. Horace Walpole wrote in 1772 in correspondence with Sir Horace Mann that East India Company adventurers in India had starved millions by 'monopolies and plunder, and almost raised a famine at home by the luxury occasioned by their opulence raising the price of everything, till the poor could not purchase bread!'(11) But it was not only nabobs who were judged thus; the new breed of merchant, the monopolist, the big businessman, caught the hostile eye whatever his line of trade. 'Indian nabob, Caribbean sugar planters, African slave traders, and government war contractors', we are informed, were grouped together in the popular opinion as the enemy 'assailing insular and agricultural England'.(12) Of these economic manipulators, the East India Company profiteers happened then to be the most noticeable and most newsworthy. To some observers their outstanding representatives, such as the fabulous Clive, the universally offensive Richard Smith, or the kinglike Hastings, appeared not just greedy but destructive of all foreign culture which they encountered and plundered, and in the end self-destructive. Horace Walpole tells off the links in the chain (loc. cit.):

> Conquest, usurpation, wealth, luxury, famine - one knows how little farther the genealogy has to go! If you like it better in Scripture phrase, here it is: Lord Chatham begot the East India Company; the East India Company begot Lord Clive; Lord Clive begot the Maccaronies, and they begot poverty - and all the race are still living; just as Clodius was born before the death of Julius Caesar. There is nothing more alike than two ages that are very alike. (1772)

Walpole wrote these words less than fifty years after Defoe had held up the merchant as the hero of civilized living. The calamitous speed of this moral downturn, all encompassed within a single lifetime, and as widespread and complete as it is sudden, with the man of trade, hero no longer, presiding destructively at its centre, is what Walpole draws attention to. What a nightmare has issued from the Augustan dream!

Since Walpole stresses, as many others also did, the malign role of the East India Company in this process of decivilization, it is necessary to remind ourselves of what it was that took place in India and why it mattered so much to contemporary moralists. Circumstances, in brief, had placed the East India Company in the position of virtual ruler of much of India by the end of the third quarter of the eighteenth century; that was the trouble. The Company had gone there to trade, taking cloth and silver from England and bringing back spices and silk in return, then had established trading depots, and fortified them, which had led to its building up a defensive force; subsequently it had driven out the French, begun to administer the territories it at first visited as a mercantile concern, and finally, impelled by pressures both outside its control and within, had assumed overall dominion in a country otherwise crumbling into disintegration before its eyes. Thus the sub-continent, a kingdom, had sunk into a company's hands. Not to exploit the gainful possibilities of such an event would have been too much to hope for or expect. Company spokesmen and defenders did what they could to put a sympathetic construction on the anarchy of the middle years of the century in Indian experience.(13) But no benign interpretation, the critics insist, could palliate the enormity by which a band of foreign merchants, granted permission to open trading posts in Madras, Bombay and Calcutta, turned themselves in a brief historical period into the masters of the whole territory. It was their abuse of this power which shocked people, not only its unauthorized acquisition. Nations had been extirpated, the stories circulated, had been sold into slavery, had been refused rice in the midst of famine so as to keep the price of foodstuffs artifically high; here is the sinister commercial note creeping in. With this revelation to combat it, we can understand how the cherished assumption that commerce works beneficently, of late anyway getting a little ragged at the edges, and that the merchant is his society's moral pattern, came to be discredited and disproved at last. Burke correctly forecast that Hastings would be acquitted, but used his trial as an occasion for stating in memorable form the concept of trust, which, he maintained, should lie at the centre of all forms of exercised power, including economic power; but so obviously did not.

Burke and Sheridan, as we shall see, put the case against irresponsible commercialism at its most resonantly sweeping so far, but they are neither of them, of course, radicals. They hold to the view that, properly managed, commerce works for the good of humanity. Others, though, went deeper. Samuel Johnson, amicably disposed to Hastings personally, would not join in the condemnation of East Indian officials,(14) yet noted and commented on the dissolving action of commercial life, breaking up the clan and family loyalties for which, as he expressed it in 1772, 'in a country so commercial as ours, where every man can do for himself, there is not so much occasion' ('Boswell's Johnson', ii, 177). But Johnson as he describes it stresses how the effect of the rise of individualism which is so bound up with the growth of a capitalist economy, is to separate and divide. 'You have first large circles, or clans; as commerce increases, the connection is confined to families. By degrees, that too goes off, as having become unnecessary, and there being few opportunities of intercourse. One brother is a merchant in the city, and another is an officer in the guards. How little intercourse can these two have' (ibid.). From division to antagonism is a short step. Boswell records how Johnson took the view against Goldsmith that commerce not luxury was the morally corroding principle at work in society (ii, 218).

The general recognition of this seamier side of commercial endeavour by the third quarter of the eighteenth century is enough to highlight for us how challenging or old-fashioned is Adam Smith's conception and framing of the issue in 'The Wealth of

Nations' (1776). When Smith reminds his readers that commerce should be 'among nations, as among individuals, a bond of union and friendship',(15) he is putting aside as accidents the incidents history may produce of the contrary operation. When he derives from the combined force of the self-seeking instinct of every individual merchant his attractive pattern of harmonious interlocking purposes, he is putting the best construction possible on economic appetite. It is an almost aesthetic idea projecting itself as a scientific law, and very redolent of neo-Augustan thought; it reminds one of the baroque concept, a condition of vital rest sustained by the equal opposition of forces. But the proposition is rather a hypothesis than a demonstration. And in feeling, Smith belongs to the optimistic years of Defoe and Hume, not the disillusioned 1770s and 1780s. Far below this hopeful sketch of what should be, he is constrained to admit, falls the conduct of the officials of the East India Company, and to extricate his theory from its own refutation he brings out his celebrated distinction between a sovereign and a mercantile role; not that it was an idea unheard of before Smith.(16) Whereas a sovereign studies the good of his subjects, Smith writes, the commercial attitude is intrinsically one of gain-seeking at the expense of other men, and so cannot be also caring of them. For this reason 'merchants and manufacturers neither are, nor ought to be, the rulers of mankind'. Smith does not dwell on the radical implications of this judgment. But Coleridge would press them to their limit.

Burke's less theoretical attitude to the East India Company was also more morally downright. Agreeing with Smith that the Company had abandoned its mercantile role in India,(17) he nevertheless launches on his own part the profounder charge that its servants had inflicted on the subject races of India an injustice greater than any other in their history,(18) or any history, and that they had implicated the whole English people in their misdeeds, now called upon to pronounce judgment on them, in their chief representative, Hastings, as perpetrators of a national dishonour. The case, for Burke, is not limited to mercantile mismanagement but stretches out to become one of corruption; and it is not a mercantile company which Burke wants to try for this crime, but a mercantile nation, whose members, some by actual guilt and the rest by contamination, are found to have exceeded all previous extremes of depraved extortionate greed. Burke continually stresses the wider reference. Opening his speech on Fox's East India Bill on 1 December 1783, that is at the outset of the scandal, he says that the debate on which Parliament has embarked 'will turn out a matter of great disgrace, or great glory to the British nation. We are on a conspicuous stage, and the world marks our demeanour' (iv, 4). Closing his speech on the Nawab of Arcot's debts on 28 February 1785, he reminds his listeners: 'do what we please to put India from our thoughts, we can do nothing to separate it from our public interest and our national reputation' (iv, 320-1).

For all this, Burke, we find, when he proceeds to open out his argument, is not concerned to impugn the mercantile character itself. He is convinced that he is dealing with a case of corrupt behaviour, not with the breakdown of morality, though a case which involves the whole of English life, and suggestive of a larger dereliction if not duly weighed and condemned. We must show a willingness to accept Burke's constant reference from the East India Company back to Parliament, then outwards to the nation as a whole, and further outwards to mankind, as implying a belief in the existence of some effective standard of commercial practice and moral feeling, some norm, and some acceptable criterion of conduct, though perhaps one which men had a tendency to violate, and from which the East India Company's servants were the aberration. Throughout, Burke refuses to condemn merchants as a class.(19)

Perhaps this belief that commerce was still benign, or at least in itself neutral, was still the general view, on balance; but other suggestions start to make themselves heard. Sheridan, speaking in February 1787 on the fourth charge against Warren Hastings, that he had inflicted 'insupportable hardships' on the person and family of the Wazir of Oude, discerns a characteristic meanness in the behaviour of the Company's servants, a consonance between what they are, men of trade, and what they stand accused of, pettiness of mind, though pettiness on a grand scale:(20)

> Alike in the political and the military line could be observed *auctioneering ambassadors* and *trading generals*; - and thus we saw a revolution brought about by *affidavits*; an army employed in *executing an arrest*; a town besieged on *a note of hand*; a prince dethroned for the *balance of an account*. Thus it was they exhibited a government which united the mock majesty of a bloody sceptre, and the little *traffick of a merchant's counting house*, wielding a truncheon with one hand, and *picking a pocket with the other*. (1787)

It is an interesting connection which this piece of rhetorical flourishing suggests, but not one which Sheridan follows up in the remainder of his speech, or elsewhere in his writings, and it is perhaps to be judged as no more than the old familiar contempt for trade in a new form. Yet when a nabob, Sir Oliver Surface, Charles Surface's uncle, appears in Sheridan's play 'The School for Scandal' (1777), the dramatist makes him the only good hearted and non-mercenary eighteenth-century worthy of the whole picture gallery of family portraits, the only one with sufficient remaining merit to his name not to be deserving of having his picture summarily disposed of for what it will fetch; the only one exonerated, if one sees the auction in IV, i as a judgment passed on the whole of the preceding century. The question still remained: how to curb the corrupting process? Before even that could be attempted, how to isolate and recognize it? Was not the rage for gain, its apparent source, the merchant's distinguishing mark? Then the commercial instinct itself must enclose the seeds of evil. 'I call Man an *aurivorous animal*,' writes Horace Walpole in 1783, judging that 'modern rapine' has become 'more barefaced' than its equivalent ever was in the past, and he goes on to add that modern nabobs plunder the Indies with open hands, not 'under the banner of piety like the old Spaniards and Portuguese' (Walpole, ix, 400). Walpole in saying this is not attempting to pinpoint man's freedom from superstition, needless to say, only his ferocious and uncontrollable modern appetite for gain. The profit motive has replaced the cross.

Walpole writes with concentrated hostility, for effect. But one cannot say he exaggerates. Even the lighter literature of the time shows traces of this latest alienation from men of trade. When George Colman makes Mr Freeport, the main figure in 'The English Merchant' (1767), a boldly generous lover and man of business, we recognize the early eighteenth-century attitude holding out; even the name is borrowed from Steele's 'The Spectator'. But when he comes up to date in 'The Man of Business' (1774), a whole new slant, instanced in the new title, is suddenly evident. Here, social events and relationships have become startling and unexpected, and the world has drastically changed. The two sides of Temple Bar have changed hands. Gay sparks have taken to business; merchants and bankers have become 'your principal persons of pleasure now-a-days'.(21) The Indian adventurers Golding and Tropick reveal themselves as subtle entrepreneurs, a new slippery breed. We are in a faster, sleazier, less rooted world. In Samuel Foote's comedy 'The Nabob' (1772) Touchit summarizes the Indian adventure: friendly merchants beg to be allowed to carry on a beneficial commerce with an inoffensive people, then turn them out of their lands and take possession of their money and jewels. (22) Foote had already attacked war profiteers in 'The Commissary' (1765), showing in that work, his nineteenth-century editor justly points out, 'a squanderer and a fool' but in the later nabob character 'a villain of a higher aim and deeper stamp' (p. 181). The anonymous Popean satire 'The Nabob: or, Asiatic Plunderers' (1773) stigmatizes the profit motive itself as corrupting (p. 42):

> Low-thoughted Commerce! heart-corrupting trade!
> To blast pure morals and true Virtue made:
> So *Plato* thought, so *More*, and *Montesquieu*;
> The voice of Heav'n confirms their judgment true.
>
> (1773)

The early capitalist reference to Sir Thomas More and the pre-capitalist reference to Plato are both rare at this date. Adding a note on Montesquieu, the writer brings us back to current issues (loc. cit.):

> This last Author says, that commerce refines indeed manners, but always corrupts morals. What idea of christianity must Indians conceive from our traders? What notions must the Africans entertain of our humanity in purchasing slaves of such who never injured us? What Religion (and can morals exist without the worship of Deity?) is seen in *Madrass*, and particularly in *Bengal*, or in the *West-Indian* Islands? Such is the fruit of commerce every-where. (1773)

One could not find the mistrust of the times more succinctly expressed, anticipating Coleridge. And notice the implication which is pressed upon the reader. The merchant is guilty for being a merchant: such is the point the writer has nearly reached. General opinion, though tending towards the sceptical with each succeeding year, was as yet less extreme than this, holding perhaps to the official view, so to call it, expressed in George Wallis's play 'The Mercantile Lovers' (1775): that trade was still the bulwark of the British nation and not less so because there exist 'a few despicable wretches who have accidentally stolen into that honourable body' (V, iv). Yet even here the case against monopolizers has a contemporary if melodramatic ring. Testy condemns Swash as one of those who 'pour'd forth the scanty produce of the land to a foreign shore - tore from the indigent, the very staff of life - avaritiously grasp'd at the king's bounty - and purchas'd wealth at the expense of your humanity' (IV, ii). So the despicable wretches appear to be getting quite powerful.

In such literary pieces the new unfriendly glance thrown on men of commerce is not to be mistakenly equated with the contemptuous prejudice of the conservative thinkers of the seventeenth century. Rather it is a freshly awakened suspicion with plenty of contemporary indications at its disposal; for instance, the slave trade. There are, of course, many more pieces than are discussed here, and though many of them are minor works of literature which offer little opportunity for profound discussion,(23) they testify to the wary spreading hostility of the age. Naturally, some writers prefer to see the excesses as exceptions to normal practice, for it is simpler to be shocked than to re-think an accepted opinion. An example might be John Ferriar, who launches an attack on slavery in his play 'The Prince of Angola' (1788), based on Southerne's 'Oroonoko' (1693), but looks forward to a time when 'commerce shall no longer serve to multiply the causes of political discord, and to extend the miseries of war', and when 'the merchant shall renew his proper character, and cease to act as a plunderer and a pirate' (p. ix). But what is a merchant's proper character? That was exactly the difficulty. A plunderer and a pirate had come to seem uncomfortably close descriptions, in the opinion of many. Thus, by the time he wrote, Ferriar's sentiment could be criticised as merely pious. More attuned to reality in that age appeared Adam Smith's verdict that a merchant could not be caring of those with whom he dealt; Dr Johnson's diagnosis of the severing and disruptive action of commerce; Burke's contention that the immorality of its merchants was for England a national issue of extreme urgency and seriousness.

This radical critique of the merchant, or rather of capitalist man, does not reach full expression until the Romantic and Victorian periods in English literature, and perhaps later still, for example in the writings of Coleridge, Dickens, and Lawrence, and not with universal agreement even then; but what the literature we have looked at does show is a significant shift in that direction. Something had gone deeply wrong, writers found, with the merchant whom Defoe had idealized, had gone wrong more or less immediately after Defoe ceased writing, and had gone wrong most of all in India. India is worth stressing, for the greater éclat of the slave trade and the overwhelmingly contentious Industrial Revolution have combined to obscure its significance for us as an issue in the history of moral change; yet, at the time, and chiefly because of Burke, it attained the status of a national moral touchstone. There had been nothing like it in recent history; it was pushed and contested as the indictment of a civilization. Burke himself insisted that those who listened to him should see Hasting's trial as the whole country calling itself to account for the 'anarchical interregnum', as a recent historian calls it,(24) from 1757 onwards, when so much of India was yielded to British hands. He argued that moral breakdown in India must mean moral breakdown in England, if condoned; and told his listeners in Parliament that the culprits, apart from one or two arch-criminals, were their friends and relations.

What then, men were now asking, with increasingly serious concern, which they had not asked before, was this malign germ of commerce that appeared capable of transforming human beings into devils? In his poem 'The Task' (1785) William Cowper turns the issue over, and at last isolates the practice of the formation of alliances of interest between calculating men as the evil principle; especially commercial alliances, alliances with a view to trading profit drawn from other men. Such relations, he says, are artificial; and they dessicate and exile the feelings. Cowper's theory is that social man in his natural condition resembles a 'flow'r/Blown in its native bed'.(25) But when he is associated and 'leagu'd' with other men by royal warrant, as in the case of chartered boroughs, or by the principles of self-interest, or by the bond of warlike action, they resemble in their compelled but unvital comradeship plucked flowers, separated from their proper source of being, and bound together with artificial ties. Such flowers, compressed, defiled, fade rapidly and die. So boroughs and privileged burghers turn hurtful by their very combination with one another which is designed to safeguard and protect men, denying more vital relations, and become 'only fit/For dissolution', and so merchants in their turn (26)

unimpeachable of sin
Against the charities of domestic life
Incorporated, seem at once to lose
Their nature; and, disclaiming all regard
For mercy and the common rights of man,
Build factories with blood, conducting trade
At the sword's point, and dyeing the white robe
Of innocent commercial justice red.

(1785)

Already in these lines, we note, the industrial revolution is glimpsed. Cowper's distinction between man as a spontaneous living individual enjoying natural social ties, and corporate man alienated from his fellows, is profoundly suggestive and prophetic. His emphasis on denaturing system, denying the free interplay of feeling, forms the starting point from which Blake, Coleridge and Dickens, facing even greater threats to human life than those of the eighteenth century, were to analyse the spirit of capitalism more radically than anyone but Cowper had yet thought it necessary to do. And even in Cowper, of course, it is not an analysis we are being offered; what he gives us is little more than an interesting suggestion.

5 THE RESPONSE TO INDUSTRIALISM 1790-1830

Cowper's hint in 1785 that institutionalized commerce corrupts is reaffirmed with a fresh, almost revolutionary intensity of distaste by Romantic writers who were experiencing, in the widespread industrialization of English life, a degree of subjection to organized commerce which Cowper of course did not know, and can hardly have dreamed possible. Revolution, and revolution of all kinds, is after 1789 the new sense which is in the air. The single issue of manufacturing industry, though morally posing no new question that mere commerce had not posed before it (that is, how to harness and civilize the gainful instinct) is recognized as a far more profound and urgent matter than commerce as such had ever been. Its social manifestations such as systematized labour, a mass proletariat, often unemployed, often starving, and huge growing cities far outstripping their provision of basic services, to say nothing of more spiritual needs, loom threateningly over a society mentally unprepared for such rapid shiftings and new growths of energy and the equally rapid vanishing of age-old patterns of behaviour, and such new intense needs, and thus not in a condition to make ready sense of them. The disintegration, writers sense, is a mental as well as a physical phenomenon. The traditional attitude to trade, that it works enhancingly, as we saw in the previous chapter, is still present in Adam Smith, who nevertheless finds himself having to explain cases where it seems not to apply as not authentic examples of trade. But more and more in the aggressive economic theories of Smith's followers, that is in Bentham, Malthus, Ricardo and the classical school, the opposite strain is the one that comes to be heard and emphasized: that the workings of trade and industry operate as if laid down by unchanging laws; and as the workings are crushing in their impact, so the laws which drive them are conceived to be rigorous and unavoidable.

All these, the material and the theoretical features of their awesome enigmatic new age, engaged the pens of the imaginative writers at the end of the eighteenth and the beginning of the nineteenth centuries. If one looks for unity among the Romantics, rather than in theories of nature or the imaginative process it may be found in the judgment that, in a more inward sense than ever before, English life has become engrained with commercialism; that in their time commercialism has reached some kind of crisis. It may be found too in the tone of voice, often desperate, in which this recognition is made. This access of urgent anxiety, it may be, is in the long run the most significant development of all, for it is a definitely new phenomenon; not the perennial controversy of each new generation, but the first-time response to something historically original. It disturbed, therefore, profounder fears than previous developments had touched. Burke, for example, had proved able to survey the commercial anarchy of India with indignation during the impeachment of Hastings, but also firmly; merchant honour, he maintained, still existed, grossly though it had been betrayed. After Hastings's acquittal his confidence left him.

In Blake's writings can be seen that reversal of optimism about capitalist endeavour which, I have suggested, characterizes the transference from the eighteenth-century frame of mind to the mood of the nineteenth. In his early play 'King Edward the Third' (1783) he describes how King Edward looking back on England from his wars in France sees

> commerce fly round
> With his white wings, and sees his golden London
> And her silver Thames, throng'd with shining spires
> And corded ships, her merchants buzzing round
> Like summer bees, and all the golden cities
> In his land overflowing with honey.(1)

We might be reading Thomson or Young. But Blake's later estimate is exactly opposite. In 'Vala, or the Four Zoas' (1797) the cruel productions of Urizen are set forth in the imagery of industrial and manufacturing England, whose energy, Blake says, is not fostering but exploiting, and which comes over as a malign and hostile encroachment on the sources of life.(2)

> First Trades & Commerce Ships & armed vessels he builded laborious
> To swim the deep & on the land children are sold to trades
> Of dire necessity still laboring night & day till all
> Their life extinct they took the spectre form in dark despair
> And slaves in myriads in ship loads burden the hoarse sounding deep
> Rattling with clanking chains the Universal Empire groans.
> (1797)

Only fourteen years separate the two poems, but, as we can see, in attitude they could not be more different. In the interval ships have become for Blake armed vessels or human shuttles burdening the hoarse ocean instead of corded merchantmen decorating a silver river and filling the land with honey and gold. In an earlier passage of the same section of 'Vala', Blake had specified that the sons of Urizen are condemned because they have changed the arts of life into the arts of death, rejecting the use of simple tools for complicated machinery; that is, he condemns them because they industrialize. And the same point lies behind the shift of vision here, from stately sailers to slave transports.

Blake's objection, if we seek to isolate his principle, is to the bondage imposed by the machine when it goes beyond simple function into intricate working, and also to mechanization, and to the spirit behind mechanization, which makes out of an implement that ought to serve man's needs his effective ruler. The hammer, axe and saw therefore are approved because man controls their operation, but not their abandonment for complex machines (p. 47):

Then left the Sons of Urizen the plow & harrow the loom
The hammer & the chisel & the rule & compasses
They forgd the sword the chariot of war the battle ax
The trumpet fitted to the battle & the flute of summer
And all the arts of life they changd into the arts of death
The hour glass contemnd because its simple workmanship
Was as the workmanship of the plowman & the water wheel
That raises water into Cisterns broken & burnd in fire
Because its workmanship was like the workmanship of the
shepherd.
(1797)

The replacements for these despised ancient instruments of labour, complicated industrial machines, are condemned by the poet as inimical to life. They operate (p. 47) so as to

perplex youth in their outgoings & to bind to labours
Of day & night the myriads of Eternity, that they might file
And polish brass & iron hour after hour laborious work-
manship
Kept ignorant of the use that they might spend the days of
wisdom
In sorrowful drudgery to obtain a scanty pittance of bread
In ignorance to view a small portion & think that All
And call it Demonstration blind to all the simple rules of life.
(1797)

Though Blake's imaginative writing resists more than most poetry the imposition on it of a specific message, when he turns to the functioning of commerce and the natural operations of a commercialized society he is explicit that its latest expression is an inroad on life, a denaturing. He writes with regard to art that market values threaten true genius by favouring saleable mediocrity in its place, indeed that commerce is 'so far from being beneficial to Arts, or to Empires, that it is destructive of both, as all their History shows, for the above Reason of Individual Merit being its Great Hatred'.(3) When he adds explanatorily that 'Empires flourish till they become Commercial, & then they are scatter'd abroad to the four winds' (ibid.), we may judge how sharp the intensification of feeling, and especially hostile feeling, is getting. For Blake's phrasing adds violent revenge, in 'scatter'd abroad', to an eighteenth-century commonplace never before expressed with such relishing animosity. None of this could be inferred from the English scene he so approvingly depicts in 'King Edward the Third', a depiction inspired by literature rather than life.

One could say that this sharper hostility to developing capitalism, as well as being Blakean, is that of the Romantic period itself: for we meet with it after 1800 whenever literature deals with social change, the spread of credit, the fluctuations of trade, the effects of war, class antagonism, necessitarian economic analysis, or any other aspects of the industrial and accompanying social and intellectual revolution of the times. The change in feel is like a rise in temperature; and we can sense this alteration in emphasis, and by now perhaps in assumptions too, if we think of the social and economic pronouncements of Defoe, profound enough yet fixed, even blissful, in their confidence that more mercantile activity will and must produce a better society, and compare what Coleridge has to say, and from what contrasting experience he draws his judgments and observations, and what deeper recognitions of the evil results of gain-hunger than were available to Defoe, when he considers the apparently desperate economic condition of his time. No writer of the age shows a tenser awareness than Coleridge of the capitalist temper of his generation. His prose writings from 1795 onwards constitute a sustained and deeply serious enquiry into the nature of the society of his time, particularly into the causes and manifestations of its extreme economic dividedness; and it is the case that for Coleridge, as for Blake, capitalism in its industrial form appears wholly destructive of the sanctities of life. A constant theme in his work is his jealousy of its invasion of spiritual well-being; even more, perhaps, his bitterness against the justifying and institutionalizing of selfish materialism by political economists in some inflexible theory of exploitation as a natural law.

But Coleridge, like Dryden before him, adopts varying positions on specific issues at different times during his life, declaring in 1795 that commerce is 'useless except to continue imposture and oppression',(4) then in 1800 tolerating it as necessary, even a blessing (op. cit., iii:i, 144), and in yet later essays, such as 'On the Constitution of Church and State', assimilating it as almost an integral element in the body politic. It is the property of vital thought to develop. Coleridge's development is towards moderation from an extremer hostility. He is consistent, though, in relating growing commercialism to declining faith and vanished culture and decayed aristocratic honour, and in the historical sense which he brings to bear on the issue, which is of sovereign importance. All man's true needs could be supplied, he declares in 1795, though commerce were 'now unknown' (op. cit., i, 223), and he proceeds to instance among the 'vast and various' evils which the rise of commerce has brought in 'Cities Drunkenness, Prostitution, Rapine, Beggary and Diseases - Can we walk the Streets of a City without observing them in all their most loathsome forms? Add to these Irreligion' (loc. cit.). If this appears to us in its context too general an indictment to be useful, cities for instance hardly offering themselves as automatic equations with commerce, it later proves to be penetratingly specific and uncompromising. Singled out for condemnation are Clive, Hastings and the East India Company, whose profits cost eight million lives; property is judged to be scarcely allowable; and value is denied to what the England of which James Thomson so proudly wrote has done and become during two centuries. Instead Coleridge reaches back to a phase before the commercial revolution had got under way to find an England sound in her moral and social organization. He calls the natural action of commerce exploitative and fraudulent, not aiming at a mainly witty stroke like Dryden, who had designated it living off the spoil, but pressing his argument with a completely serious intent. All those engaged in trade, he says, are subject to the corruption here isolated, and no trader, no commercial man, may regard himself as free from its contaminating influence. Let any such person, Coleridge demands (loc. cit.):

> look around his shop? Does nothing in it come from the desolate plains of Indostan? From what motives did Lord Clive murder his million and justify it to all but his own conscience? From what motives did the late rice-contracting Governor famish a million and gain from the Company the Title of Saviour of India? Was it not that wicked as they were they increased and preserved the commercial Intercourse? It has been openly asserted that our commercial intercourse with the East Indies has been the occasion of the loss of eight million Lives - in return for which most foul and heart-inslaving Guilt we receive gold, diamonds, silks, muslins & callicoes for fine Ladies and Prostitutes, Tea to make a pernicious Beverage, Porcelain to drink it from, and salt-petre for the making of gunpowder with which we may murder the poor Inhabitants who supply all these things. Not one thing necessary or even useful do we receive in return for the horrible guilt in which we have involved ourselves. Africa and the West India Islands, on these fearful subjects I shall observe nothing at present. I hang my head when I think of them, they leave an indelible stain on our national character - all the waters of the Ocean cannot purify, all the perfumes of Araby cannot sweeten it. (1795)

Coleridge's dense factual reference in a passage of this kind, which draws into the discussion Indian trade, African trade, West Indian trade, the luxury goods market, genocide, silk manufacture, the commerce in tea and in saltpetre, are, along with the sweep of his vision, and his depth of feeling, all a considerable advance on anything similar to be found in Goldsmith; though it is Goldsmith's kind of insight, obviously, into immoral commercialism, which is being extended here; but so extended as to be quite re-formed. Actual knowledge and information are what authorize Coleridge's judgment, and confer on it its unusual weight. He rises above his age in his moral bearings, but does so because he has first submitted himself to be sunk in and master of the actual facts of its existence. His embracing rhetoric, at least in these early writings, pronounces worthless the entire commercial culture of modern England and Europe, and leaving aside his at times quirky sense of sin ('Tea to make a pernicious Beverage') there could be no more determined reversal of the commonplace Augustan boast. For Defoe, commerce had worked to unite scattered humanity, enlarge the possibilities of life, glorify the struggling trader and benefit his fellows. But for Coleridge his function actually disables the trader from moral action and stamps him as a public enemy.

This judgment was later softened, though not reversed. In 1800 Coleridge accepts that mercantile enterprise may contribute to welfare, and in fact recommends that a renewed 'vigorous trading and commercial spirit in France would, at first be a benefit and stimulus, even to our commerce; but it would be still more importantly beneficial, both to us and to the quiet of all Europe, in a political light, by giving the death-blow to Jacobinism' (iii:i, 142). The social conservative steps in to hold the radical critic in check. Here is a departure from five years before, when all forms of commerce had seemed to Coleridge forms of iniquity. Yet the insistence remains: the success of commerce, he says, does not in itself constitute a nation's welfare. Coleridge argues for the conceding of priority of importance to the development of English agriculture over that of commerce in any plan designed to ensure England's economic and political health; a Foxite position intended to counter Pitt's commercialist leanings in state policy. In 'A Lay Sermon' (1817) some years later Coleridge seeks for the cause of England's disastrous condition, and comes to fix on the overbalancing of the commercial spirit during the preceding century and a half as the corrupting excess, on trade's too pervasive expansion into all departments of life unrestrained by the counter-influences of religion, culture, honour; this evidently reduces considerably the absoluteness of the original contention that commerce was per se unnecessary and bad, and admits commerce as a natural activity in its due place (iv, 202ff.). And later still in 'On the Constitution of the Church and State' (1830) he includes the commercial spirit in its widest signification which embraces the professions and distributive bodies as common elements in the social community which combine to form its principle of progression; and in opposition to this force for movement Coleridge places all the landed and agricultural interests. These, he says, cluster into a contrary body and represent a contrary principle of permanence. Both congregations of interest are organic and both are essential to harmonious development and stable being. In this analysis commerce, once alien, now supplies energy and change, and has become integral with the national life.

Bearing in mind this movement towards commerce from a starting point of flat rejection, we are tempted to see Coleridge as realizing over the years that he must come to terms with a historical change too confirmed to be stopped, like Scott. And there may be truth in the suggestion. But in fact his is nothing like so equable a reconcilement. Essentially he remains hostile. The corrosive spirit and avoidable destructiveness of commerce, substituting interest for charity in the relations between men, will not pass with his humanitarian Toryism, and he is far too conscious of its prevalence as political economy, then newly fashionable, and in the form of a theory much more pernicious than in any other form, to reach an intellectual position from which he can offer it a wholehearted welcome or acceptance. With momentous insight, laying the foundations for Carlyle and the later generations of thinkers whom Carlyle so deeply influenced, he actually connects public distress more acute than any known to earlier history, which is succinctly attributed to the results of money-making run wild, with the prevailing thought of the science of political economy, an orthodoxy indifferent not because of greed, but on abstract theory, to the suffering required by the proper operation of its recently discerned laws. Coleridge's criticism of Sir James Steuart, who, the poet objects, forgets the individuals composing it when he writes about the nation's welfare, and in fact confuses welfare with wealth (iv:i, 299-300), is criticism not just of one deficient individual thinker, but of the political economist as a type. It is, we are given to understand, characteristic of such men, thinking so purely and so cruelly, to overlook real lives in their unfeeling abstractions. To bring out what he means Coleridge narrates the story of the simple vine dresser, economically speaking admitted to be useful only when he produces more than he and his family consume, but otherwise, Coleridge ironically declares, echoing a judgment of Steuart's, 'no loss to the state' if swallowed suddenly by an earthquake (loc. cit.). To this rather sweeping criterion of value Coleridge objects that what makes up the real meaning of a man's life, all that is included in true use, spontaneous growth, affection, vital enjoyment, intelligent learning, is missing from its range, and from the economist's estimate, and cannot but be missing because of his quantitative standard and his morbid concern with material excess, which between them exclude all spiritual experience. Here is how Coleridge frames the opposition of values (iv:i, p. 300):

> The poor vine-dresser rises from sweet sleep, worships his Maker, goes with his wife and children into his little plot - returns to his hut at noon, and eats the produce of the similar labour of a former day. Is he useful? No, not yet. Suppose then, that during the remaining hours of the day, he endeavoured to provide for his moral and intellectual appetites, by physical experiments and philosophical research, by acquiring knowledge for himself, and communicating it to his wife and children. Would he be useful then? '*He* useful! The State would lose nothing although the vine-dresser, and his land were both swallowed up by an earthquake!' Well, then, instead of devoting the latter half of each day to his closet, his laboratory, or to neighbourly conversation, suppose he goes to the vineyard, and from the ground which would maintain in health, virtue, and wisdom, twenty of his fellow-creatures, helps to raise a quantity of liquor that will

> disease the bodies, and debauch the souls of an hundred --- Is he useful *now*? --- O yes! --- a very useful man, and a most excellent citizen! (1809)

When the political economist rationalizes trade cycles as things 'finding their level', and describes as mere deviations in a pattern the economic lurchings from slump to boom, and back again, which Coleridge with greater human sympathy wishes to call 'Revolutions' (vi, 202), he forgets that people are not material things, and thus have not the same degree of resilience and resistance as rocks and water, justly described in terms of physical laws (vi, 206).

> After a hard and calamitous season, during which the Wheels of some vast manufactory had remained silent as a frozen water-fall, be it that plenty has returned and that Trade has once more become brisk and stirring: go, ask the overseer, and question the parish doctor, whether the workman's health and temperance with the staid and respectful Manners best taught by the inward dignity of conscious self-respect, have found *their* level again! (1817)

The real puzzle of an evil mode is how good men can be persuaded into adopting and perpetuating it, not how or why some men may choose to be bad. It is a problem which moralists have never solved but to which Coleridge finds his attention drawn by the desperate state of English life, as he conceives it. Explaining the paradox that many industrialists are 'Gentlemen of enlarged minds and real benevolence', yet run a system as evil as that on a slave plantation (iii:iii, 155), Coleridge suggests that the taint, the corrupting germ, perhaps originates in the industrial disposition itself, in the values it encourages and in the relations it naturally and inexorably enforces between men. It occurs to him (iii:i, 156) that there must be 'something in the nature of the cotton mill, I know not whether it be steam or bad air, or the scintillations of *lucre* amidst the precious flocks,' that can

> work up into activity the worst parts of our nature, and deface the best, so that the *warp* of human kindness (to speak in the idiom of the trade) shall become, as it were, lost in the *weft* of sordid gain, and the *man* be no longer recognized in the *manufacturer*. (1818)

Coleridge by 1818, as the range of his observation here shows, has moved far beyond the subject of commerce as such into that of industrialism; hence our discussion must be similarly widened. For the gainful instinct, the present study's essential theme, is at the core of both the commercial and the industrial debate in creative literature. It is the case, though, that in the literature of the nineteenth and twentieth centuries the representation of the merchant pure and simple, if he was ever that, dwindles into a less important aspect of the analysis of capitalism, and gets pushed to one side, as in life, by new capitalist types: the manufacturer, the industrial magnate, the financier. These, therefore, are the characterizations to which the discussion must give prominent place; otherwise it would soon cease to have relevance.

Increasingly, to repeat, the merchant fades from significance; but the main point at the present moment is perhaps his affinity, morally and socially, with his successors, not their departure from him into some new order of social function. Coleridge himself sees no essential difference between industry and commerce; neither do his contemporaries. When his subject is factory exploitation he is reminded of slavery and of the misdeeds in recent memory in British India, and insists on the moral connections between the new outrages of commerce and the old. Scott too, as we shall see, stresses this continuity between the centuries. Dickens gives the merchant a distinct new significance in Mr Dombey, but, considering Bounderby, Rouncewell, Merdle and Veneering, one might say that not even in Dickens does the old order re-attract important notice more than briefly. The tide is now running strongly the other way.

Coleridge's revulsion from trade has led to his being called misguided on the economic question, for example by John Stuart Mill; but the noteworthy thing is how widely shared was the general attitude, if not their specific judgments, which his essays express. Wordsworth, less theoretical, is not much less hostile to the capitalist and the industrialist, if sometimes willing to be impressed by them also. And so are Shelley, Byron and Keats, none of whom attempt the painful effort of accommodation to an industrial capitalist economy which is evidenced in some of Coleridge's later essays. Admittedly Scott is more tolerant, though no enthusiast, but it is Scott who is the special case. All these writers need to be discussed, as do certain others of the period, but none of them exhaustively, if it is remembered that the condition of society they respond to in their distinct fashions is conceived as a revolutionary state of things; that is, that Coleridge's is a representative gravity of alarm. Wordsworth's deep concern at the industrialization of England, and at her reduction of all considerations to that of cash profits, may be less obvious than Coleridge's, because he offers less straight argument. And he is given to introducing commerce into his poems with no odium attached to it, on numerous occasions; it is one of the things people do for a living. (5) Then again such poems as 'Greenock' and 'Steamboats, Viaducts, and Railways', two of the 'Itinerary Poems of 1833', admire the capacious energy of industrialism, as did Carlyle and Dickens and other writers later in the century; and Dickens and Wordsworth share other resemblances. (6)

But in his main discussion of industrial capitalism in book 8 of 'The Excursion' (1814) Wordsworth gives us a fuller and explicitly critical picture. The Wanderer describes (book 8, lines 133-42) England's wholesale changes in which once deserted spots are now towns thick with houses, wild country is vanishing, and

> the shores
> Of England are resorted to by ships
> Freighted from every climate of the world
> With the world's choicest produce. Hence that sum

Of keels that rest within her crowded ports,
Or ride at anchor in her sounds and bays;
That animating spectacle of sails
That, through her inland regions, to and fro
Pass with the respirations of the tide,
Perpetual, multitudinous!

(1814)

If the sound of such lines is Augustan, reminiscent of Savage, super-added in those which follow is a sense of human cost which is new. Wordsworth goes on to assess the price of all this achievement and sums it up as an 'outrage done to nature' far more serious than the half-delightful decadence of too much culture apprehended by Young and Thomson and their contemporaries from the safe ground of pre-industrial England. He brings home to us the mutilating facts of life of the industrial night shift usurping sleep, in which men, maidens and youths, mothers and children, boys and girls indiscriminately replace each other without ceasing in the many-windowed factory (lines 183-5)

where is offered up
To Gain, the master-idol of the realm,
Perpetual sacrifice.

(1814)

Though the Wanderer exults in the 'intellectual mastery exercised/ O'er the blind elements' (lines 201-2) which industrialism symbolizes, no counter-impression is strong enough to obliterate this vision of the unacceptable sacrifice of men's lives for the sake of profits. Wordsworth is not writing a diatribe, however; the other side of the case is put by the Recluse, who objects that poverty, beggary and disease all existed before the industrializing of commerce brought about mass factory labour. At this point, the crux and sensitive moment in the whole discussion in an argumentative sense, but not, perhaps, poetically a matter to dwell on, the discussion is cut short. The effect of truncating it is to strengthen the critique, not the defence, for it leaves in our minds the image of factory labour which Wordsworth has already established, and which is the most expressive symbol possible: that of a cotton child, creeping along the road, pale, covered white with flecks of cotton dust, dead in the eyes, breathing with difficulty (lines 309-15). Wordsworth underlines what he wishes us to feel by not arguing for it, in the end, but by simply depicting it, and letting the depiction carry its own message.

Coleridge generally in his writings on the subject, and Wordsworth in this kind of portrayal, isolate the aggressiveness of modern trade as its chief feature. It was indeed one of the characteristic elements of the new sense of things that markets could now be created where they had not existed before, and might not have sprung up on their own account; that the production of commodities could be forced; that trading opposition could be crushed out of existence, not just overcome in the way of traditional mercantile rivalry; and that the world, rather than being merely drawn on, as in the past, even if greedily, could be compelled and bent to serve the energetic manufacturer's purpose in a wholly new order of exploitation.(7) An extra cruel potential is thus conceived as now being added to greed. A penetrating but little-known early analysis of the destructive effect which industrial competition has on social culture and national welfare, and even international well-being, in fact a scathing attack on Hume's notion, praised by Adam Smith, that the commercial spirit has been socially liberating in its effect, is delivered in Charles Hall's interesting essay 'The Effects of Civilization on the People in European States' (1805). Hall's revelation is that industrialism has split a once unified society into two intrinsically opposed entities or classes, the rich and the poor, as mutually destructive to each other in their forced relation as 'the algebraic terms *plus* and *minus*' (1850 edition, p. 54); and also that the competitiveness which has become a fact and condition of life is actually psychologically disabling in its effect (p. 113).

> Hence, a violent struggle is excited; every man strains every nerve; every man's interest becomes opposite to every man's. Hence, eager competitions, sharp contentions, frauds, oppression. Hence, the source of all matters that render life anxious and unhappy. (1805)

Hall's is an extraordinarily alert and vibrant analysis of industrial psychology, especially considering the early date of its appearance; when it came out Carlyle was only ten years old. And Robert Southey is a social reporter who gives us ample evidence of this development in national morals in early nineteenth-century Britain both in his social descriptive work 'Letters from England' (1807), a kind of pessimistic Defoe's 'Tour', and then more diffusely in the argumentative essays which make up 'St Thomas More; or, Colloquies Upon Society' (1829). So also do Hazlitt, Cobbett and Lamb when they attack the ruthlessness and selfishness of economic science and the mean-spirited nature of commercial morality. (De Quincey's is a lonely opposition voice.) In Southey perhaps, of these writers, we have the fullest instance after Coleridge of that disastrous expectancy which a close survey of industrial conditions in those years, and of the spirit and belief informing them, induced in thinking minds. A warning outcry against a dangerously over-commercialized Britain is the message of his 'Letters from England' (1807), a work pretty clearly written with Goldsmith's 'Citizen of the World' (1762) and Montesquieu's 'Lettres Persanes' (1721) in mind; both of which, it will be recalled, had also warned against commercialism. Southey's travelling Spaniard is astonished by the aggressive selling spirit of London's shopkeepers who cover dead walls, vacant houses and temporary scaffolding with printed bills and 'lose no possible opportunity of forcing their notices upon the public'.(8) He sees the reduction of all things to their money value; the possibility that Burlington House, Piccadilly, may be pulled down for speculative building causes the rents to rise as if the venture had actually taken place (p. 71). Everywhere is seen the extreme mixture of great wealth with great poverty, a violent enigma. He is horrified by what Birmingham has done to its inhabitants, who press and contend for work which they know will kill or cripple them in a few years' time (p. 197), shocked by the African guns made there which burst apart when fired and 'mangle the wretched negro who has purchased them upon the credit of English faith' (p. 198), and still more shocked by the fact that all persons seem to accept this trade as natural, express no detestation of its perpetrators and exploiters, and instead accept them into their houses, mingle with them, and envy and praise their success and their wealth. For such exploiting cruelty, which makes old style plunder look like benevolence, Southey searches his mind for an appropriate image. Finally he tells us (p. 107) of a shrub in certain of the East Indian islands

> which the French call *veloutier*; it exhales an odour that is agreeable at a distance, becomes less so as you draw nearer, and, when you are quite close to it, is insupportably loathsome. Alciatus himself could not have imagined an emblem more appropriate to the commercial prosperity of England. (1807)

The point, Southey reiterates, is that the universal acceptance of commerce and its corrupt methods, and of its extreme and boundless aggressiveness, are a feature of the age. We might compare Burke and Smollett, if we wish to highlight what it is that has changed in the life span of the industrializing generation. Those writers attack commerce, it will be remembered, for its villains, for its excesses, and for its malpractices; Southey attacks its practice, attacks its ordinary men who are doing their ordinary respected work. Manchester men, the Spaniard finds, cannot be persuaded that they are mistaken in their values, success in trade having dazed them, and he terms them spellbound (p. 209):

> I thought of the cities in Arabian romance, where all the inhabitants were enchanted; here Commerce is the queen witch, and I had no talisman strong enough to disenchant those who were daily drinking of the golden cup of her charms. (1807)

Perhaps even more movingly than the profundities of Coleridge this despairing outcry of Southey sums up the new sombre frame of mind. Gone, and gone for good in English experience, is the insistent hopefulness of eighteenth-century commercial writing: the idea of the benign self-interest of Adam Smith, Defoe's magical renewal and growth, Burke's affirmation of mercantile honour. Southey's contrary assessment is of an England everywhere riddled by commerce, everywhere poisoned. 'Literature, arts, religion, government, are alike tainted, it is a *lues* which has got into the system of the country, and is rotting flesh and bone' (p. 368). The affinity between such thought as this and Coleridge's position on commerce needs no stressing, though the violent language, such as the image of 'lues' meaning plague or syphilis, is Southey's own, but a new note comes through in 'Colloquies Upon Society' (1829);

a muted repetition of the protest, but with some glimpses of new hope. Here Southey points out that though neither the Napoleonic wars, nor the 1688 Revolution, nor the seventeenth-century Rebellion, nor the Reformation, all comparable crises with industrialism, had proved so hard to work through as this latest disruption to social peace, yet manufacturing commerce might come to furnish the remedy for its own evils in due time. It might furnish its own 'euthanasy' (1829 edition, ii, 245), at a period in the future when other nations will have learned to compete in world markets, and Britain's foreign trade will have consequently declined, and with it the mad rush into an ever-expanding and apparently insatiable overseas market for products and commodities. After euthanasy may then be seen palingenesia or the 'restoration of national sanity and strength, a second birth' (loc. cit.). Little proof of this historical resilience is offered by the writer, but for all that it remains a curiously powerful hint, like an avowal of faith in life in the darkest moment of a period of despair.

For all their specific criticism, we notice that Coleridge, Wordsworth and Southey rather attack the spirit of their age than its outer forms. They are particularly severe on the rationalizing of appetite. A new creed of selfish necessity, narrow, theoretical, heart hardening, pushing under and crushing out of sight the ideals of service and care, is, they recognize, or believe they recognize, now the widespread central assumption of the times. And it seems like a creed of death, and productive only of a faithless and hopeless materialism for the future. What Coleridge opposes to Steuart's economic criterion, in his estimate so thin and brittle an ideal of life, is spiritual excellence, the sanctity of individual free experience, and he denies, as we have seen, that economic so-called laws have any just claim to a validity which overrides such value as that. His argument is directed at Steuart, but is not limited to that philosopher. It bears no less forcibly on the population law of Malthus, according to which suffering falls on the fringe poor inevitably and unchangeably, as naturally as the law of gravity draws objects to the ground, and on Ricardo's iron law of wages, which denies that wages ever can or do really increase; formulations of despair both.

In this opposition to rigid thinking, or thought which issues in rigid practice, Coleridge does not speak for the older Tory poets alone, but for all the Romantic writers. Against political economy, the effective theology of industrial England, almost all the creative writers of the time can be said to be united. It is their shared and even defining feature. They strive to re-centralize the human issue in an abstract and theoretical debate. They object against political economy that its tenor and mode are careless of life. Typical of this kind of hostility, though the idiom is his own, is Cobbett's insulting scorn of 'beastly Scotch feelosofers' whose idea of wealth is 'the *fewer* poor devils you can screw the products out of, the *richer* the nation is'.(9) De Quincey is the exception to the norm here. Much of his life he spent popularizing Ricardo, who seems to have had on his mind the effect of luminous redirection which John Stuart Mill was to receive from Wordsworth, and De Quincey attempts to spread his discovery by publishing a number of instructive discussions of Ricardian economics cast into dialogue form for easier consumption among general readers;(10) though, of the two, Ricardo provides the lighter reading. Yet even the committed De Quincey is found denying Malthus his fashionable proposition that food increases arithmetically but people geometrically, and asserting the same rate for both.(11) This is to take the inevitability out of Malthus, and to some extent restore man's self-respect by restoring his sense of control over his own affairs. It is just this human softening, or heart wisdom, this solidarity with the men of the field and the mill, the cellar, the factory and the mine, which stamps the imaginative critique of capitalist civilization and thought in its most brutal and triumphant manifestation yet. It for the moment unites Tory with radical writers, haters of change, like Coleridge, with the advocates of fresh action, like Shelley, in joint defence of the sufferers from commercial greed and exploitation and against the exploiting money-men and their intellectual backers, or sycophants, as they perhaps seemed, the theorists of self-interest.

Typical of the later Romantic voice is Hazlitt. He is marked on commercial and political themes by a radical distaste for upper-class pontificating, and anger and indignation against patronage, especially moral patronage, offered to the voiceless poor, as when he questions whether Jeremy Bentham sitting down to his psychological dissertations after a prelude on the organ, or gazing through his study window at a fine prospect when at a loss for an idea, can know anything of 'the principles of action' of rogues and vagabonds.(12) Hazlitt denies that laws are valid when made by the rich for the poor; he includes economic laws, or so-called laws, and revels in the facer, if we may adopt his own term,(13) which Malthus delivers to Godwin's argument for a future of rational perfection by his revelation that unchecked sexuality would lay it in ruins in the shortest possible biological period of time. The law of perfectibility is discredited by the law of population; one renders the other ludicrous; both are dangerous in their indifference to real men and women, to real experience; is either really a law? One is reminded when reading Hazlitt in this mood of the subversive and weighty laughter of Dickens. Hazlitt is very cutting and unfair, but because he exaggerates, not because he invents, when he scoffs at Malthus for lecturing the poor on moral regulation and telling them somewhat ungraciously that they are doomed to starve by the laws of nature and God.(14) And he has a serious point to make: hardness of heart is productive of 'radical errors in reasoning'.(15) Not to feel, he claims, to put it differently, is to be disabled from social philosophy; here is the Romantic emphasis again. More of the same is to be found in Hazlitt's 'Hints on Political Economy' (1826) and in his 'Outlines of Political Economy'. The drift and tacit assumptions behind all this argumentation, not its technicalities, are all we need to note for our present purpose, for it is necessary not to stray far from the present book's chosen topic; and the political economist is not the merchant. The argumentation matters nevertheless because Hazlitt sees Malthus, Ricardo and the rest as putting the mercantile and industrial case. He sees political economy as the equivalent of the manifesto of a heartless system. He sees the men of commerce, and their counterparts in high positions of power, as benefiting from it. He sees the labouring population as permanent losers in the class and money war, which is what social relations have degenerated into. The essays in which he says all this will have been read by Carlyle, who came to London in 1824, and there is some of Hazlitt in the early Carlyle, perhaps.

In Hazlitt and in the younger Romantics generally (Lamb is an exception) we search in vain for that historical consciousness, that willingness to return to origins, which aims to substantiate the Tory theory of cultural and moral deterioration; in its place we encounter radical vehemence. Thus the indictment of selfish commercialism is still present, still enforced, is even intensified, in their writings, even if unaccompanied by reverence towards the past. Byron in 'The Age of Bronze' (1823) rewrites the terms on which, he discerns, poetry is now properly to be composed; glory, wealth, freedom, old themes, are to be looked for in old volumes, he says, whereas the theme for modern England is the single one of financial greed. It is the universal vice. Britain's landlords sacrificing all to raise rents are matched in Byron's portrayal by the Church, weeping for her tithes, but not weeping for anything else, by war profiteers, by commercial men exploiting everyone everywhere, by financiers pulling the strings of state and controlling individuals and empires. In so broadly frontal an assault, mere merchants are not to be separated from other capitalists. The Jews, the argument runs,(16) that is financiers,

> parted with their teeth to good King John,
> And now, ye kings! they kindly draw your own;
> All states, all things, all sovereigns they control,
> And waft a loan 'from Indus to the pole'.
> The banker, broker, baron, brethren speed
> To aid these bankrupt tyrants in their need.
>
> (1823)

The Congress of Vienna is scathingly dismissed as botched world jobbery. Coleridge might have agreed with this, though not with Byron's praise of the Luddites seven years earlier.(17) And he could have actually applauded Byron's diagnosis of a spirit of government more concerned with profits than with lives in his sarcastic 'Ode to the Framers of the Frame Bill' (1812). Hanging every machine breaker, Byron here suggests, will make economic sense:(18)

The rascals, perhaps, may betake them to robbing,
  The dogs to be sure have got nothing to eat---
So if we can hang them for breaking a bobbin,
  'Twill save all the Government's money and meat:
Men are more easily made than machinery---
  Stockings fetch better prices than lives---
Gibbets on Sherwood will heighten the scenery,
  Shewing how Commerce, how Liberty thrives!

(1812)

Coleridge parts company, perhaps, with the allegiance behind this kind of judgment when Byron's working-class sympathy shows through, as in his House of Lords speech on the same topic and of the same date, yet even Byron is in general too ironic and varied in his imaginative interests and outlook to feel the class antagonism more than momentarily. That is, on a general estimate it is not an important strand of meaning in his greatest poetry. 'Don Juan' (1819-24) has pungent lines on avarice, whose cash, not love, rules the grove, 'and fells it too besides' (Everyman 'Poems', iii, 350), but its subject is the whole sum of human experience. Hence when Byron turns to look at it he sees an England commercial through and through, ruled by the ethic of the counter, and then he attacks it forcefully, but he does not often turn to it.

In Shelley the note is more insistent and politically more explicit, almost more programmed. He brings to bear not the slow historical awareness of Coleridge or of Scott, but a rhetorical view of the past, what we might term the Ozymandias view of political and commercial empire, which serves to highlight the present in just the rousing and dramatic fashion he desires. The eighteenth-century origins of such a frame of mind are obvious, yet it is not a view destined to end here in melancholy; rather, in anger and political action. Thus in 'Queen Mab' (1813) the Fairy begins by pointing out the ruined palaces of Palmyra, Nile's pyramids, Jerusalem's temple, Rome and Sparta now a 'moral desert' in which a cowled monk has succeeded Cicero and the great Socrates. (19) Shelley categorizes his own society as intrinsically corrupt, corrupt because mercantile (op. cit., p. 729):

Hence commerce springs, the venal interchange
Of all that human art or nature yield;
Which wealth should purchase not but want demand,
And natural kindness hasten to supply.

(1813)

Industrial imagery is drawn on for the denunciation of manufacturing England; men are depicted as pulleys, as wheels of work, as articles of trade (lines 76-8). England's money economy is repudiated (lines 79-80) in the judgment that

The harmony and happiness of man
Yields to the wealth of nations, (1813)

in which the emphasis is contrived so as to fall scornfully on 'wealth', the enemy of life. Nor is the reference to Adam Smith casual; 'Queen Mab' rejects the whole eighteenth century. For example, Shelley may be said to radicalize Gray's vision of futile humanity when he tells us that many a Cato, Newton or Milton has submitted to a lifetime spent making pins, which brings to mind Smith's account of the division of labour. He may too perhaps recall Edward Young's celebration of the universe as a great exchange in his notion that 'the very light of Heaven/Is venal' (lines 177-8), and in the image of fellowship and the instinctive duties bought and sold 'as in a public mart/Of undisguising selfishness, that sets/On each its price' (lines 186-8). If such a recall, or rather recasting, is being attempted, the near century which has elapsed between Young and Shelley has brought in, we see, a destructive emphasis, a cynically discordant tone, and changed the application of the sentiment to its exact opposite.

Shelley apologizes for 'Queen Mab' as a juvenile piece, but it does not appear that its view of commerce as a weapon of tyranny is cast off or significantly revised in his later writing. In 'The Mask of Anarchy' (1819) the voice of the Earth calls on Englishmen to shake off their chains of dew - despotic gold, fraudulent paper coin (stanzas xliv, xlv) - and then repeats the charge that paper money is robbery, a forged title deed to the earth's inheritance. These lines may look abstract to us, but they would have struck home with a sharp relevance at the time of writing; in the year 1814 twenty-seven banks had failed and gone out of business, with untold damage to lives and livelihoods, in 1815 twenty-five, in 1816 thirty-seven.(20) The Mammon figure of 'Oedipus Tyrannus, or Swellfoot the Tyrant' (1820) satirizes governmental finance. 'To the Lord Chancellor' (partly published in 1839) levels charges of bought and sold justice, trampled on truth and 'heaps of fraud-accumulated gold' (stanza ii). In these poems the animus and collocations of 'Queen Mab' are repeated without significant recasting: they are, that commerce is a constituent part of tyrannical fraud in a world strengthened in its negations by time and use, powerfully established, and ruthless in seeking to preserve itself, but nevertheless destined to be replaced in the end by freedom and love. Nowhere does this apocalyptic vision transform itself into the historical probing of Southey, Coleridge, or Scott. Shelley writes not so much to dismantle the elements of society and understand their workings a little better, as to demolish and destroy them, and rebuild the entire social establishment afresh and in a new pattern.

Other Romantic writers are equally hostile, if less politically tense. The only mercantile appearance in Keats is that of the two brothers in 'Isabella, or the Pot of Basil' (1818), a characterization however savage and final:(21)

And for them many a weary hand did swelt
  In torched mines and noisy factories
And many once proud-quiver'd loins did melt
  In blood from stinging whip;---with hollow eyes
Many all day in dazzling river stood,
To take the rich-ored driftings of the flood.

For them the Ceylon diver held his breath,
  And went all naked to the hungry shark;
For them his ears gush'd blood; for them in death
  The seal on the cold ice with piteous bark
Lay full of darts; for them alone did seethe
  A thousand men in troubles wide and dark:
Half ignorant, they turn'd an easy wheel,
That set sharp racks at work, to pinch and peel.

(1818)

'Noisy factories' and 'torched mines' remind us that the brothers figure not as merchants but as merchant manufacturers. This is a consciously nineteenth-century touch; Keats is adding to his medieval source an industrial colouring for which, in a later stanza, he apologizes to Boccaccio, admitting that such terms hardly suit his 'piteous theme'.(22) The contemporary reference adds a shock and clinches the moral judgment Keats invites us to make. The brothers are not merchants on the one hand, and then murderers in addition, two different things. They are murderers because they live by commerce; their very trade is death dealing; Lorenzo is a victim among thousands. Nowhere could one find a starker or more absolute condemnation of the whole capitalist category.

Romantic writers as a general rule, it will be seen, and certainly Romantic poets, do not expand into reasons, sources and origins when they condemn industrial commerce in verse; they condemn. This is a change from Pope and Thomson, and from the Augustan practice generally, which is to argue its point of view through to a conclusion, and prove the truth of it if it can. But Coleridge and Southey show themselves quite ready to discourse argumentatively in prose, we have seen. And another example of the same willingness to theorize is Charles Lamb. In an important essay on the clerkly virtues, which as a lifelong servant of the East India Company we may suppose him to have thought deeply about, Lamb attempts to place the mercantile character in a historically intelligible light. His formulation is both hostile and representative. Defoe he characterizes as a 'Philosopher of meanness',(23) and 'The Complete English Tradesman' (1727), Defoe's bourgeois manual, as deserving indictment for its vile debasing cast. What gives this attack significance for us is not the fact, which it demonstrates clearly enough, that tastes alter, but the historical generalization which Lamb offers along with it. He declares roundly that the orderly, temperate, submissive, advantage-seeking ideal clerk embodies 'those frugal and economical maxims which, about the beginning of the last century (England's meanest period), were endeavoured to be inculcated and instilled into the breasts of the London Apprentices, by a class of instructors who might not inaptly be termed *The Masters of mean Morals* (op. cit., pp. 128-9). 'England's meanest period' is the beginning of Coleridge's century and a half of the overbalancing commercial spirit. Like Coleridge, Southey and Shelley, Charles Lamb rejects the eighteenth century as the merchant's era, as the flourishing time of calculation and materialism, and takes pride in his sense of the moral distance separating him from the world of Defoe. Defoe had upheld trade as adventurous and renewing. But to Lamb it represents the systematic murder of the spirit of man; to Lamb, and to most of the creative writers of his time.

The exception is Scott, an artist open-minded enough to hold back from instant condemnation, but without yielding to the new because it is new, and to look at the developments of capitalism from both sides; but even Scott is not their spokesman. Literature does not reflect at a high level the new evangelical impetus given to the notion of godly profit, so that little if any dissent in creative writing of the first order is to be found from Lamb's view that the commercial revolution of the seventeenth and eighteenth centuries had narrowed and hardened the national character and brutalized its soul. Here is one reason perhaps why in the novels of Jane Austen trade and tradesmen are shunned as impolite acquaintance by genteel characters, though not similarly despised by the novelist:(24) that by 1800, for three or four generations past, English life was felt to have become tainted by a calculating spirit, a spread of meanness, a trading soul. Naturally, to this must be added too the perennial distrust of men of commerce found in Fielding, Wycherley, Jonson and others, which fears them as a threat to established aristocratic preserves. Men of trade figure less than prominently in the novels of Jane Austen, therefore; but always to the fore, or at least always present, if unexplored and unargued out, compared with what we find later in George Eliot, is her sense of the economic basis of genteel living and fine consciousness, of money's rule over the spiritualities of human existence, and of the moral challenge posed by a materialistic and acquisitive world to the uncorrupted heart. The opening chapter of 'Mansfield Park' (1814) is filled with this mercenary sense of things English, and it is typical. Yet how much of the ironic undertow in the novel, we might ask, is traceable to the fact that a contrast seems almost to obtrude itself upon us between the decorous Sir Thomas Bertram, embodiment of proper conduct, and Sir Thomas Bertram the West Indies planter, and therefore presumably slave owner, quelling a spot of bother at the producing source of his wealth and respectability, while his sensitive dependants tremble at the moral riskiness of putting on a play about flirtation without his concurrence? Not to allow an irony here is to convict the novelist of obtuseness, as Kingsley Amis does,(25) but it is certainly hard to see an explicit one in the texture of the novel. If we wish to find a more documented examination of the industrial and manufacturing type of the Napoleonic years we must look at, for example, Maria Edgeworth's 'The Manufacturers' (1803); but this is a story too brief to penetrate to any deeper theme than that of gentility.

What Jane Austen does not attempt, for all her sharpness in observation, and hinted judgments, is any gesture towards a delineation of how her condition of society came into existence; precisely the centre of interest in the writings of Scott. And since Scott's output is so huge, and also since his characteristic effects tend to be a product of the gradual accumulation of scene upon scene, and of the contrast of portrayal, not of argument, so that one can only propose to make a point of any substance about him in an extended way, he demands a great deal of space. Much has to be left out here, therefore, and a great deal more severely compressed. But the point to be brought out is no less than that the growth of capitalism, an aspect among others equally or more important to him of the growth of modern Britain, forms one part of Scott's subject; and though Scott's respect for his material is such as to hold him back from forcing any theory of his own upon it, so that the mercantile delineation may sometimes appear casual, it is nearly always present, and quite frequently takes a central role. Growth; the pain of historical birth; the sense of an unfolding process; these, not praise or blame cast on the doings of earlier men judged by some momentary criterion of conduct, are the distinguishing features of what Scott's fiction offers us. The past is described as it was, as nearly as that recognition can be made, but with a view to what it was to become, and from the standpoint, but not the moral point of view, of the present; thus a spaciousness and distinctness of interest both characterize the fiction.

The at first minor figure Wilkin Flammock, a bourgeois miller in Scott's twelfth-century novel 'The Betrothed' (1825), is one who, it becomes plain, will increase in substantial power and inherit the future whether Norman defeats Saxon or Saxon routs Norman and manages to regain control of England, the ostensibly important issue of the whole story; though probably Scott had in mind the creation of the composite English character from a merging of his commercial code with Saxon faith and Norman chivalry. It would hardly distort the novel to see Flammock as its unexpectedly dominating presence. Not jousts and greensward heroisms form the central interest of 'Ivanhoe' (1819; twelfth-century England) but the essential supremacy of financial power in a dynastically and socially troubled period, a theme bearing an obvious relation to Scott's own time. In 'The Fair Maid of Perth' (1828; fifteenth-century Scotland) honest bourgeois and artisan repel the honourable but insolent aristocracy; these terms of analysis are Scott's own, as may be seen especially from chapter xx, and his entire symbolism - Ramorny's right hand severed, Henry Gow's impregnable home-made armour - seems to endorse the conquest of a decadent by a growing ethic; seems to, but suggests rather than positively declares the historical consequences of the story. In 'Quentin Durward' (1823; fifteenth-century France) Scott explores the calculating egoism of Louis XI of France, calling him the Merchant King and showing how he hires mercenary soldiers, levies taxes to pay for them in lieu of service, and governs his country by the method of the counting house, all of them aspects of the mode of the future. This is to hold up for us the mean side of the commercial outlook, and we get the other side in 'Anne of Geierstein' (1829; fifteenth-century Switzerland and France), in which the Swiss successfully defend their commerce and freedom, the two being inextricable blessings in their eyes, and assert the honour of a mercantile nation against tyranny and contempt from older warlike peoples. Behind the political oppositions and religious debates in 'The Monastery' (1820; sixteenth-century Scotland) and its sequel 'The Abbot' (1820; the same), and perhaps operating through them, are glimpsed the pressures of economic insecurity at a time when old methods of livelihood are fallen into disuse and new capitalist methods are on the increase: Sir Piercie Shafton takes to Catholic adventuring to repair a shattered estate, while the monastery shrinks to vanishing point as a centre of life.

We would expect these economic dwindlings and new growths, if indeed Scott offers them as phases in the capitalist story, to take on firmer definition as he approaches the modern period; and they do so. Important themes in 'Kenilworth' (1821; late sixteenth-century England) are discovery, risk and adventure, the character marks of the Elizabethan age, and more than just engaging anecdotes, emblematic incidents in the larger tale, are the facts that Sir Walter Raleigh spoils a cloak but makes a court fortune (chapter 15), and that if the queen refuses to pay a royal visit to the village of Woodstock and thus draw to it a throng of attendants, entertainers, chapmen, sightseers, adventurers, hangers on and rascals, and give it something to live and profit from, it will die (chapter 7). This is the depiction of a society whose economic energy is still largely directed by court favour. 'The Fortunes of Nigel' (1822; seventeenth-century England) displays for us a new mercantile code replacing aristocratic honour, and the striking figure in the earlier parts of the story before things degenerate into escapade is not King James, not the Duke of Buckingham, not Nigel himself, but the banker George Heriot. Heriot is certainly no hero, nor idealized in any way, but he has a solidity of presence due to Scott's recognition that he, not the traditionally impressive political characters of those days, stands truly at the centre of power in a world disintegrating yet recomposing itself along new economic lines. In 'A Legend of Montrose' (1819; seventeenth-century Scotland) military interest replaces clan loyalty, and contractual responsibility the concept of romantic honour. Another of those summarizing originals in which Scott is prolific, the mercenary soldier Dugald Dalgetty, embodies this new spirit, which is really the commercial spirit, though here cast into the world of clan warfare, and behind Scott's laughter lies acceptance and perhaps respect, for Dalgetty opposes to snobbery and moral objection against his values the fact of his continued survival (chapter 23). But one cannot make out an author on Dalgetty's side.

In 'Peveril of the Peak' (1822; seventeenth-century England) a new commercial and an old semi-feudal outlook jostle each other uncertainly. Uncertainty seems to be the theme. A sign of men's anxiety is that all who can afford it eat off silver plate, keeping it beside them not locked away in some business vault, for treasure is more secure than a goldsmith's receipt. But 'let there be a demand for capital to support a profitable commerce, and the mass is at once consigned to the furnace, and, ceasing to be a vain and cumbrous ornament of the banquet, becomes a potent and active agent for furthering the prosperity of the country' (chapter 14). The speaker of the lines is Bridgenorth, the commercial expert in the novel; but possibly Scott had in mind the practice of the East India Company of his own day.(26) In 'Old Mortality' (1816; seventeenth-century Scotland) civil war holds back development; Scott makes the capitalist point by appending to the story proper, which of course deals with quite other matters as its main subject, as do several or most of Scott's novels, an account of the revival of agriculture and its attendant economic and cultural life following upon King William's prudent tolerance after 1688 and 1689 (chapter 37). 'The Pirate' (1822; Shetland in 1700) shows us a traditional economy under threat from more up-to-date mainland Scottish methods of organization, labour and cultivation, which stand for modernity here, though elsewhere in Scott's work Scotland is the backward contrast to progressive England; and the rover era as attractive but already outdated, a temporary historical phase now past its relevant period. Scott as usual contrasts loss and gain on both sides, sensitive to old and new but neither brash nor nostalgic. In 'The Bride of Lammermoor' (1819; eighteenth-century Scotland) the wealth shift from aristocrat to entrepreneur and to artisan is projected, is indeed shown to be already all but complete. William Ashton has plotted Ravenswood from his inheritance, and on the other side Ravenswood's tenants have won their battle for independence, full property rights, and the denial of old payments (chapter 2; chapter 12). Caleb Balderstone, Ravenswood's servant, refuses to accept the new dispensation and causes plenty of mirth by his insistence on old social forms; an insistence also oddly touching and impressive. 'The Black Dwarf' (1816; eighteenth-century Scotland) records the passing of the bandit economy of the border and its replacement by constraint, by regular livelihood, and by financial responsibility. 'Rob Roy' (1818; eighteenth-century Scotland) turns on the contrast, not new in Scott, between commercial credit and warrior honour, the latter ousted with some loss of spirit and of poetry, but not uselessly regretted, and in 'Waverley' (1814; England and Scotland during the 1745 rebellion) the message remains the same: Jacobite ambitions and dreams, such as those of Fergus and Flora MacIvor, born out of a departed time and expressive of a finished world view, are irrelevant to a Britain now irreversibly capitalist. They are doomed and heroic together. Scott makes this a commercial as well as a predominantly political stroke when in chapter 72, 'which should have been a Preface', he remarks, we are reminded of the economic progress of Scotland since the events of the narrative proper, which has outstripped that of all the other countries of Europe. Scott here describes as fact, we may say, what Smollett forty years before had sketched as possibility. Between these two novels we may place 'Heart of Midlothian' (1818; mid-eighteenth-century Scotland). From a stormy opening this novel moves to a tranquil close, from the depiction of a subsistence economy with hard fare and cruel rent exactions to the almost luxury of experimental farming 'according to the best ideas of the time' in what Scott describes as the 'Highland Arcadia' of Dunbartonshire (chapter 45). Too earnest and too engaged with real issues, like all of Scott's fiction, to be called fanciful, the novel yet reads like an idyll of the modern world thankfully attained out of a dark past. Scott brings out what the clan and livelihood changes of 'Waverley' mean for ordinary human beings, not the heroic leaders of mass movements but the unheroic led, in his short story 'The Highland Widow' (1827; eighteenth-century Scotland). Here Hamish Bean chooses wage labour as an enlisted soldier since his father's freebooter life has become closed to him, but his mother dreads the accompanying 'subjection to strangers, and the death-sleep of the soul which is brought on by what she regarded as slavery' (chapter 3); and she brings about their destruction by her inability to adapt to a new world. No economic fable, the tale perfectly illustrates Scott's sense of the plight of helpless beings on the one hand, yet, on the other, the necessity of economic change. It would be a trite juxtaposition did not the vitality of the portrayal deepen it for us.

'Guy Mannering' (1815; Scotland in the third quarter of the eighteenth century), rather concerned with law than with commerce, nevertheless explores in its discussions of free trade and smuggling (chapter 5), the gipsies (chapter 7), the revenue question (chapter 9) and Dandy Dinmont's hunting livelihood (chapter 25) the pressures of an energized volatile economy, and as well as the large-scale disintegration of the old ways it is the introduction of Mannering's new Indian wealth, we are shown, which is one of the disturbing, yet also renewing, factors. 'Redgauntlet' (1824; late eighteenth-century Scotland) records the slow encroaching removal and take-over, by business method, of erratic enterprise, for example in the way salmon are caught by tidal nets rather than speared as of old; and a similar methodizing of the mind. The two aspects of this change, business and godliness, go together in Joshua Geddes and his Quaker colleagues. Alan Fairford's Bar thesis, whose legal examinations are based on Scott's own experience, is entitled 'De periculo et commodo rei venditae'; not Scott's subject, who wrote a thesis on the disposal of the bodies of executed criminals. He has changed this detail to bring his story more into line with his commercial theme. The ambitious greed of the nabob era is delineated in 'The Surgeon's Daughter' (1827; Scotland and India in the late eighteenth century), a class of which Richard Middlemas's exploits appear to serve Scott as an illustration and pattern; Mannering, also of Indian experience, is a military not a commercial man. Middlemas lives a rascally and unscrupulous life thoroughly equalling the notorious doings of the East India Company's servants during the high age of the nabobs. He absconds from the British community, serves with the Nawaub of Bangalore, then plots to betray the Nawaub back to the British and seize the Nawaub's army for his own use in the process; and selling his fiancée to the pleasure-loving son of Hyder Ali is a single treachery which he throws in by the way as a means of ensuring his success in this politico-military fortune hunting. However, the detail proves too much for Hyder Ali, who causes an elephant to stand on Middlemas's chest to show his general disapproval of such intrigue. All this is a long way from economic analysis, it will be objected, possibly, yet behind Middlemas's character and through his story flit the shades and doings of Clive, Hastings, Francis, Sulivan and Benfield, the grand men of the East India Company of the eighteenth century, none of them distinctly named or recalled; and in its details such as the duel, the sale of Menie Gray, and the extortion of money, aspects of the Hastings impeachment are brought to mind.

In 'The Antiquary' (1816; eighteenth-century Scotland) Scott brings out the gap between commercial morality and humane values, noting the cruel side of the market attitude to need and human relationships. 'St Ronan's Well' (1824; early nineteenth-century Scotland) darkly suggests the wasteful vanity of fashionable life in a new spa town, and perhaps of the commercial prosperity it is built on and helps to further, and seems to judge it summarily at the end when Mowbray pulls down the spa and returns the town to the condition it enjoyed, or endured, before capitalism had been heard of. But though Scott puts the suggestion to us, of course, this is not by any means his judgment on the matter; it is what Mowbray does to his property after a disrupting and unpredictable series of misfortunes; and Mowbray's has become an unsettled mind, we read; the issue is left ambiguous, and alive.

Looking at the novels in the order of their historical chronology, like this, not of their composition, enables us to recognize how thoroughly Scott covers the whole course of capitalist development to his own day, but stops short at manufacturing industry as if to leave that to others,(27) and as if it is his concern to recapture the process by which a medieval economy was transformed over centuries of slow deflection and counter-influence into the familiar organization of nineteenth-century England and Europe. 'The Talisman' (1825; twelfth-century Syria), 'Castle Dangerous' (1832; fourteenth-century Scotland), 'Woodstock' (1826; seventeenth-century England) and 'Count Robert of Paris' (1832; eleventh-century Constantinople) do not enter into commercial discussion; 'Woodstock' perhaps surprisingly. These are on the whole insignificant exceptions to the truth that commerce is not only an informing theme in Scott's fiction but frequently the real subject of stories which look quite other in their dress and language. It would be out of place in a summary discussion of this sort to show how Scott's consciousness of the subject works, to try to go into the subtle thematic manifestations and reinforcements of the commercial idea in those novels such as 'The Fortunes of Nigel', and 'Redgauntlet', in which capitalist enterprise plays a central role; there would not be space enough.(28) And the point to be emphasized here, how consistently relevant an issue capitalism shows itself to be in Scott's fiction from first to last, is adequately suggested by the underlining here offered of Scott's marvellously comprehensive and capacious vision of human development.

If we ask, probing further, what lies behind this continuous depiction, and where Scott's governing interest shows itself, and in what, we shall find he is concerned throughout, and above all, to illustrate what really happened in the distant and strange times and places, but vitally connected with the life of his own era, which he selects for the settings and subjects of his romantic adventure stories. A serious concern with true issues lies behind the escapades. In the scrupulously documented 'Kenilworth', 'The Fortunes of Nigel' and 'Peveril of the Peak', for example, all of them reconstructions of the early phase of the establishment of capitalist activity, he records how it looked and felt when a pre-modern economy underwent the transformation into a modern one in sixteenth- and seventeenth-century England. And he does the same for Scotland as for England in what we may describe as the Scottish equivalents to those novels, 'The Bride of Lammermoor', 'Rob Roy', 'Waverley' and 'Redgauntlet', setting them a hundred years later in history because, for Scotland, the same developments came a hundred years or so after their appearance in England. All these are examples of the historian's wish to get the story right, which may be seen operating too in the same way in each of the other novels. Another answer might be that Scott, while never forgetting the otherness of the past, yet sees in it an analogue of the present, and draws forth in departed manners a pattern of existence which the reader can identify with and even recognize as an image of his own. Scott himself is open about this contemporary reference, declaring for instance in the preface to 'Ivanhoe' that it is necessary, for exciting interest in historical fiction, 'that the subject assumed should be, as it were, translated into the manners, as well as the language, of the age we live in'. And we may see how such a principle works in fact when, in 'The Betrothed', Wilkin Flammock, more a captain of industry, incidentally, than a miller, complains of riots in York and Bristol and threatens to take his skill and wealth out of the country to some more peaceful part of the earth (chapter 26); for this comes upon Scott's first readers a bare decade after the Luddite disturbances and obviously is intended to gain in impact from the circumstance. In 'Ivanhoe' the Jews control all England's ready money, make 'immense profits' out of her natural wealth, and elude control by inventing the bill of exchange (chapter 6). All three were live issues in England in 1819, when specie payments had been stopped for twenty years and paper money was being blamed for ruining country banks. 'Ivanhoe' and 'The Betrothed' are both twelfth-century stories. But they are twelfth-century stories written with the nineteenth century in mind, and from its specific base of experience, and by a writer deeply concerned with exploring the connectedness of human life from age to age, and with scrutinizing earlier manifestations of social effort for what they were in themselves, and for what they might tell him of the issues of his own day. Such nineteenth-century awarenesses figure habitually in Scott's historical reconstructions, and are particularly to be observed in the imagery.(29)

Of the commercial spirit itself Scott avoids judgments of exclusive partisanship, and instead occupies a morally involved but on the whole neutral position, unable to deny the loss capitalism has brought in its train, nor its improvements, but chiefly aware, it would seem, of its irreversibility as a historical fact. It is important that we read Scott in such a way as to give to this openness of treatment and judgment of his of the complexities of the economic question its due recognition, for it is the evidence of a capacity of sympathetic vision, of historical sympathy, extremely rare in the period or in any period, and because the case against commerce, like the case for it, but more temptingly than the case for, is easily made from Scott's pages; too easily in both instances, in fact; they cancel one another out.(30) Scott's feelings appear just as harmonized as his judgment. Reading 'Rob Roy', we sense, perhaps, that he yearns after the poetry of the clan, the loyalty beyond contract, the sword and buckler economy. Some yearning is doubtless there. But no less strong is the feeling that such modes are finished. Besides, Scott sees a new poetry in sturdy realism, and it is not to cast him as a narrow modernist to recognize that in the construction of relevant contrasts with others and with the world around them which makes up their respective stories Wilkin Flammock, Arnold Biederman and Henry Gow are important because they last, because, like the contract-signing soldier Dalgetty, they are attuned to the reality of their time; and that Rob Roy and the Children of the Mist appeal to the yielding reader's fancy, as they do, because they are about to vanish. Yet nothing will make Nicol Jarvie as glamorous as Rob Roy. The harmonious final position Scott takes up comes from a balance of opposite or various responses, every one of which acknowledges some original facet of truth in the picture being drawn of a moment in the life of man.

We can place Scott with Southey and Coleridge, and to a lesser extent Lamb, as a writer profoundly conscious of the long-drawn-out historical movement of which his age was the latest period and expression: the epoch of commerce and manufacture. This historical perception of the era of capitalist development is important, for it is a very recent sense. For instance, it is an era now in Scott's lifetime glimpsed, certainly, but not yet named; that is to be Carlyle's achievement. There is no similar awareness in Burke; there had been a sort of apprehension of it in Goldsmith. Scott claims a place far above both Coleridge and Southey, and therefore above all other creative writers in his age, in his information about the workings of capitalism and about its different historical manifestations, yet lower in hostility of judgment on it; and one is tempted to look for a connection between these two facts. Perhaps the key is to be found in the receptive, dramatic nature of Scott's kind of fiction, so ill-suited to aggressive or judgmental moralizing. He does not quarrel with history but accepts it. He recreates its moments of change and pinpoints their critical economic and other developments, making them the focus or centre of interest of romantic stories which are decisively affected by the economic condition they illustrate, and hence are not just romantic, and always he chooses for analysis the major turning points in western, or British, history to supply his material. For instance, he notes as important the onset of egoistic calculation, the transfer from a static to a dynamic economy, the rise of new wealth, the shift of old. I stress acceptance of the unchangeable past in Scott, and of the irreversible new, but that is not to say that he champions capitalism. His imaginative sympathy with the chivalrous honour which capitalism has destroyed is obvious on every reading of his stories, and to every reader. Yet it is the case that he stresses the need to accept the real, not to take refuge in wishing or dreaming. Thus his openness to the facts of history and to life, or, to put it differently, his acceptance as a writer of what must be accepted by all real living men and women in their daily lives, whether it is congenial or not, which is a maturity of response almost Shakespearean in its nature, is what makes him stand out. With his compassion for the sufferers from centuries of mercantile and manufacturing growth, he yet remains submissive to the forces of change which no complaints can reverse, and perhaps a believer in progress.

His steady refusal to engage as novelist in the discussion of contemporary capitalist endeavour, fascinating though the phenomenon must have seemed to him as the outcome of what he had spent so long a time exploring, sifting and assessing, looks tantalizingly curious and unexpected, yet strong-minded at the same time. Perhaps Scott realizes that industrial and manufacturing England is a subject too vast and mobile for a single writer to tackle and comprehend satisfactorily, and leaves it unexamined, grappling instead with a historical aspect of the topic which he makes no less relevant and alive. At any rate, in his pages the Romantic age discovers its condition by paying systematic attention to its forming origins and course of development; and what he personally does not find time to explore, the up-to-the-moment aspects of an industrialized national way of life, his Victorian successors in fiction exhaustively do.

6 FROM INDUSTRIALISM TO BIG BUSINESS 1830-1900

In tracing the capitalist theme through Victorian literature we find ourselves, for the first time in this discussion, being largely though by no means exclusively confined to writing in prose; for poetry, after Shelley's death in 1822 and Byron's in 1824, and notwithstanding Coleridge's and Wordsworth's much longer lives, hardly touches in a direct sustained form the industrial and economic facts of life in nineteenth-century England. An obvious exception has to be made to the generalization for such a poem as Tennyson's 'Maud' (1855), and Browning's very different study in the commerce of spirituality, 'Mr Sludge the Medium' (1864). Still, the generalization can stand. Indeed, when William Morris in the 'envoi' to his 'The Earthly Paradise' (1868-70) disclaims any ability as poet to deal with the real facts of life in his time and offers the reader only escape from them into a less challenging country of the mind,(1) he only puts into explicit language what the poets of the age for the most part appear silently to assume. Yet it may be fairer and more useful to put the matter the other way round. Perhaps we can see the important Victorian poets not as writers who lose their nerve when called upon to face the actual conditions of living in the world they inherit, but as writers driven by an intense recognition of them to explore other sources of meaning than the money acquisitiveness of advanced industrial capitalism: Tennyson identifying with the themes of Arthurian chivalry, Morris bringing up to date the heroism of the sagas, Browning exploring Renaissance Italy, Swinburne myth, the pre-Raphaelites medievalism; in other words, we might see the poets of the Victorian age as secondary Romantics. And the Romantics, it is to be added, 'did not dismiss the world of the industrial revolution from their consciousness; they appealed to other values, of Shakespearean or Greek poetry, against that world'.(2) It is a difference, however, between nineteenth- and eighteenth-century verse that capitalism was deemed to be not a poetic subject after Wordsworth, a shyness of the imagination which would have appeared incomprehensible to Dryden or Pope. A similar difference can be posited between the poetry of the nineteenth century and of the twentieth; for after nearly a hundred years of neglect T. S. Eliot rehabilitated capitalism into poetic discussion; and in Pound, Auden, and later writers it has become as familiar a theme as it ever was traditionally, and as we would expect it to be.

But if in poetry Victorian writers to an extent ignore the dominating fact of their age, in prose they do not; but instead, in the literature of the middle third of the nineteenth century, rather extend and deepen the Romantic analysis of capitalist civilization till that analysis of events fails any longer to explain the nature of an always developing social condition and has to be left on one side to make way for a fresh appraisal. This new spirit is felt after the 1860s and 1870s, when the corporate capitalist or manager, or manipulator of the international money and commodity market, no longer the individual producing merchant manufacturer, takes over as the main literary embodiment of the type; when the working-class voice begins to be heard; when socialism becomes a relevant and significant force of thought; when a tenser world outlook undercuts English confidence; and when, along with these developments, if not because of them, nervousness enters literature. Not all of these are directly capitalist themes. But present in and behind them all is the economic pressure, influencing livelihood and social relations, influencing the terms of approval and disapproval, influencing moral existence; another modern perception. Thus the elements are slowly prepared for the capitalist discussion in the writings of Shaw and Conrad, Lawrence, Pound and Auden.

More modern and perhaps more subtle recognitions, then, in time push aside the Romantic response, but writers in the early Victorian years still seek to understand a phenomenon new to history by recording industrial expansion, urban distress and class enmity, and by describing unfamiliar social relationships and types and new work and traffic. They aim at clarifying the moral and social meaning of the new world they describe, not just its significant physical manifestations, and strive to influence events by containing revolution, castigating an inhuman ethic and holding up to the age a realistic reflection of its notions and appetites and therefore of its true nature. It is in the moral assumptions behind such writing that we recognize the influence of the Romantic poets, an influence occasionally explicit, like that of Wordsworth in Frances Trollope's novel 'Michael Armstrong, The Factory Boy' (1840).(3) Scott does not seem to figure in any literal way in this kind of imaginative bequest, and perhaps more preparatory for the Victorian social problem novel is John Galt's interesting and original, but in the end, and by the highest standards, unsatisfactory 'Annals of the Parish' (1821); a novel in the form of a journal diary given thematic life by its rising stress on the industrial transformation of the narrator's small world around Dalmailing and Glasgow, and on its human cost, and on its benefits. The same is true of his novels 'The Provost' (1822) and 'The Entail' (1822), both of them equally good pictures of the economic turbulence in southern Scotland during her industrializing years, and very readable; but limited. What makes Galt unsatisfactory, coming at the critical juncture which he does, both for life and for literature, is his unwillingness to generalize. For by the 1820s and 1830s some largeness of thought and defining effort regarding England's condition had become necessary.

Really an application of Romantic insights into spiritual and imaginative truth, into human brotherhood, and into love, a demonstration of why these values mattered and what they were in an age which felt itself cast away from familiar norms and seduced by the glamour of material conquest, needed redirecting on to the industrial Victorian scene. A writer had to be found who could mould the perceptions of Blake into a kind of statement that such as Dickens could assimilate and use. Obviously Galt is not up to this kind of endeavour. It is because Carlyle actually succeeded in offering this new light to his contemporaries, and nobody else did, that he mattered to them so much; for he seemed to the early Victorians, especially those dissatisfied with inept Christianity and with arid Benthamism, the one thinker who promised to work out an adequate explanation of the developments that bewildered and alarmed his generation. More, Carlyle's is an explanation of events which is highly critical but finally accepting of them, which even celebrates what it finds alarming in the tendencies of its time. His is a significant voice, then. He stands as a sage, not a poet, who helps his fellows to define what they have become. His relevance to them drew its strength from the facts that he moves a stage further on from Romanticism, that he lashes his age, and that he endorses it. These are advantages which make it no surprise that he engrossed a zealous following in his lifetime. Carlyle's analysis of English life, for example in 'Signs of the Times' (1829), stresses its mechanism, recalling Coleridge and Wordsworth, but bites into the Victorian experience when in the very opening pages of 'Sartor Resartus' (1833-4) he blames the universal reliance on 'our mercantile greatness, and invaluable Constitution', a lower vision of excellence, for pushing out what is a higher vision, the cultivation of disinterested wisdom and pure science. Yet at the same time and in the same argument he recognizes that the energetic pursuit of commercial supremacy is at least a vision of sorts, and being a real ideal can compel men's allegiance. Thus it is not to be thoroughly damned. Idlers are damned. Here is an instance of how Carlyle manages to gather his age to himself while rejecting it. When he invents the term 'Industrialism' for the spirit of the age, he means by it something positively enhancing and purposive, if limited and by itself shallow, not something to be feared and attacked tooth and nail, though it soon became a pejorative word in common usage. But there is nothing pejorative intended by its original coiner (book 2, chapter 4):

> Cannot the dullest hear Steam-engines clanking around him? Has he not seen the Scottish Brassmith's IDEA (and this is but a mechanical one) travelling on fire-wings round the Cape, and across two Oceans; and stronger than any other Enchanter's Familiar, on all hands unweariedly fetching and carrying: at home, not only weaving Cloth, but rapidly enough overturning the whole old system of Society; and, for Feudalism and Preservation of the Game, preparing us, by indirect but sure methods, Industrialism and the Government of the Wisest? (1833-4)

Feudalism is the opposite of Industrialism here, an irrelevant, vapid and self-indulgent ideal of living, at least in its decadent nineteenth-century form, solely for the sake of enjoyment. Carlyle scorns this as moral triviality.

The attitude may tempt us to connect him with Defoe and with Bacon, perhaps validly; but overriding so theoretical a link is the other side of Carlyle's mind, his undistorted awareness of how industrialism is actually working, of its social and human cost, and his condemnation of that price as unacceptable. All his major writings emphasize the supremacy of true life over mere material advance, and, going further, isolate the profit hunger of industrial capitalism, and its money valuation of all of men's activities and of men's relations with one another, as the corrupting element and deadly yeast in the social mass. Carlyle's admiration of practical energy is one thing, and looks one way; his stripping off of outer ceremony to show the brutalization of the essential relation between man and man in the industrial age, looks quite another. It never allows him to relinquish his hold on the idea that capitalism in its latest form has decisively altered man's condition, and for the worse so far. This, the Romantic writers had judged before him; but we see it in Carlyle with increased documentation and a new ambivalence of attitude, more prepared to concede where concession is possible in spite of a profound genuine anger.

What the basic relation of man to man now appears to have turned into, in Carlyle's opinion, his long essay 'Chartism' (1839) makes plain, perhaps plainer than the same message even in 'Past and Present' (1843), his better-known work. In 'Chartism', which we may therefore concentrate on, the sense of lost bearings is piercing; the cause of the failure of English life is precisely judged and placed; the sense of pride, nevertheless, in an achievement unmatched by other nations then or earlier, is unmistakeable. It is a very Victorian mixture. English commerce, we read, stretching its fibres over the earth, is propelled outwards to the ends of human existence by the demon Mechanism, which at home oversets and hurls workmen and known methods of labour and material interchange in all directions, so that a condition has been reached in which 'the wisest no longer knows his whereabout'.(4) The social and intellectual disarray here perceived is simply, Carlyle says, the result of trying to compress value and obligation down to one pure commercial relation, to the nexus of cash payment and the law of supply and demand. This is an outrage on the complexity of life which human nature throws off with violence; for, Carlyle goes on, in the famous reminder, there are 'so many things which cash will not pay', and demands 'entirely indispensable, which have to go elsewhere than to the shops, and produce quite other than cash, before they can get their supply' (op. cit., p. 383). What is articulated here is the impossible state of a society which is trying its best to live according to an over-simple ethic, the ethic of competition, and which as a result is destined for revolution, the outcome and other side of pure competition unchecked by any other restraining influence. Coleridge is very close to this sort of writing. Carlyle's vision, his discovery, his contribution to the debate, is of the imminence of revolution which is why his influence as a thinker fades as the nineteenth century advances and the threat of revolution recedes from immediate expectation. He makes the point with such impact in 'Sartor Resartus' and 'Chartism' that its re-exploration in 'Past and Present' (1843) and in 'Latter-Day Pamphlets' (1850), and in his other essays, need not detain us in the present discussion; though it is never just a repetition of old ideas we find in Carlyle. We may also spare an analysis here of Carlyle's hero ideology, a historical non-starter.

Carlyle's importance, in short, is a defining rather than a solving one. He gives the Victorian age the formulation it needs. He names England's transformation from a commercial into an industrial society. He disposes the random events of the centuries of English life into a progress, his secularized Calvinism proving helpful here, and describes it as a progress towards a goal no one person or generation of the English race foresaw, until (x, pp. 400-1):

> in the middle of the eighteenth century they *arrived*. The Saxon kindred burst forth into cotton-spinning, cloth-cropping, iron-forging, steamengineing, railwaying, commercing and careering towards all the winds of Heaven - in this inexplicable noisy manner; the noise of which, in Power-mills, in progress-of-the-species Magazines, still deafens us somewhat. Most noisy, sudden! The Staffordshire coal-stratum and coal-strata lay side by side with iron-strata, quiet since the creation of the world. Water flowed in Lancashire and Lanarkshire; bituminous fire lay bedded in rocks there too, - over which how many fighting Stanleys, black Douglasses, and other the like contentious persons, had fought out their bickerings and broils, not without result, we will hope! But God said, Let the iron missionaries be; and they were. Coal and iron, so long close unregardful neighbours, are wedded together; Birmingham and Wolverhampton, and the hundred Stygian forges, with their fire-throats and never-resting sledge-hammers, rose into day. Wet Manconium stretched out her hand towards Carolina and the torrid zone, and plucked cotton there; who could forbid her, that had the skill to weave it? Fish fled thereupon from the Mersey River, vexed with innumerable keels. England, I say, dug out her bitumen-fire, and bad it work: towns rose, and steeple-chimneys; - Chartisms also, and Parliaments they name Reformed. (1839)

This is not just felicitous; it is luminous. Carlyle has comprehended events, has seen that they form a process, and says so because, perhaps alone at the time, he has been able to make the connection. He names the process because he understands it in its historically inevitable determination, and therefore has the insight which enables him to relate the unimaginable contemporary phenomenon to its forming origins and make sense of it for his deeply concerned but bewildered contemporaries. It is a perception not found in Scott, too deep for Galt, and unavailable to

Coleridge, and is Carlyle's stroke of genius. That his understanding of what he is talking about is as thorough as need be in the 1830s is shown by his almost casually thrown-in reference to steeple chimneys, a phrase and idea echoed by Froude fifty years later,(5) which, if we allow it to register, really says everything; by his admission, in 'fish fled thereupon', and similar phrasings, which suggest the enormity of the violation of the natural order which industrialism has occasioned, of a past irreversibly severed from the life of the present, and from future experience, and placed like Eden for ever out of man's reach; by his willingness to equate the importance of power mills with political radicalism and with learned journals, and indeed his identification of them all as the forming elements in the one historical event of which all men are conscious; and by his explosive imagery. All this testifies to Carlyle's complexity of awareness of the revolution in affairs which is his subject.

Carlyle's gifts to his generation and to posterity were two: first, this inestimable one of naming the common condition as it now was; and second, a feature of his writing which has perhaps received less allowance than it deserves, his positive excitement and receptivity, severely qualified, certainly, but basically affirming, as the passage quoted just now makes obvious, the imagined benefits and mountainous deeds of the industrial revolution. The latter sentiment helped to bring Victorian writers out of the Romantic dead end, as it would have been for them, since the conditions of the England of the Romantic poets had now changed, of shocked rejection; and succeeding literature as a consequence is full of echoes of Carlyle, and Carlyle's ideas. For instance, Dickens, and the industrial novelists Disraeli, Elizabeth Gaskell and Charles Kingsley, and others, not to mention Matthew Arnold and William Morris and later writers, inherit and popularize his analysis of things, and particularly assimilate his mixture of criticism with wonder, for instance with regard to Manchester, the shame and wonder city of English industrialism, and what Manchester symbolized. But we are not to follow up in the present chapter every tremor of that influence, every reflection of industrial commerce, every fictional merchant in the entire literature of the Victorian age. There is too little space. Nor is there need. The main lines are what matter. And in Carlyle we meet the first articulation of a new way of seeing, the progression from a Romantic to a Victorian statement of experience, and the creation of a terminology of debate which could be expanded and adapted by other writers in succeeding years.

To acknowledge Carlyle as basic to the Victorian discussion is not to claim for him that he is its centre. Dickens is central; and after Carlyle's pioneer work, without which Dickens could not have seen things as he did, it is to the novels of Dickens that we must turn for an imaginative portrayal of the individual capitalist and the capitalist world, and its spirit, and its relation to the rest of human society and to life in general as they were viewed and felt during the first generation or so of the Victorian age.

The kind of revelation that Dickens can offer, but Carlyle cannot, is that contained in the imaginative rendering of experience compared with an account of it. Not that Carlyle is merely theoretical; but it is the naming of the life of his times which he is concerned to fix as accurately as he can, whereas Dickens conveys its texture, and shows us, not what we should think of it only, but what being a merchant feels like, or an industrial magnate, or a financier, or a factory hand, or a business manager, or a dependant or victim or opponent of such persons in England in the middle years of the nineteenth century. His writing is thus closer than Carlyle's to rendering the real experience of men and women.

An important aspect of this reflection of his times that we find in Dickens is that it develops; the portrayal changes. It does so because the outer scene itself undergoes a constant modification, and Dickens reflects that, and because Dickens's imagination is continuously creative and renewing in itself and never contents itself with reproducing in a later book the knowledge which has already been won in an earlier, and no more. From the 1830s to the 1860s he reflects the new outgrowths of developing capitalism which were its prominent features, such as speculative companies, railway building, union action, economic over-expansion, international finance, while at the same time isolating special aspects of the subject in each novel; the two aims are part of each other, of course. He throws in contrary delineations which prevent us from forming a too simple judgment on his handling of the issue, as well. And such many-sidedness does not, as we half suppose it might, hold Dickens back from a firm response. The main developing line of his portrayal shows the reverse to be true, with its deepening hatred of, if not his capitalist society itself, at least its foremost representatives and furthering agents, the men who live for personal aggrandizement and profit.

The line runs from the miser Ralph Nickleby of 'Nicholas Nickleby' (1837-8) through the merchant Dombey in 'Dombey and Son' (1846-8), the manufacturer Bounderby in 'Hard Times' (1854) and the financial crook Merdle in 'Little Dorrit' (1855-7) to the rentier speculator Veneering in 'Our Mutual Friend' (1864-5), the names themselves sufficiently expressing Dickens's growing sense of alienation from what such men live for and represent. If we find on examining them that the representations get progressively less awesome, that Dombey and Bounderby are potent creatures, but Merdle a weakling, and Veneering ludicrous, we are not to suppose that Dickens as he gets older has come to accept his exploiting age more tolerantly than before, even though he always writes of it as a critic rather than a true foe; in the later fiction all of society is his target, and its pathetic idols are part of his indictment. Here in the growing rift between Dickens's ideal of conduct and his understanding of the personality of the money man, and in his realization that all life was being encompassed within the range of influence of the latter even as he wrote, is the side of him which led Shaw to appraise him as an unconscious revolutionist.(6) But to consider only this adverse reaction, like Shaw, is to simplify, and Dickens is not a simple novelist. Almost as important as the capitalist villains already mentioned are his characterizations of the ironmaster Rouncewell in 'Bleak House' (1852-3), the business manager Clennam and honest ex-banker Meagles in 'Little Dorrit', not to mention Pickwick in 'Pickwick Papers' (1836-7), the Cheeryble brothers in 'Nicholas Nickleby', Solomon Gills in 'Dombey and Son' and Jarvis Lorry in 'A Tale of Two Cities' (1859), all generous and responsible persons, and all inescapably men of trade and of business. What do these representations tell us? They tell us that Dickens may be against capitalism purely considered, as against any purely considered system, but is not against all capitalists. He is a vehement critic therefore rather than a revolutionist.

Coming closer to the fiction itself, we find that Dickens brings us with a smack straight into the Victorian world. His eighteenth-century origins as novelist only show this new original feature the more strongly. 'Nicholas Nickleby' (1837-8), for example, takes up where Smollett leaves off, asking about modes of livelihood for friendless individuals or families in a competitive world, but in its full sweep reflects a more catastrophically upset state of society than any in the fiction of the eighteenth century. Everyone is now at risk. Bankruptcy is the story's opening event; and before the Nickleby fortunes have been recoverd, Nicholas ending his career, incidentally, as a successful merchant, Mantalini has been ruined, Ralph Nickleby has lost ten thousand pounds, equivalent to a resounding bankruptcy, and Nicholas and Tim Linkinwater have spent days helping to clear up the failure of a Cheeryble correspondent in Germany (chapters 21, 54, 40). Bankruptcy is rare, though not unknown, in Jane Austen and Scott, but is normal experience in the fiction of Dickens and his contemporaries, and is, of course, no more accidental there than the tempest which opens Shakespeare's play of that name. Bankruptcy is the symbol of the life of the age.(7)

Recognizable as a distinct Victorian businessman, as well as wicked uncle and Jacobean miser, Ralph Nickleby inaugurates the United Metropolitan Improved Hot Muffin and Crumpet Baking and Punctual Delivery Company, a fraudulent money-making scheme, and introduces Kate Nickleby to Lord Frederick Verisopht and Sir Mulberry Hawk at a discount party (chapter 19). Other examples in the early novels of this up-to-date sense of capitalist activity, and of Dickens's moral suspicion of it, are the entrepreneurial Daniel Quilp of 'The Old Curiosity Shop' (1841), Scrooge of 'A Christmas Carol' (1843) and Tigg Montague in 'Martin Chuzzlewit' (1843-4) with his Anglo-Bengalee Disinterested Loan and Life Assurance Company. The last-named enterprise, an updated version of the muffin venture of Ralph Nickleby, is modish, sudden, and most of all respectable-looking. It has newly plastered, newly painted offices, newly fitted up and fully furnished, and with no real commercial activity to back up all the appearance of business, no substance behind the show. This glances at Dickens's depiction of the Veneerings twenty years in the future. Already, even so early, Dickens's analysis of his society is seen to be essentially complete; the picture he draws is of an age unpredictable and protean in its economic manifestations, spiritually cut off from its roots and lacking in self-knowledge. And his major portrayal, beginning with 'Dombey and Son' (1846-8), authenticates this judgment on the empty ignorance of the commercial creed, the economic egotist, and the money man. Carlyle's influence is evident and pervasive here, but Dickens's reach, and what he makes of his borrowings, are what impress us, not what individual nudges he may have received from other writers. The Dickensian effect is all-important. When Mr Dombey comes to think the commercial relation all that matters between men, Dickens, expressing the process of his self-contemplation and refusal to participate in the world as it is, draws into the texture of his narrative the wide Augustan imaginings on trade of a century earlier, a tired eighteenth-century ideal actually taking on new life in the age of Cobden and Bright,(8) and the idiom of 'Genesis', and by mixing the two styles creates a weighty mockery whose suggestions are contemporary, old-fashioned and prehistoric at the same time (chapter 1):

> The earth was made for Dombey and Son to trade in, and the sun and moon were made to give them light. Rivers and seas were formed to float their ships; rainbows gave them promise of fair weather; winds blew for or against their enterprises; stars and planets circled in their orbits, to preserve inviolate a system of which they were the centre. Common abbreviations took new meanings in his eyes, and had sole reference to them. A.D. had no concern with anno Domini, but stood for anno Dombei - and Son. (1846-8)

Dombey here is more than a haughty old trader; he stands for an accredited system of things, a way of being. He is the mercantile eighteenth-century type of man living on into the nineteenth century, whose new conditions he fails to recognize and adapt to. The novel is full of reminders of this departed world of the eighteenth century with its hard-to-use machines and unsaleable instruments, and its ponderous ideas. But Dickens is no keener on the new men: Carker for instance, or the Director of companies, who, if he chooses, can buy up 'human Nature generally' (chapter 36). Dickens disliked the eighteenth century, and Dombey is odious because he is an eighteenth-century type; or rather, strikes Dickens as in some elements characteristic of the human inadequacy of the upper- and upper-middle-class culture of the eighteenth-century period.(9) But his condemnation of Dombeyism, the spirit of mercantile pride and gain, remains Dickens's judgment on the capitalist world even of his own day; in spite of the improving railways.

His successive novels, after 'Dombey and Son', cut deeper into the issue without softening their hostility. By adding Gradgrind, the theorist of selfishness, to Bounderby, its practical example, in 'Hard Times' (1854), though Gradgrind has also worked in the wholesale hardware trade, Dickens adds extra modernity and penetration even to the picture drawn in 'Dombey and Son'. The times are seen as having become in late years all of a piece, and worse, a creed now offering to confer righteousness on the pursuit of appetite and competition, not a particularly stressed feature of Dombey's world view, receiving sanction as the natural law of things. Bounderby, savagely worse than Dombey, and a brutalization in all aspects, is no throwback as Dombey is, but the precise type favoured and cast up by the industrial era. The analysis proceeds, consequently, in 'Little Dorrit' (1855-7). Here is brought out the prevalence of a now almost impersonal money hunger, so generally established has it become in the system of society, a condition of life in which personal affection seems lost sight of, and, among other loosening ties, that of financial accountability seems generally neglected and disused. Ralph Nickleby, Dombey and Bounderby all dominate the men and women around them, and inhabit vividly actualized worlds; but the worried, insignificant personality, almost a denial of personality, which is bestowed on Merdle, and which symbolizes his mean function of paper profiteering, is criticism not of a single man but of a whole civilization given over in its basic conviction to self-seeking and non-function; for Merdle, we are reminded, is his age's representative.(10) More than acute character drawing is in view here, though. A little-remarked side of 'Little Dorrit' is its careful build-up of the story of the process and progress through all social levels of an economic expansion, followed by over-expansion, followed by slump,(11) a wonderfully thought-out and unobtrusive mirror image of expanding capitalist Britain in the mid-Victorian years. But the range of view has begun to widen further still. Doyce, we read, is in repeated demand for engineering commissions abroad, while the proud English banker Meagles, who has retired from work, and the people of England generally, even down to the lower-class Plornishes, continue to become more and more insular and to refuse to accept the international realities. One of these unpalatable truths is that other ambitious nations are beginning to flex their economic muscles while Britain is in a daze of self-congratulation. And Meagles is a smug type well caught by Clough in 'Amours de Voyage' (1862), a poem written in the same period;(12) he is destined to reappear in a more sinister form as the marine insurer Podsnap in 'Our Mutual Friend' (1864-5). Such a development betrays in Dickens, on one level, a deepening gloom at the state of capitalist England, though it may be just England rather than capitalism in general he feels gloomy about, and continues in 'Our Mutual Friend' with its attack on money parasites who do nothing for the money they enjoy, and, if they have none to call their own, try to live on the profit they can extort by any means whatever out of other people.

Looking over the entirety of Dickens's work, then, we see it as first of all a coherent indictment of the impoverishment of life potential under industrial capitalism, and recognize that each novel grows out of and adds to the sinister vision of the one before. The money world has become all but the whole world in 'Our

Mutual Friend', but intrinsically is just a natural continuation of the society that lives by the credit fraudulence of 'Little Dorrit', itself an out-reaching from the community split into open economic war of 'Hard Times', the tyranny of money egotism of 'Dombey and Son' and the business free-for-all of 'Nicholas Nickleby' and 'Martin Chuzzlewit'. Looking again, we find that Dickens is much less stark; otherwise he could not have kept his popularity among a nation which he exclusively lashed with such vehemence. As with Carlyle, the fact is that Dickens speaks for his age because, for all his angry words, he is able to find something in its inmost convictions which he can approve of and share. He can see magic in the commerce of 'Dombey and Son', advantage in the railway, power in Coketown and in the northern iron country, hope in capitalist endeavour abroad, and a worthwhile livelihood in commercial activity of any kind, large or small, in any place and at any time, provided that a genuine task is being performed or service offered or product made; provided something is being done. As with Carlyle, he embodies the age he criticizes. Still, there is a difference between this and approving of it. If anything in Dickens gives the reader cause for anxiety it is the lightweight nature of his positives, given his powerful and complex understanding of capitalist aggression and money tyranny. Ruskin saw Dickens's hero in the ironmaster Rouncewell, but Rouncewell is a hero unprobed, set against the lethargic and the undoing, and judged heroic because he is otherwise. We may ask what but their fictional roles distinguishes Rouncewell from Bounderby; certainly not the nature of their work. Rouncewell, then, is a hero taken for granted. Being himself outstandingly self-made, Dickens could always take for granted the benign possibilities of capitalism, it may be, but when he looks closer into its workings he comes to like what he finds there less and less. Again we are reminded of Carlyle, and of the whole early Victorian age the two writers express so well. Nothing is more Victorian than such a blend of critical pride; especially characteristic is the pride, for sharp criticism had come before, and was to intensify afterwards, but only then, during the second third of the nineteenth century, and even in those years with an anxious tremor towards the close, did industrial England feel assured in its ascendancy over the rest of the world.

Disraeli, Kingsley and Elizabeth Gaskell claim attention as critics of commerce and industry whose fiction, like Dickens's summary novel 'Hard Times', expresses the Carlylean denunciation of reckless gain; and also reveals to us their basic affirmation of the industrial achievement which characterized their age and had made it what it was; this last, perhaps, least of all in Kingsley. What is to be said of them is that they certainly bring into literature indignantly the new facts of social experience, Disraeli in 'Coningsby' (1844), 'Sybil' (1845) and 'Tancred' (1847), his condition of England trilogy, Elizabeth Gaskell in 'Mary Barton' (1848) and 'North and South' (1854-5), and Kingsley in 'Yeast' (1848) and 'Alton Locke' (1850); and that their reformist zeal is authentic, but that they are all of them more critics than rebels, and visibly, even in their indignant writings, impressed critics at that. The full social question as these novels individually reflect it is far too large a subject for us to enter upon a discussion of it here, though not particularly a complex one; and perhaps too familiar to need repeating.(13) Our interest lies in the fact that, with any amount of stern criticism, and any number of serious revelations of suffering and injustice, all caused by its natural operation and unchecked drive, Disraeli and Elizabeth Gaskell are both writers who endorse capitalism decisively and approve of the capitalist type; and Kingsley, though more argumentatively unimpressed and anti-capitalist than either, and incidentally a worse novelist, never quite carries through his criticism to outright rejection. Disraeli's Sidonia, the son of a fictional Rothschild,(14) his Millbanks, the father a Lancashire manufacturer, the son a member of the reformed Parliament, all in 'Coningsby', and his manufacturer Trafford, calling Robert Owen to mind, in 'Sybil', in intention distinctly overshadowing the implications of the scandalous revelations of those novels, make up a full-scale presentation of the capitalist and entrepreneur as hero, an optimistic gloss on the accepted type of the age. In 'Sybil', Trafford's model village is nearly crime-free. In 'Coningsby', Manchester workplaces are magical. Not all the horrors of Wodgate can hide this basic thrill. Elizabeth Gaskell's development is from the indignant 'Mary Barton', a gesture towards a working-class rendering of events, to the opposite point of view in 'North and South', which, Higgins notwithstanding, idealizes the self-made industrialist in Thornton, first culturally polished, then morally chastened, and at last given the girl and the girl's money, and elevated by the author into the position of an all-round hero of her time. Thus the novel's real movement is Margaret's towards trade, not Thornton's away from it, which represents Elizabeth Gaskell's real outlook in life.(15) Kingsley is more radical. He certainly approves of strong-minded effort, and is perhaps the most Carlylean novelist of all in his capacity for being impressed by convinced material energies, but he sees beyond mere achievement to the need for spiritual illumination. 'Yeast's' Lord Minchampstead, one of the Dissenting nouveaux riches who has recently turned himself into a Church of England man, is a practical reforming and modernizing landowner, Prospero to the country Calibans, and is zestfully described, but Lancelot Smith thinks past his profit-motive ideal to the Christian-Carlylean notion that men have forgotten God and must rediscover him before all else, if they are to put the state of the country right. 'Alton Locke' (1850), through the Chartist Crossthwaite, further highlights for us the limitedness of the self-help myth, stressing the number of noble gentlemen who have fallen into drunkenness and suicide because nobody would give them a helping hand. It is interesting to see Kingsley's socialist note added here to Shelley's radical solidarity with the unvoiced of history, itself an extension of Gray's leveller sentiment in the famous 'Elegy'. Kingsley shows us he can hit quite hard when he wants to. His portrayal of the tailoring trade in 'Alton Locke', and of the general condition of English society in his time, is of an exploiting world, of economic Darwinism, though the term is of course not his own and could not be, and of all the early Victorian writers his socialist critique comes closest to being an outright rejection of the whole structure of capitalist enterprise and civilization.

To summarize and be explicit about it, what these early Victorian writers offer us, as Dickens supremely does, is a working out of the Romantic inheritance of moral indignation at unchecked economic competition, and an evidence of the dissemination and acceptance of Carlyle's belief in the improving function of productive effort and of work. Dickens chiefly extends and deepens these commitments; the secondary social novelists add their important and interesting contributions, not by any means agreeing with each other about what is important, or seeing the same things, or wanting the same action taken to improve matters; but agreeing in their souls about the existence of a hope which their gloomy words may sometimes appear to belie.

Elsewhere in literature at large the optimistic conviction, in its turn, as the century progresses, provoking yet other minds to question its judgment of events with more fundamental opposition, and to find its certitude offensive, is echoed and re-expressed. There is no simple opposition being argued out here, of course, no pattern in the matter, only continuous exploring revaluation and re-inspection and echoing of the assumptions of social life. Heathcliff in 'Wuthering Heights' (1847) is a self-made man. Robert Moore, the hero of Charlotte Brontë's 'Shirley' (1849), a novel set in Napoleonic times, is another, a Napoleon, or rather a Coriolanus, of commerce; not that this novel offers blanket praise of a class. In their sum of meaning, all the commemorations in Samuel Smiles's 'Self-Help' (1859) add up to an expression of the ideal, as the title tells us, especially those of the men of business and industry in chapters 2 and 3; yet Smiles offers his celebration in a nostalgic manner, as if by the 1850s there was less assurance and more need for reassurance in the air; and perhaps the appearance of his book proves the fact.(16) Similar anxiety may explain the worship of success, especially evident in the third chapter of volume 1, which pervades Macaulay's 'History of England' (1849-61), and exalts the commercial and technological achievements of the nineteenth century above the civilization of the sixteenth and seventeenth centuries with a dogmatic certitude of mind which appears to argue some kind of paralysis of the historical imagination. Such writing, Marx protests, is a subordination of objective to interested history.(17) Material valuation; the idealizing of effort irrespective of function and end; an emphasis on willpower: these are the signs of the work priority in the hands of less subtle thinkers than Carlyle. Thomas Buckle's 'History of Civilization' (1857-61) declares that 'of all the great social improvements the accumulation of wealth must be the first',(18) a reflection back, but with marked loss of fineness of thought in the transference, to Smith's distinction in 'The Wealth of Nations' between productive and unproductive labour.

Naturally, such simplifications met with opposition. A lifelong opponent and corrector of the inert cast of mind which gives rise to them was Matthew Arnold, who in 'Culture and Anarchy' (1869) brands mechanical thought such as Macaulay's as philistinism or hebraism, and opposes to it hellenism, the Greek ideal: luminous beauty. Arnold's social and cultural writings are too wide-ranging, too complex and too voluminous to go into in detail; but basically his criticism is of a late-Victorian England stifled by the value deriving from materialistic capitalism and reduced generally in its mental horizon, of an England created in the image of Podsnap; and it is also interesting that it should be Greece, not Rome, as it would have been a century earlier, that he chooses to offer to his countrymen as their ideal of true civility. This Greek affinity is a nineteenth-century preference, strongly present in Shelley and Byron before Arnold's time, and also seen in his contemporary Kinglake's 'Eothen' (1844), which enforces the cultural contrast between Greek and English life in explicitly capitalist terms. (19) Another Arnoldian critic is Thomas Hughes, both of whose Tom Brown stories stress the mental limitedness and moral and social danger of judging of welfare solely by the criterion of material gain, as when Harry tells Tom Brown in his Oxford study in 'Tom Brown at Oxford' (1861) that the devil of profit is 'the devil that England has most to fear from' (chapter 10). In 'Tom Brown's Schooldays' (1857), we recall, Hughes had charged railway directors with spending millions on bribing the country's doctors to recommend all their patients who could afford it to take a change of air (chapter 1).

To these critics of commercialism we may add Tennyson, who describes in 'Locksley Hall' (1832) the fading of the vision of benign commerce, a dream held over from more innocent days, and then in 'Maud' (1855) condemns the capitalist organization of society as war under the guise of peace in which the millionaire has become 'Britain's one sole God' (Part III, vi, 2). It is the concern of this poem to generalize the indictment made of villainous greed, to see 'that old man, now lord of the broad estate and the Hall', who 'Dropt off gorg'd from a scheme that had left us flaccid and drain'd' (Part I, i, 5), and whose successful duplicity has led to the suicide, if it was suicide and not something worse, of the narrator's ruined father, as a representative of the age, as a type and mark which all men aim at and admire, and would wish to be. Such are the real lines of action and desire, aggressive, outdoing, mutually exploiting and destructive, and in reality not in any important feature different from the confessed antagonism of a stage of war, of a society still hypocritically congratulating itself on its civility and its maintenance of peace (Part I, i, 6-10):

Why do they prate of the blessings of Peace? we have made
them a curse,
Pickpockets, each hand lusting for all that is not its own;
And lust of gain, in the spirit of Cain, is it better or worse
Than the heart of the citizen hissing in war on his own
hearthstone?

But these are the days of advance, the works of the men of
mind,
When who but a fool would have faith in a tradesman's ware
or his word?
Is it peace or war? Civil war, as I think, and that of a kind
The viler, as underhand, not openly bearing the sword.

Sooner or later I too may passively take the point
Of the golden age - why not? I have neither hope nor trust,
May make my heart as a millstone, set my face as a flint,
Cheat, and be cheated, and die: who knows? we are ashes
and dust.

Peace sitting under her olive, and slurring the days gone by,
When the poor are hovell'd and hustl'd together, each sex,
like swine,
When only the ledger lives, and when only not all men lie;
Peace in her vineyard - yes! - but a company forges the
wine.

And the vitriol madness flashes up in the ruffian's head,
Till the filthy by-lane rings to the yell of the trampled wife,
While chalk and alum and plaster are sold to the poor for
bread,
And the spirit of murder works in the very means of life.
(1855)

Others cheat the sick for profit, the poem goes on; a Mammonite mother kills her child for a fee; the new-made lord at the Hall descends from a coal plutocrat who wrung his profits from the labours of poisoned workers; everyone is involved in a money corruption, a profits fever; commerce has become all in all. Tennyson's specific charges can be very penetrating, as shown by the last two lines quoted here, which reveal a kind of exploitation for money familiar enough in Victorian England and earlier, but not much emphasized in the literature. Only the fact that he has to put them into the mouth of a person unbalanced, and thus a suspect witness, or at least one dramatically different from the poet himself suggests that the extremity of the rejection of English civilization here uttered is something about which he feels a little uneasy. It is from this universal condition of hypocritical cruelty and fraud that the 'Maud' speaker seeks purer action in honest militarism; in the Crimean War! The two narrators of 'Locksley Hall' and 'Maud', we remind ourselves, are imagined personages, and not to be identified with the poet. But elsewhere Tennyson speaks against commercialism in his own voice.(20)

Sharing the theme are Elizabeth Barrett Browning's 'The Cry of the Children', a watery repeat of Blake, and 'A Song for the Ragged Schools of London', a plea for more consideration for the victims of commercialism; and some of the lyrics of Thomas Hood. Two opposed studies in the self-help and success ideal are Jabez Clegg, the hero of Mrs G. Linnaeus Banks's 'The Manchester Man' (1876), a sub-Smilesian mercantile idyll, and Tom Tulliver in George Eliot's 'The Mill on the Floss' (1860). Tulliver is shown to us as a young man of 'good commercial stuff' (book 5, chapter 2) and solid character, not moulded like Clegg on 'the spooney type of the Industrious Apprentice', but deeply entered into and sympathized with, and thus brought to life; then condemned.

With Matthew Arnold and George Eliot we begin to move out of Dickens's period, but the Dickensian presentation of capitalism is of itself sufficiently capacious and reconsidering to comprehend to some extent all the points of view so far expressed; it is an indication of how central he is to the literature of early Victorian England. A novelist not included in the comprehension of Dickens, though, is Thackeray, and clearly George Eliot is another, so to fit those writers into the texture of the discussion is to begin to progress onwards in an important way from the Dickensian analysis. Thackeray stands outside the range of influence of Dickens both by his experience and by his method as novelist. His examination of commerce reaches back in basic assumptions to the classic English contempt for vulgar trade in Fielding, Wycherley and Ben Jonson. He is incurious about industrialism, as is George Eliot, and in the context of the present discussion this reduces his significance, perhaps drastically; but there is nothing indecisive or vaguely seen about what he actually does give us. His unmitigatedly hostile view of the man wholly involved in commercial pursuits is summarized in Osborne senior, the sadistic, black-browed merchant tyrant of Russell Square in 'Vanity Fair' (1847-8) but with Thackeray, as with Fielding and Jonson before him, the real target of the satire is human greed and folly. And these are vices which are not confined to men of commerce, though given fuller scope to develop themselves in their style of life than in another, but nevertheless remain, so to speak, permanent marks in the grain of human character, and are treated as such. When Dobbin's schoolfellows laugh at him because his father is a grocer, Thackeray is not entertaining us with child's play; the same savage cruelty, worse because adult, is visited on the bankrupt merchant Sedley later on in the story. In both cases Thackeray is dealing with cruel commercial snobbery and hatred, but is not specially concerned with them as commerce; rather, as examples of how vicious people can be to one another when they try. Indeed, in the latter instance he underlines his moral rather than documentary purpose by expressly sliding over the technicalities of the crash.(21) Yet he succeeds in conveying piercingly enough the financial instability of the Napoleonic era, a period in which mercantile double-dealing and fortune hunting and social climbing were brought into greater prominence than usual by a political and economic crisis of international significance. This sense of historical development is brought up to date in 'The Newcomes' (1853-4), a novel whose title suggests its theme. Newcome, named after its prominent family, once a country village, is now a manufacturing town; Newcome's merchant-banker sons, rising on the strength of its industrial prosperity, have grown in wealth and power while their colonel brother, the hero of the tale, declines into insignificant obscurity, ruined by his humane and generous temperament in a world which can find no place for it, the world of the commercial-minded and the self-seeking. Capitalism on an international scale enters the story in the Anglo-Continental Railway and in the Bundelcund Bank, based in offices in Sydney, Singapore, Canton and London, a shaky financial empire run by the Indian speculator Rummum Loll which finally collapses and drags uncounted innocent people to ruin in its fall. All this comes before Merdle in 'Little Dorrit'.

Thackeray's Indian and European backgrounds provide the material from which he can take this raised world view of capitalist action, but, on the disabling side, it also perhaps holds him back from knowing industrialism. Sensibly, if so, he keeps away from the proletarian theme.(22) But with George Eliot, who also declines to enter on industrial delineation in any detail, though not to acknowledge its overwhelming significance in the national life, things are different; indeed, she makes this precise recognition the basis of her exploration of county and country town life, and this brings to the subject a new deep perception of issues. In 'The Mill on the Floss' (1860) she singles out the fact of industrialism, especially urban industrialism, as the defining feature of modern life, and goes on to term it, as it really was, but had not often been called, the real under-structure of genteel culture, as if to bring the whole fine world of Jane Austen down to earth (book 4, chapter 3):

> But good society, floated on gossamer wings of light irony, is of very expensive production; requiring nothing less than a wide and arduous national life condensed in unfragrant, deafening factories, cramping itself in mines, sweating at furnaces, grinding, hammering, weaving under more or less oppression of carbonic acid - or else, spread over sheepwalks, and scattered in lonely houses and huts on the clayey or chalky corn-lands, where the rainy days look dreary. This wide national life is based entirely on emphasis - the emphasis of want, which urges it into all the activities necessary for the maintenance of good society and light irony. (1860)

This is certainly a pugnacious challenge to decorous prejudice, yet the novel itself proves to be a story about a shopkeeper economy, in which saving Gleggs are compared with prospering Deanes, and both distinguished from risky Tullivers, and the grand implications, once made, are left to lie in the reader's mind and register there, but do not seem to enter into and change the stuff of the novel or the way it is handled. The initial sense is of great power left unused, as if George Eliot had sat down to write another but more intelligent 'Cranford'.

What relation is the reader to supply between the industrial insight and the non-industrial story? What significance are we to see in Bob Jakin; is he a commercial traveller, or is he Autolycus? The questions are important ones, and the answer seems to be that George Eliot the novelist writes about what she knows, or rather remembers from her personal experience, and thus knows best; that this is the life of the society of the county and of the country town, usually remote from, or as yet only touched by, hard-core industrialism in any density of presence; but that she recognizes, nevertheless, and brings into her fiction the economic primacy of industrial and urban activity over rural experience. Thus the novels are relevant, but nostalgic. 'The Mill on the Floss' in fact presents with some force an examination of the cost in spiritual and emotional underdevelopment of the success of a self-made man. 'Silas Marner' (1861) is also strengthened, not weakened, by its omission of industrial action and industrial society, strengthened because the omission is consciously made and explicitly declared, and so is not really an omission at all; rather, it is a deflection of attention which keeps the major fact always in view. Hoarding, if not money-making proper, is the subject of the novel, an obviously related topic to capitalist endeavour; and Raveloe, where the action all takes place, is specifically set among the quiet midland counties of England, unprogressive, hidden, 'aloof from the currents of industrial energy' (chapter 3). Aloof, Raveloe may be. But, as becomes obvious when the story unfolds, it is not unconnected with and not uninfluenced by those currents. And again we are conscious of much that could be said, of the author's held-back energies, in the muting of the topic.

If we doubt George Eliot's full knowledge of what is meant by the replacement of a rural by an industrial national life, 'Felix Hold, the Radical' (1866), with an authority pointing forward to Lawrence, settles the doubt in two or three magisterial paragraphs. Here at the outset is delineated exactly that change from an old rural to a modern pacey industrial life which is the story of the industrialization of so much of England in the nineteenth century. It is a change described as unfolding before the eyes of an imagined traveller who passes through the midland counties, but, in real terms, and at the time of writing, one experienced in their daily and yearly life by the real inhabitants of those and other areas (introduction):

> But as the day wore on the scene would change: the land would begin to be blackened with coal-pits, the rattle of handlooms to be heard in hamlets and villages. Here were powerful men walking queerly with knees bent outward from squatting in the mine, going home to throw themselves down in their blackened flannel and sleep through the daylight, then rise and spend much of their high wages at the ale-house with their fellows of the Benefit Club; here the pale eager faces of handloom-weavers, men and women, haggard from sitting up late at night to finish the week's work, hardly begun till the

Wednesday. Everywhere the cottages and the small children were dirty, for the languid mothers gave their strength to the loom, etc. (1866)

Despite its historical setting in the 1820s, this has a distinct modern feel to it such as is not found in 'Dombey and Son' or 'Hard Times'. Even so, George Eliot captures the process before the past has gone out of sight, and keeps for her story's subject her preferred rurality. For the moment, we are reminded, old encloses new, and 'the busy scenes of the shuttle and the wheel, or the roaring furnace, of the shaft and the pulley, seemed to make but crowded nests in the midst of the large-spaced, slow-moving life of homesteads and far-away cottages and oak-sheltered parks' (loc. cit.); thus Treby Magna succeeds in remaining a market town and 'Felix Holt' a pastoral story. In large part so does 'Middlemarch' (1871-2) too. It turns out the same sort of archaic rural-genteel social mixture, with an industrial presence that never threatens to dominate, yet, for all that, is a novel bleakly undeterred in its dissection of the capitalist mode of life. Every contrast - with the crass but feeling manufacturer Vincy; with Featherstone, the unrepentant miser; with Caleb Garth - tells against Bulstrode, the novel's capitalist type, a bank manager of criminal origins and power-hungry, damped-down money greed. Perhaps George Eliot has for the most part chosen not to become involved in providing all the technical details of some industrialized process of work and life based on mine or factory or dockside or yard because, as she demonstrates so convincingly here and in 'Daniel Deronda' (1876), she can give us the essence of the matter without them. Her view of the moral quality of capitalist, especially financial-capitalist, activity comes through unmistakably in 'Middlemarch's' contrary depictions. Garth and Bulstrode, like Doyce and Merdle in Dickens, are the two who form the true opposition, and it is an impressively extreme one. Against the embodiment of ignoble capitalism, Bulstrode, who subordinates all to the securing of his own profit, Garth stands out as an ideal businessman whose specific condition of excellence, we are told, is his incapacity with money. That is to say, in Garth's scheme of values business activity is a function more than admired, but 'it must be remembered that by "business" Caleb never meant money transactions, but the skilful application of labour' (chapter 56). There could be no more final judgment on the money side of gainful effort than the valuation implied in these two contrasting portraits; it throws out profit hunger, capitalism's motive force.

In the polite world of 'Daniel Deronda' (1876) all threatens to reduce to commerce and commercialism, and Deronda's search for true purpose, for the secret of the meaning of his existence, and for the virtuous life, is given extra significance by being set in a world context of the dishonourable waste, by men and women in general, of money and energy and life. A bankruptcy forces Gwendolen Harleth, whose surname, suggesting harlot, intimates the theme, to abandon her fashionable recreation of gambling and find some authentic means of livelihood for herself and her family;

and she then finds that the subtle pressures of civil intercourse, or more roundly the death dealings of snobbery and etiquette, are no less a buying and selling matter than the action of the market place. It is doubtful if the novelist loses point by her concentration on a single finely educated sensibility, that of Gwendolen, struggling to find a moral means of keeping herself which is also socially acceptable, and by her neglect of the factory and the slum, which appears to make the novel's range narrow, since Deronda's quest is intended to widen it. Anyway, the background to Gwendolen's story is a worldwide struggle to find and hold on to fortune, to maintain social positions originally based on or bought by made money, like the Harleth's, which till it suddenly vanishes is dependent upon 'colonial property and banking' (chapter 6), or the Arrowpoints', which derives from 'some moist or dry business in the city' (chapter 5), or on acquired wealth, itself originally similar in creation; and also to acquire social respect, and increase it if possible, as the badge of acceptance into this materialistic and externalized society. The question here, in other words, is whether in so exploiting a world human worth can fulfil and sustain itself against the pressures of physical need. The private story is seen to epitomize a public issue. George Eliot is explicit on this, making 'Daniel Deronda' an incomparably more pertinacious and hard-hitting exposure of economic hypocrisy, or moral commercialism, in her society, than the novels of Jane Austen, who perhaps implies it here and there. For example, we are told that the importance of Gwendolen Harleth's 'small inferences of the way in which she could make her life pleasant' (chapter 11), at a time when 'the soul of man was waking to pulses which had for centuries been beating in him unfelt', of her slim thread of consciousness amid the world of public issues, is that girls are the point and purpose of those issues. 'In these delicate vessels is borne onward through the ages the treasure of human affections' (loc. cit.). In other words it is not a private mistake that is to be avoided, but a matter of universal significance that Gwendolen should choose right; though she chooses wrong.

It is interesting to see how closely George Eliot plots her course over Jane Austen's territory, but with how much more tenacious an awareness, as she does so, of the massive pressure of economic forces in the later age. Another parallel, no less striking and important, though much less commonly remarked, is with Dickens. Grandcourt holds that the Jamaican negro 'was a beastly sort of baptist Caliban' (chapter 29), and 'embraced all Germans, all commercial men, and all voters liable to use the wrong kind of soap, under the general epithet of "brutes"' (chapter 48); he tries to neutralize and eradicate his defunct relationship with Mrs Glasher by paying her an allowance into the bank; he would have made an effective ruler in a difficult colony by exterminating rather than cajoling 'superseded proprietors' (chapter 48), as George Eliot ironically puts it; he uses the odious Lush to inform Gwendolen of the contents of his will, and regards marriage itself, we are told, as a contract or a sort of commercial transaction, of which he has fulfilled his side (chapter 54) even if Gwendolen has failed in hers. Leaving aside his contempt of men of commerce, Grandcourt's psychology here is strongly reminiscent of that of Mr Dombey. And when George Eliot remarks of him that 'there is no escaping the fact that want of sympathy condemns us to a corresponding stupidity' (chapter 48), she is offering a judgment which covers the two of them with equal justice. It would be instructive and interesting to follow this connection through, perhaps; but here there is no more space.

Whereas a novelist, unless such as Thackeray, will tend to enter with sympathy into any individual merchant or manufacturer or financier he portrays and to complicate his disapproval, if it is diapproval he intends to feel, by understanding him, a moral essayist or historian writing on the subject of capitalist civilization is freer to offer an absolute judgment either way. Macaulay is one example of this. Marx is another. And a third is Ruskin, who, after the imaginative density of the fiction of Dickens and George Eliot, appears to us to offer a discussion slightly disembodied, though lucid, like an atmosphere more or less emptied of human content and living smells. Ruskin's has been a much celebrated contribution to the social discussion of the profit motive; but his true place is only to bring up the rear of the Romantic analysis. There is little new in what he says. To his simple message that commerce is intrinsically corrupting Carlyle and the eighteenth-century moralists have contributed substantially, obviously, yet Ruskin's expressive emphasis on the inalienability and unpurchasableness of life is his own, and has a particular reference which he does not fail to bring out to the condition of mass industrialism and mass urban living which to his generation was proving so much more familiar and urgent a problem than to the age of Coleridge and Southey. 'The Stones of Venice' (1851) is thus an exercise in art criticism which has a distinct contemporary purpose; the stones of Venice are touchstones; all other architecture and culture, including modern culture, are to be judged by them. Additionally, a parallel is proposed between Venice, a society untouched by enthusiasm of soul, Ruskin says, and activated into exertion only when the secret spring of her commercial interest was touched, and commercial nineteenth-century Britain, which similarly misinterprets life; and, he adds, particularly in its industrializing aspect, mechanizes living creatures.

In 'Unto This Last' (1866), casting out the claim of political economy to be able to provide a rule of life because of its wish to ignore men's affections, Ruskin insists that service must be the merchant's ideal, as honour is the soldier's. He refuses to grant precious metal any value except such as naturally accrues to it from its enhancement of life, and formulates his renowned definition of wealth as not treasure but life itself, pure and simple.(23) The same priorities recur in 'Time and Tide' (1867), in which Ruskin suggests doing away with the profit motive by making retail shopkeepers salaried officials, which might work wonders if it were ever tried, and they also recur in 'The Crown of Wild Olive'

(1870), with its recommendation of good things well made, wise work and educated taste over cipher gains. Ruskin tells us that he drew his conviction of commercial honour from his understanding of the practice and character of his father, a wine merchant who liked to be first in the market but never cheated anyone, and from his 'extremely low estimate of the commercial mind as such' from first-hand observation of it among his father's business associates and their families.(24) Presumably it is true enough that he took his impressions from life. But it is no accident that Ruskin should be so vehement in his attack upon the political economists, Coleridge's favourite target; for what we really see in him is the terminus and summation of the moral opposition to commerce of the Romantic writers, almost a return to it in theoretical purity, and the final statement of the humane case, the point beyond which it cannot go. I mean by this that nothing more is to be done in an economic discussion in which wealth has been redefined as people; there is no point in arguing the case; Ruskin is saying no to the nature of things. His limitedness of outlook on the subject of capitalism, given the time at which he wrote, may perhaps be suggested by the drift of his 1870 Slade lecture, advocating imperialism. This is the speech which inspired Rhodes with his African dream.(25) What is now ready for appearance in English literature, as in English life, by the close of Ruskin's writing career, is determined opposition to the capitalist class, as a class, by the exploited class and the writers sympathetic to it, not civil disapproval of them as misguided greedy men by liberal humanists; that is, what is due to appear is the Marxist note. As it happened, the outer world now began to reveal such changes and startling new threats to a once secure England that literature found altogether more urgent problems on its hands than the question of the myopic moral vision of political economists.

By Victorian writers so far, we have seen, the commercial profession is looked on as still something personal, still a matter of individual responsibility, still something for which, if it goes wrong or works exploitingly, someone somewhere is to blame. The generalization may simplify the late work of Dickens, whose novels from 'Bleak House' onwards project a more organizational view of economic cruelty, in the sense that Merdle and Veneering are less menacing in themselves than the world which sustains them, but is nevertheless just. But from 1870 or so the concept of big business begins to make its presence more emphatically felt in literature. Big business is conceived as not just large companies or enterprises, like Dombey's, but a complex or network of such enterprises, or even a general state of things. It is a system made up of multiple organizations impossible to pin down in any one place, crossing the boundaries of country and continent, owing moral allegiance to nowhere in particular, and assimilating individual responsibility into so cloudily corporate a structure that no single person can be found to be guilty of anything that is done or not done at any one time. Walter Bagehot in 'Lombard Street, A Description of the Money Market' (1873) observes that London bankers, once a prestigious breed, were disappearing and that the 'world had become so large and complicated' of late that you could no longer be sure of who people were, nor of their means and allegiances.(26) Evidently the wider sense could work not as an enlarging but as a cramping pressure. Froude counselled Britain in 1870 to turn the colonies into her back garden and the colonial settlers into her new peasantry, hoping thus to rehumanize a world lost to honourable motivations.(27) The plan may be naive, but Froude's perception of moral seediness at large, his world-weary sense, is important and new, and is one sign of the beginnings of modernity, the second psychological phase of industrial living.

We should note the significance of this change of tone, whose cause is more important than it seems, and is to be long-lasting in influence. Competitive capitalism had horrified the Romantic writers and Coleridge had asked wonderingly how decent men, merely for profit, could act so barbarously to their workpeople as to enslave, poison and kill them in order to safeguard a return on investment. Then after a generation, to the first Victorians it had seemed to threaten the continuance of social order. Revolution seemed around the next corner. But revolution did not happen. And by that generation's children competitive industry was accepted as no longer a new thing but a part of life, and, if painful, more the kind of pain that was caused by a permanent ache than by a fresh wound. Further, and 'Maud' testifies to this developing attitude, it began to be expected that business would exploit and defraud, that such was the way businessmen operated, and men learned to expect to have to be on their guard against them. In the 1860s and later state legislation, aimed at curbing and inspecting business activities and providing for the victims of industrialization, started to come into widespread effect, and the implication of such a development in the history of the growth of moral attitudes to capitalist enterprise, as Harold Perkin reminds us, is profoundly significant. It is, that the Smithian assumption of benevolent individualism, which had lain behind the free trade theory, was in the process of being replaced by its contrary assumption, the Benthamite stress on selfish individualism. The latter was now seen as a force requiring to be controlled and compelled into useful and beneficent channels, and not as flowing naturally into them; a century of finding out how industrial capitalism actually worked had been needed to force through this major shift in attitude. After it the view that capitalist ambition was something to be suspicious of, not trustful in, was so to speak officialized.(28) Other signs of the new age are the emergence into English literature of the Marxist critique, for example in the writings of William Morris, and a more real expression of the life of the working class in the novels of Gissing and others. Such developments in information, and in scepticism and counter-aggression, point forward to the capitalist world described with such profound loathing in Conrad, Wells and Lawrence, and systematically opposed in the writings of Shaw and the mid-twentieth-century socialists.

What distinguishes even a writer as early as Trollope from Dickens and Thackeray is his fragmentary perception of the beginning of this new phase; he is still Victorian, but discernibly late Victorian. It is very fragmentary, at the same time. Trollope's Barsetshire stories turn their back on the industrial and commercial side of English life, as an aside in 'Doctor Thorne' (1858) admits.(29) Little will be found in the Palliser novels but the gossip of politics, and many of Trollope's commercial depictions yield little in the way of fresh insight. Yet he brings a more detailed, less exotic knowledge of economic activity in Europe, New Zealand, Australia and America, which, along with his recognition of its direct involvement with the economic life of England, marks a change from the earlier literature. It is a change easily overestimated, yet there. Melmotte and Hamilton K. Fisker are the new types in 'The Way We Live Now' (1874-5), updated versions of Merdle and Rummum Loll in Dickens and Thackeray, and the new detail and cynical tone in Trollope's description of them and their enterprises are what strike us. For instance, Melmotte's uncertain past is to the point; he is of no country. He is wanted by the police in foreign places but England is still willing to take him in; that is, it is Melmotte who takes England in (chapter 4). When such points can be made of the workshop and ruler of the world, the period of high Victorian British pride has given way to a new sardonic outlook. But in Hamilton K. Fisker Trollope illustrates that the new world is just as corrupt as the old. His scheme for a Vera Cruz railway enterprise will make fortunes, he reminds those who are to conspire in it with him, before a 'spadeful of earth' has been moved (chapter 9), and it will do this even if it crashes, he points out gleefully and boastfully (chapter 10). Trollope suggests that such a course of action, namely fraudulent conspiracy, is what all the world now lives for: the Beargarden; the literary circle; the professions; the political set. But the problem is what to make of such extremity of disapproval, outrunning even the denunciations of Carlyle. Does Trollope mean it? Nine years later he tells us he did not.(30) Perhaps for us the novel's real interest lies in its reflection of a new slick world, not in its judgment. 'John Caldigate' (1878-9) is another example in which new international commerce figures. Here, as well as moneylending, the fortunes of gold prospecting and its risky supply industries, and Australian sharp practice, all unexcitedly set down as if now part of normal life, form a love story's props and setting.

Like Trollope, Charles Reade is a novelist who sees the world developments of capitalism as significant of his time, and reflects them in his fortune-chasing novel 'Hard Cash' (1863); but Reade seems to hover uncertainly between knowing whether to blame and wishing to be impressed by them. This is no longer like Carlyle's tense dual vision; it is a new wavering, and shows in his ambiguous portrait of the banker Richard Hardie bravely standing apart from the mania of a shares scramble, then joining it and being bitten by it, then cheating ruthlessly in order to escape ruin. Reade emphasizes Hardie's alacrity and steadiness and his massive deceit,(31) and also the latter's consonance with the general morality of the times, and in doing so captures the universalizing, one might say the normalizing, of fraud in the second half of the nineteenth century as literature portrays it. There is more than just a quick retort being dramatized when a novelist can write of a bank clerk discovered in the act of feathering his personal nest without regard to moral consideration or human feeling: ' "Stuff and nonsense," said Skinner, "I'm not a viper; I'm a man of business" ' (chapter 51).

More instances of this global view of capitalism and the new cynicism it provoked are to be found in Stevenson's 'The Wrecker' (1881), Meredith's 'One of Our Conquerors' (1890-1) and Hardy's 'A Laodicean' (1881) and other novels, Stevenson's Loudon Dodd has attended the Muskegon Commercial Academy, where imitation cheating is the sole lesson taught, then meets the real thing in the world outside. In spite of its larger horizon and increased sense of possibility, which Stevenson conveys with spirit, this worldwide setting is revealed to be a seedier, meaner, more raffish and miserable place than any provincial town in Dickens or George Eliot, a sort of wonderland turned sour. There is neither need nor space to go into the slippery main story line which illustrates this judgment, but the point is, Stevenson tells us (epilogue), that it is a story typical of our times. It has

> a cast so modern: - full of details of our barbaric manners and unstable morals; full of the need and the lust of money, so that there is scarce a page in which the dollars do not jingle; full of the unrest and movement of our century, so that the reader is hurried from place to place and sea to sea, and the book is less a romance than a panorama. (1881)

'Nostromo' is foreshadowed in such a specification, but this kind of hyperactive raffishness sums up the general sense of the era. Meredith expresses the same unrest in all his novels and portrays in Victor Radnor, the conqueror in 'One of Our Conquerors', the 'incorporeal power of immense Capital, dramatically acquired and magically manipulated'.(32) 'Beauchamp's Career' (1875) has similar reverberations.

The pastoral Hardy is anything but just pastoral, we find, looking again, but rather intently scrutinizes the slippage and realignments, village small, worldwide, and involving the private individual remote from the centres of energy just as much as the trader, industrialist and financier more in the public eye, of an economy troubled to the depths of its organization by a new order of capitalist pressure and ambition. The references are there if we look for them. And it is plain from the presentation of his stories that Hardy intends their economic contemporaneity, or, in the historical tales, the economic foundations of their energy, not to be missed. For example 'A Laodicean' (1881), expressing the moral tremor of the 1880s revalues and devalues bequeathed concepts of which one is the entrepreneurial ideal, and is expressly subtitled 'A Story of Today'. Paula Power is the Laodicean, whose father, we are informed, an engineer-artist of heroic ancestry, made 'half the railways of Europe' (Book I, chapter 11) and a tunnel skilful enough to diminish the chivalric castles;(33) but Hardy's whole point is that this paragon of the early period of industrialism makes no appearance in the story over which his image hangs so pervasively and influentially. He is dead and belongs with the dead and with him has died the superior aspect of industrial capitalism. In its place Hardy draws the movement's decadent aspects: sub-contracting which demotes workmanship below profit-making (book 3, chapter 11); unscrupulous competitiveness, such as William Dare's; perverted scientific skill like Abner Power's, the railway contractor's morally warped brother. Indeed in the last-named personage Hardy gives us an extremely modern type. Abner Power is a sort of satanic counter-image of his brother, a businessman-engineer-inventor turned anarchist. The characterization anticipates some in Conrad, particularly the conspirator figures of the novel 'The Secret Agent' (1907), and a similar portrayal appears in Henry James's 'The Princess Casamassima' (1886), though here the portrayals are many rather than one, so the psychological complications we are being offered are less dense.

Such a congregation of roles as Abner Power's, in late-Victorian fiction, illustrates how extremely involved the discussion of the capitalist issue has become in literature by those years. Over the centuries, we may remind ourselves, we have seen a constant amplification and enlargement of the range and depth of understanding with which capitalist endeavour has been perceived and written about, an ever-complicating definition of it; and here we arrive at the most enveloping perception yet. To the writers of the age of Shakespeare the issue presents itself as more or less a question of what the right attitude must be to the antagonizing matter of buying and selling; this is not to say that writers then saw the issue as simple, or easy of solution. In Defoe's apprehension over a century later mercantile imperialism is added, and credit expansion. Then Carlyle, after another century, and speaking for the attitude of his whole age, includes the industrial manufacturer and the social revolutionary in the discussion of capitalist enterprise. Alone among Victorian English writers, it might be added by way of parenthesis, Disraeli sees and lists this historical transformation of roles in a little-noticed aside in his novel 'Sybil'. (34) And now, discussing the commercial theme in the fiction of the 1880s, we are led by the logic of the subject into a consideration of political conspiracy and economic colonialism, for instance behind Abner Power's offer to Dare of an opening in Peru or Australia or Canada as his business agent (book 5, chapter 11), and in his own life story: he has been involved with a group of anarchists in Geneva, has invented some new form of bomb, rendering the assassin's dagger obsolete, has in consequence been wanted since that time by 'all the heads of police in Europe' (ibid.) has disfigured himself in a sabotaging accident, has emigrated to Peru and entered into business in the guano trade, and has afterwards extended his capitalist-conspiratorial contacts to other countries in the world.

All this Hardy grasps and brings out, but he manages it very economically, keeping the economic suggestions less emphatic than sex and romance, his main themes. But in his other novels too, persistently, he brings out the corroding effect of economic change or forces on social living. In 'The Mayor of Casterbridge' (1886) Farfrae renovates Henchard's grown wheat, which has made the dough of the latter's customers 'as flat as toads' (chapter 5), and saves Henchard's commercial credit, then stays to compete with his beneficiary, not wishing to oust Henchard, and believing there is room for both of them, but drawn into destructive rivalry by the nature of the business relationship itself. Melbury and Winterborne in 'The Woodlanders' (1887), to make the same point in the opposite way, successfully co-exist because their businesses, timber works on the one hand, the apple and cider trade on the other, are not in competition; Melbury can take the floating labour of the neighbourhood in winter and spring, Winterborne in the autumn; and they can even exchange equipment without loss or sacrifice on either side. This is an antique stationary organization outlasting its time, as is hinted in the presence of Felice Charmon's husband, a northern ironmaster representative of the newer ruthless capitalism, but not in this case brought by Hardy into opposition with the life of the immediate locality which supplies him with his subject; there, however, for all that; a presence. World capitalist enterprise and small-town trading are reflected in 'The Lady Icenway' of 'A Group of Noble Dames' (1891) and 'Fellow-Townsmen' of 'Wessex Tales' (1888), but capitalist pressures show still more forcibly in 'Tess of the D'Urbervilles' (1891), and on every social level, though, once again, unobtrusively throughout. Alec D'Urberville, vulgar son of a 'mushroom millionaire' (chapter 30), struggles unavailingly to find a role and purpose in life, or perhaps to live up to his new gentility. The Trantridge villagers are forced to drink inferior beer in Chaseborough every Saturday night, monopoly brewers having gained control of the once independent inns (chapter 10). Angel Clare and Tess drive the milk cart to the London train so that 'strange people that we have never seen' (chapter 30) may drink it at their breakfasts on the following day. A steam threshing machine travels on hire from farm to farm and exhausts the workers in the immemorially natural tasks, now natural no longer, turning them into machine slaves. Depopulation, migration and economic change are thus more than in the air; they are the facts of social experience, crushing realities Hardy describes openly and boldly, and all with the emphasis on denaturing and violence of process, as when he refers to the large towns drawing the workers from the land like water flowing uphill 'when forced by machinery' (chapter 51). We see a capitalist predator in Marcia Bencombe's father in 'The Well-Beloved' (1897), founder of the Best-Bed Stone Company, which has swallowed up all but one of its rivals. 'Jude the Obscure' (1895) describes a society composed, or rather by now discomposed, of even more pronouncedly rootless, disinherited, and economically turbulent and disorganized elements, a world in disarray. Their fidelity of reflection of the mood and structure of life in the late nineteenth century is what stands out in these portrayals, not their archaism. Hardy sees not just 'the realities of labouring work', but 'the harshness of economic processes, in inheritance, capital, rent and trade, within the continuity of the natural processes and persistently cutting across them. The social process created in this interaction is one of class and separation, as well as of chronic insecurity, as this capitalist farming and dealing takes its course'.(35)

While such writers reflect an international network of economic competition, the world build-up, so to call it, towards total capitalism, or total anti-capitalism beating capitalism at its own game, George Gissing's distinction, though Gissing too brings in the wider scene, is to concentrate on England, and draw out the effects of a century of competitive commerce on the community which, first industrialized, offered at that time the best summary of its natural workings. Gissing takes us on from Dickens and further from hope. His protest against three generations of injustice is not in itself an original theme, but it does take on originality from the intense alienation with which Gissing advances it, alienation, it seems, from all camps in the class war. Gissing's is not reforming criticism. He warns against hoping for improvement from the poor themselves, brutalized beyond the power of springing back, or from the system, or from organized or principled opposition to the capitalist domination of England, and in 'Workers in the Dawn' (1880), 'The Nether World' (1889), 'The Whirlpool' (1897), 'Demos' (1886) and elsewhere seems to take a professional's pride not only in depicting industrial and slum conditions considerably more extreme than anything in previous social-problem fiction,(36) but also in refusing to colour his description by romance or poetry or any saving message of social hope. This monochrome fidelity is well seen in 'The Nether World'. Usage, the novel says, has reduced the working class to animals in harness (chapter 2):

> It was the hour of the unyoking of men. In the highways and byways of Clerkenwell there was a thronging of released toilers, of young and old, of male and female. Forth they streamed from factories and workrooms, anxious to make the most of the few hours during which they might live for themselves. Great numbers were still bent over their labour, and would be for hours to come, but the majority had leave to wend stablewards. (1889)

The tone is intentionally disturbing, it is evident; for such beasts one may feel contempt or perhaps pity but not sympathy. So Gissing seems to say. The description of the brutal pleasures of the populace on a bank holiday outing later in the story reiterates his point. Diabolism, as in Clem Peckover, is the product of the violent down-breeding of the lower class, or Clara Hewitt's 'inheritance of revolt' (chapter 3), doomed before it starts; and meanwhile, against the background of evolutionary nemesis, details of the printing business, of cabinet making, of the potman's and barmaid's livelihood, and of the baked potato trade, lowest of the low, along with hints of the desperate deals and schemes of demoralized men out of work, such as the hopeless venture into filter making, the death in life of artificial flower manufacturing (a bitter Gissing joke), and counterfeiting, the last resource of the frustrated mechanic-inventor, fill in Gissing's exceedingly sharp sense of how, one hundred years after their initiation, out of the diminished lives and perverted affections of the mass of ordinary human beings, is being extorted the price of science, industrialism, and capitalist advance.

All this is to say that Gissing conveys the proletarian scene, and with inside knowledge; though not the proletarian sense; and as a matter of fact his evaluation of mass spiritual blight shows how closely we are approaching to the twentieth century. Indeed, one could say that the depressed condition of the common man is the real new element in his fiction. A hundred years earlier Gissing's characters would have figured in literature, if at all, as mob. Now they are present as recognized humanity. This is perhaps the biggest single extension of awareness that literature has ever made. Again, Gissing may be clear on capitalist iniquity, but is no socialist. Arthur Golding in 'Workers in the Dawn' (1880) throws himself purposefully into the workers' cause for a time, but at the end of the novel emigrates to a life of capitalist farming in America. 'Demos' (1886) warns against looking for the people themselves to improve things. 'The Whirlpool' (1897) works as a contrast between, on the one hand, the maladjusted money world of quick fortunes, metropolitan fashion, glitter, bankruptcy and suicide, and, on the other, the pre-industrial organization of Basil Morton. Morton's however, strikes the reader as a barefaced dream existence, and it is hardly brought in by Gissing as a realistic alternative to trying to cope with, and probably going under to, the intractable pressures of organized social life. He sells the stuff of life for a fair price without exploiting anyone, lives in the country in a half mansion a century or more old, stands outside the whirlpool of modern civilization and represents what cynical-sentimental late-nineteenth-century man might suppose a merchant could once have been at some unfixed period of time in the past, but could never hope to be allowed to remain any more. When Gissing can write such an analysis of men of trade as this, like Morris in 'News from Nowhere' (1890), he is attacking the commercialism of the nineteenth century so uncompromisingly as to be attacking the nineteenth century itself.

Basic to such an attack is the instinctive, but also by now solidly experienced and informed, hatred of the principle of aggressive competition, the soul of industrialism as writers saw it; and it is a feeling which takes us right back to the beginning of the century, for example to Southey's 'Letters from England' (1807). In that work, it will be recalled, Southey isolates a new kind of aggressive selling and advertising, and draws it to our attention as characteristic of the age; and the point is reiterated in the imaginative critique of capitalism right through the century. 'Thou shalt not covet, but tradition/Approves all forms of competition', writes Clough in 'The Latest Decalogue' (lines 19-20) in 1852-3 (published 1862);(37) 'tradition' is the word for us to note; it has become normal by the middle years of the century for men to think of their fellow beings as predators or as prey. Dickens stresses the same truth in 'Hard Times', and so does Kingsley in 'Alton Locke'. Bulwer Lytton's story 'The Coming Race' (1871) dreams of an underground heaven inhabited by a race of beings who do not strive, or compete, or envy, or covet; this is a very Victorian kind of heaven, a condition of existence with the pressure of the age magically relaxed. Indeed, the industrial era, and never more obviously than in our own century, is the period of all others which has produced its own anodyne to real experience, in the form of escapist fiction and art; and of course not by any accident. Cobbett, to return to the early nineteenth century, places this Edenic state, which he felt he remembered, in a period before industrialism had got truly established,(38) but to late Victorian writers, his successors, it could and did merge with the recollection of their youthful era, an unhistorical placing perhaps, but psychologically and emotionally right. Writing in 1881, Mark Rutherford describes business activity in the village of his childhood, now, he reminds his reader, a mode vanished for ever, as an accepted and common feature of life, and as a process not free from profit, but free from the antagonizing and disruptive profit motive, from competition. 'There was absolutely no competition, and although nobody in the town who was in trade got rich, except the banker and the brewer, nearly everybody was tolerably well off, and certainly not pressed with care as their successors are now.'(39) Mill attacks the competitive character of his society, discouraging spiritual achievement, inculcating sameness, and impoverishing individual life, as he judges, in all his writings, and in 'Principles of Political Economy' (1848) writes in recommendation of a stationary state. An advantage of the proposed state of society, he says, is that it would have the effect of demythologizing the success ethic; it would relax the strife, loosen the competition which has become the normal condition of life, and a disabling condition, of the majority of people. Mill's words are to the point (book iv, chapter 6):

> I confess I am not charmed with the ideal of life held out by those who think that the normal state of human beings is that of struggling to get on; that the trampling, crushing, elbowing, and treading on each other's heels, which form the existing type of social life, are the most desirable lot of human kind, or anything but the disagreeable symptoms of one of the phases of industrial progress. (1848)

By the close of the century, competition is not just attacked in literature; a replacement is found for it, and vigorously recommended, in socialist co-operation. This opens for us a huge new area of discussion, destined to predominate over all others, perhaps, in the literature of the twentieth century relating to this topic. William Morris's essay 'How We Live and How We Might Live' (1885), a Marx-inspired analysis, but also one drawing on the

English literary tradition here sketched in, rejects the condition of nineteenth-century society out of hand as perpetual war, what Morris describes as 'that other war called *commerce*'.(40) Morris means the society of the world, not just English society. To him the 'desperate scramble' (p. 6) for overseas markets is simply 'successful burglary and disgrace' or 'mere defeat and disgrace' (ibid.); and capitalism is intrinsically and irremovably a war of nation against nation, class against class, company against company and worker against worker. One sees how much more advanced Morris is, considering such a breakdown of the working elements of society, than Ruskin. He looks forward and takes in the global nature of the issue. He stresses that being poor is a cultural more than just a financial deprivation: only a certain kind of life is open to a person or a class if they are limited to certain purchases. Naturally, this applies to whole communities as much as to individuals (p. 9).

> The South Sea Islander must leave his canoe-carving, his sweet rest, and his graceful dances, and become the slave of a slave: trousers, shoddy, rum, missionary, and fatal disease - he must swallow all this civilization in the lump, and neither himself nor we can help him now till social order displaces the hideous tyranny of gambling that has ruined him. (1885)

When Morris insists on this assimilation of commerce into war he makes the Marxist analysis English and familiar, as Shaw does also, and as we read through his writings we find he hammers the point home in every relevant context. 'The Hopes of Civilization' (1885) includes a Marx-inspired historical summary of commercial and industrial change during four centuries. 'Art under Plutocracy' (1882) compares the neat appearance of a military regiment, covering its deadly role, with the organized ferocity of respectable commerce. In place of the infidel Renaissance, which for Ruskin and Carlyle had signalled a downturn in human development because of its destruction of an age of faith, Morris attacks the capitalist Renaissance, and tries to trace evidence in Renaissance architecture for the taking away of economic and cultural self-respect from the workmen who built it. Few things about the nineteenth century may strike us as so embarrassing or doomed as its willingness to dispense with the Renaissance for some theory or other. Here, Morris is obviously leaning on Ruskin; 'The Stones of Venice' is the work most recalled. It is a thinly and wistfully argued case. Yet he forecasts at least half truthfully in 'Art and Socialism' (1884), when, drawing an English analogy with decadent Rome, he declares that the poor are the new barbarians destined in the fullness of development to crush the existing order, and exulting in the prospect to come. It is interesting to see the Roman image, to the eighteenth-century as sombre as the fall of civilization itself, offering to a nineteenth-century socialist the handy opportunity to press home a fable of social reconstruction.(41)

George Bernard Shaw also lays down his socialist priorities in his early plays 'Widowers' Houses' and 'Mrs Warren's Profession', two of the 'Plays Unpleasant' (1898). Having in the first chosen to show slum exploitation to be the source of genteel wealth and morals, a familiar charge, Shaw then adds that slum improvement is also a form of exploitation and one more lucrative and pernicious than the first. Here is a new ingenious corruption in a society already thought to be rotten to its centre: the ever-surprising capitalist has learned to milk state provision for his own victims. Trench puts the matter bluntly: 'It appears that the dirtier a place is the more rent you get; and the decenter it is, the more compensation you get. So we're to give up dirt and go in for decency' (act III). Commercialized sex - not just prostitution, a private lapse, but a European brothel chain duly organized and paying thirty-five per cent return on investment - is the specific subject of 'Mrs Warren's Profession'; but the play's larger and more real charge is of a society soaked through and through in the commercial ethic of selfish greed and hypocrisy. Shaw's letters of the period back up the extremity of his condemnation here, and make plain how serious his original rejection of English capitalist society was, whatever became of it later. But Shaw's proper context, however formed by the conditions of the Victorian age, and however summarizing and completing its perception into, and through, the pretensions of the capitalist culture it also, for all the criticism of it, did not reject, is the twentieth century; and it is in the discussion in the following chapter that his output as a whole is best considered.

7 WASTE LAND TO WELFARE STATE 1900-1980

English literature during the first half of the present century expresses an expectation of the collapse of the economic system, and with it the whole order of civilization inherited from the past, now seen to be too unpredictable and indeed out of control in its fluctuations and violent competing energies.(1) Then, after the Second World War, a Keynesian reconstruction of British society, which admittedly did little to eradicate class privilege or seriously redistribute welath, held out, nevertheless, as the minimum standard of life guaranteed for all by the state, the prospect of full employment and social security; and the effects of this new dispensation show through in the concerns of literature, as a feeling of liberation from economic terror and a new openness to life and its possibilities, as well as a receding, in large part, of the capitalist discussion itself, at least in explicit terms, from the pages of the novelists and the poets. That is, we witness first an obsession with capitalism as a theme, then a kind of indifference to it. Developments in world capitalism in the late 1970s, for instance oil diplomacy and sharp inflation, have suggested that this quiet interval may be nearing its end, but there are still few pointers as to how the new insecurity, if it proves to be genuine, and goes deeply into experience and lasts, will affect English literature in the near future, as it undoubtedly will.

Given the trenchancy of his Victorian critique of capitalism, Shaw's twentieth-century analysis might be expected to go revealingly deep, yet, strange to say, his early writing is the most penetrating. As time passes its farcical bent dilutes his work's meaning, posing for us an overall problem of seriousness. It is not that there is any doubt of Shaw's theoretical opposition to the capitalist world; his essay 'Socialism and Superior Brains' (1894), rebutting W. H. Mallock, makes this plain, and it is followed by a large number of arguments for socialism of a similarly clear sort in later years. But in Shaw's plays an authentic revolutionary message is consistently undercut by paradox, and in addition his portrayal itself tends to fasten increasingly on less significant features of the commercial type. Undershaft, the arms manufacturer in 'Major Barbara' (1905), is described by himself as a 'profiteer in mutilation and murder' (act I), a capitalist devil. But Undershaft turns out to be personally charming. When the arguments begin he routs all the representatives of religious and sentimental orthodoxy and successfully upholds the material view of life. We find that we have been persuaded that all society is the villain, and have found the discovery amusing. This is a witty revelation and perhaps true, but not one likely to subvert a theatre audience, or ouselves as we read. John Tanner remarks in his 'Revolutionist's Handbook' appended to 'Man and Superman' (1903) that society approaches dissolution as money greed ruins the culture it once favoured, but in the play he marries and settles down conventionally, putting his ideas to the back of his mind where they can do no damage; is it the play or the handbook which carries the authentic utterance? One hesitates before complaining about wit, but Shaw's surprises here, unlike Wilde's, which often pack an unexpected punch, sometimes appear to empty out the significance from a serious problem; unless this is a case of solemn literary criticism getting it wrong once again. And frequently his representations of men of commerce, like John Tarleton in 'Misalliance' (1910) and Knox and Gilbey in 'Fanny's First Play' (1911), bring out their lighter side and do not carry much weight. The preface of 'The Shewing-Up of Blanco Posnet' (1911) challenges comparison with 'Little Dorrit', but, unlike Dickens's novel, lacks anger.

Shaw designates England after the First World War as 'Heartbreak House' (1919), a concern run by the industrialist-financier Boss Mangan, and here gathers up all his separate insights into one account, one explicit judgment on the man of business; so it is instructive to watch carefully while he deals with the subject, and see how he follows it through. Mangan, we learn, starts people off in commerce by lending them money so that he can buy them up cheaply when they have ruined themselves, and make their businesses pay for his own profit; but, Mazzini adds, he is an industrial financier who knows nothing whatever of manufacture and is exclusively interested in money. So far this is the orthodox capitalist predator of a hundred Victorian novels; but there are surprises in store. Later Mangan tells Ellie and Mrs Hushabye that he lacks money of his own and is a poor man barely able to make his profession yield him enough money to provide a living income. He has to survive entirely on travelling expenses and on commission, because everything is owned by 'syndicates and shareholders and all sorts of lazy good-for-nothing capitalists' (act III). The villain is exonerated. He still makes a living out of villainy, if we suppose that enticing innocent men to their own ruin for your advantage is an unpraiseworthy line of work, but other villains egg him on, and gather up his gains when he has made them, and do not return him a generous reimbursement for his skill, and so are worse than he is; and the villainy is spread wide and thin by means of such revelations until it touches everyone in the play and in the theatre, and is everywhere, and in everything, and thus reaches disappearing point. It is all very funny, and the only heartbreak is in the play's title. To a socialist 'St Joan' (1924) ought to be a tragedy; on the contrary, it is a celebration of the rise of the bourgeoisie. 'The Millionairess' (1936) and 'Buoyant Billions' (1947) are both insubstantial pleasant comedies. So modest a climax to Shaw's promised onslaught against commercial civilization of fifty years earlier cannot but be disappointing. There is some evidence that Shaw recognized this.(2)

When Shaw speaks of capitalist society in dissolution he expresses, it has been said, the judgment of a whole age. As the previous chapter has suggested, it was indeed an opinion gradually forced on the Victorian world, and widespread at its close, yet reaching its true climax only in the first decades of the present century, that the whole structure of European capitalism was approaching or had passed its peak of development, and that what everyone witnessed around them were the tremors of its imminent disintegration. Many writers, of course, belong to both worlds, which for them are just one world, the Victorian and the modern together; such is Conrad, formed out of the conditions of nineteenth-century imperialist commerce but bringing his knowledge to bear on the world capitalism of the twentieth century. Conrad's life experience, we realize, as we read his work, saw the division of Africa, the Boer War and the First World War; in ocean commerce he witnessed steam navigation, electronic telecommunication and national shipping enterprise draw together all sections of the globe into a single economic consciousness, separable, nevertheless, and separated, into its exploitable and exploiting elements. This gives Conrad his material. He does not convey the English experience; for that we have to go to Lawrence; but he gives us the contemporary world scene. And what Conrad shows the reader more and more, as he develops his recognition of the nature of the twentieth-century world, is a profound serious concern for the omnipresence of commercial ambition, of conspiracy capitalism, amounting even to economic world bondage, in the life of the men of the present day. In 'Almayer's Folly' (1895), the first novel, set in the islands of the far eastern seas, the expatriate trader Almayer prospers riskily when it is learned that the British Boraco Company proposes to establish itself in Pantai, but, when the project falls through, faces ruin. The story exemplifies Conrad's theme that an economic decision taken in one of the centres of capitalist strength on one side of the world exacts human happiness on the other as its price,(3) and not just the lives of the exploited; of the exploiters too. 'An Outpost of Progress' (1896) tells us this clearly enough. It shows that the much-talked-about civilizing mission of Europe to the underdeveloped world is a cruel joke, or worse.

What impresses in Conrad, especially in his short story 'Heart of Darkness' (1899), for instance, where he presses home the racial exploitation most pertinaciously, is the density of effect he can build up in a small space by varying his manifestations of emphasis. Here, European greed is the simple theme, but Conrad fragments his presentation of it into several individual portraits, which, taken together, indict the attitudes of a whole civilization. Marlow's aunt thinks of him as an emissary of light, but he is really attracted to Africa, he tells us, by its mystery; the shadowy figures at the Company's head office are locked in a power and profit conspiracy; the Central Station manager keeps going in the savage trade only by suspending his sensibility; the manager's uncle by brutalizing himself; the inmates of the company station pretend to be philanthropists while each secretly covets a lucrative appointment; the Eldorado Exploring Expedition is made up of men who are no better than a band of burglars 'breaking into a safe' (Section I); the pathetic Russian believes in Kurtz; Kurtz represents all Europe, an idealist corrupted by his evil heart and by the force of circumstances. Such a comprehensive analysis recalls to us that Conrad wrote when Lenin wrote; and that the basic meaning of Lenin's 'Imperialism, the Highest Stage of Capitalism' (1916), for instance, is a Conradian vision of the annexationist and plundering motives behind apparently beneficial commerce and civilizing exploration. There is a remarkable identity of moral concern between this and, for example, Conrad's representation of South American silver mining and railway building in 'Nostromo' (1904). But Conrad's distinct interest lies in the private issue of moral honour, to which economic circumstance is a context, though often a crucially defining one. 'Lord Jim''s (1900) island of Patusan, a once glorious pepper centre of the passed-away Dutch and English spice trade, now forgotten by the world, is a fitly chosen centre for the close of a story juxtaposing the limitless appetite of the men of the seventeenth century with their mean modern counterparts: Chester, the Australian wrecker, pearler and miscellaneous trader; his partner Robinson, smuggler and seal shooter; Stein the gentle merchant and entomologist; Cornelius, his incompetent manager; and Jim, flawed by a spiritual vacancy within. And 'The Inheritors' (1901) makes the same point as 'Heart of Darkness', that, more than even the suffering it inflicts, capitalist exploitation of one part of the world by another, advertising itself as beneficial, damages human survival by loosening the reliance men can place upon each other in their passage through life. In this story the Duc de Mersch has floated a company to modernize Greenland, and speaks in his prospectus of letting 'the light in upon a dark spot of the earth' (chapter 3). But Granger, finding in his hands a true report on the 'Système Groënlandais', gives us his summary of it, and Conrad in writing out this section of the story noticeably generalizes its implications, and draws to our notice the betrayal of human trust in exploiting fraud of this kind which is, in his estimate, man's ultimate failure to man (chapter 17):

> There were revolting details of cruelty to the miserable, helpless, and defenceless; there were greed, and self-seeking, stripped naked; but more revolting to see without a mask was that falsehood which had been hiding under the words that for ages had spurred men to noble deeds, to self-sacrifice, to heroism. What was appalling was the sudden perception that all the traditional ideals of honour, glory, conscience, had been committed to the upholding of a gigantic and atrocious fraud. The falsehood had spread stealthily, had eaten into the very heart of creeds and convictions that we lean upon on our passages between the past and the future. (1901)

It is the twentieth-century view of capitalist method which is brought out here, in Conrad's word, like a 'revelation', for the Victorian temper, we may remind ourselves, cherished some ideal of commercial action while it could. Looking at 'Heart of Darkness', at 'Nostromo', at 'The Inheritors', considering too Conrad's studies in the economic and moral substitution of impersonal, unfeeling forces for individual contact, and of brashness for honour, as the modern age comes into being, for example in the unsentimental 'The End of the Tether' (1902), and of his business failures such as Almayer and Lord Jim, we see that now, to Conrad, in the developing condition of twentieth-century capitalism, no ideal of general equal economic advance seems tenable.

The distinction allows us to separate him, glancing ahead to a stark future for mankind, from such as Kipling, content to stay in the immediate present or in the past; or, perhaps it is better to say, to look at his subject only in part, or through one kind of colouring medium, and not on its every side. Kipling can be clear-eyed about the moral seaminess of commerce in the boom towns of America, when patriotic sentiment does not blur his gaze. But he is strangely silent on the exploiting aspect of British imperialist capitalism in Africa, India and the far east. Thus, 'The Naulakha' (1892), located in the American west, draws an unflattering portrait of the mushroom towns Topaz and Rustler intriguing and trafficking for self-promotion and self-enrichment. But when Kipling touches on British commerce, and mixes patriotic sentiment with capitalist analysis, for example in 'M'Andrew's Hymn' and 'The Merchantmen' from the verse collection 'The Seven Seas' (1896), and in the stories 'A Deal in Cotton', 'The Mother Hive' and 'An Habitation Enforced' from 'Actions and Reactions' (1909) and 'The Devil and the Deep Sea' from 'The Day's Work' (1898), all lending themselves to an exploration of profit-making imperialism, and in a sense receiving one, only a fatally limited one, he casts a mystical glow over the whole discussion. Conrad's bleaker scrutiny is finally more chilling than this, being so much less disabled by its rhetoric. In 'Chance' (1913) he gives us du Barral's world-moving schemes, half fantasy, half business, as a parody and final debasement of the entrepreneurial optimism of the Victorian period, but also brings us up to date by his reminder that du Barral, for all his notoriety, is undistinguished and even 'perfect in his consistent mediocrity' (chapter 3); he is the tycoon of an age of democracy, a representation one step further down the moral ladder from that of Mr Merdle, though perhaps too owing a hint to uncle Ponderevo in Wells's 'Tono-Bungay' (1909). There are other Conrad novels in which similar points are made, covering the same ground, though never in repetition, like 'Victory' (1915), and 'The Partner' (1915); and I have deliberately not concentrated on 'Nostromo', Conrad's most extended and renowned discussion of the issue, which fully explores the manipulation of backward countries by American and European capital, the outcome of complicated evil when political and economic ambitions unite in struggle, and the moral hardening of the individual given up to the pursuit of material interests. This is a novel which the reader can find thoroughly discussed along these lines, indeed hotly argued about, elewhere.(4)

As a matter of fact, though Wells does anticipate Conrad in 'Tono-Bungay' on the mediocrity of the modern commercial type, searching in Wells for a satisfactory account of or distinct response to capitalist civilization is a frustrating experience; like Shaw, he writes much but says little. There is plenty of haranguing in his pages, and much talk of the future state of man, but usually the middle section of the portrayal, which deals with how the present condition of society is to be transformed into an improved version, or is to deteriorate into the opposite, the crucial section, and the one in which we have the sharpest interest, is the one left out; this may not detract from the stories as entertainment, but it does have the effect of nullifying their analysis of things. Consider how 'The Sleeper Awakes' (1899) projects an England in which proprietorial capitalism has reached ultimate monopoly, and Graham wakes up to find that he owns everything, on the one side of the picture, while at the same time, on the other side, slavery has become the fate of all but a small middle class of necessary administrators. The interesting question is how this future condition developed out of society's present state, what were its causes, and stages of growth, and what might have hindered it; but we are given a fait accompli. 'The First Men in the Moon' (1901), 'The History of Mr Polly' (1910), in their different ways, are other examples. Wells's belief rests in applied intelligence, which, he tells us in 'Marriage' (1912), 'The Passionate Friends' (1911) and elsewhere, would make short work of the mess of social existence as it is.

But it is in his criticizing and negative portrayals, his rendering of depression, poverty and lack of hope in the capitalist jungle or desert of modern life, that he is most successful. Kipps plumbs an abyss of boredom apprenticed to a Folkestone draper in 'Kipps' (1905), but, left a fortune, is uprooted and disconnected more profoundly still; here the clipped limited mental horizon of the lower-middle-class wage-earner is well observed. 'The History of Mr. Polly' (1910) covers similar ground. 'Tono-Bungay' (1909) is impressive in its supply of convincing detail, just what Wells elsewhere is in the habit of skimping, when it portrays Ponderevo's rise and fall in the commercial world. He starts in business by deceiving a firm of wholesale chemists, some pirate printers and a newspaper proprietor and then by diverting his nephew George's trust money; that is, by means of a 'damned swindle' (book 2, chapter 2). Once established he spends his profits on 'lies and clamour to sell more stuff' (book 2, chapter 3). He branches out into hair stimulant, eye lotion, lozenges, chocolate and mouthwash. He builds up his enterprise into 'a crescendo of magnificent creations and promotions until the whole world of investors marvelled' (book 3, chapter 1), and at his height owns two million pounds' worth of property and controls thirty million besides. All this has been excitingly described, while formally the author and the narrator find the story dismaying; and here we approach the problem at the centre of Wells's thought. He is far from justifying Ponderevo's activity, indeed reminds us continuously of its fraudulence, but releases in his narrative gusto a kind of sympathy with the little man who being irrepressible has made the world submit to his prescriptions, and casts a proportion of the blame for Ponderevo's swindling life on to 'this irrational muddle of a community in which we live' (book 3, chapter 1). If Ponderevo is twentieth-century capitalism then Wells finds capitalism entertaining. The critic is making his own unnecessary problems who demands singleness of response from a creative writer; but there is an awkward compromise here of which Wells seems half-aware himself.(5)

D. H. Lawrence praised 'Tono-Bungay' when it came out because it momentarily endorses his own opinion of the state of England, which was not a hopeful one;(6) but in Lawrence's own work we are offered an inwardness of recognition of the nature of English industrial capitalism quite beyond Wells's limit of perception, and, of course, not available to Conrad or to Shaw with their non-English upbringing. Lawrence, like Dickens, and like Defoe, describes his age, including its commercial aspect, with inside knowledge, with an awareness founded in early personal experience; and in his response, which is pure, like theirs, it can be claimed that we hear the authoritative voice of his generation. It is 'The Rainbow' (1915), 'Women in Love' (1920) and 'Lady Chatterley's Lover' (1928) which demand our attention, not so much 'Sons and Lovers' (1913), for, despite the latter novel's firmness against the dragging ugliness of industrial civilization, and its impressive opening summary of the historical development of systematic coal mining from the mid-nineteenth century to the time of writing, it is not really a novel of protest, and all the social movement described in the lives of its central figures is upwards, out of wage slavery, and towards security and the discovery and realization of the self.

But in 'The Rainbow' (1915) and later works Lawrence writes in order to understand and fix the capitalist type. It is not the salesman he concentrates on, like Ponderevo, nor the financier, like Boss Mangan, but the doer, the industrial and manufacturing magnate, the essential representative of the coal and iron economy of the England of his day. Ursula Brangwen's uncle Tom is the manager of a colliery in the newly-built town of Wiggiston in Yorkshire where the streets are 'like visions of pure ugliness' (chapter 12) and his house conveys the sense of 'hard, mechanical activity', and where he himself finds his only 'moments of pure freedom' in serving the machine. Ursula's growth in understanding of what it means to be him includes much that is significant in the novel. For instance, when she decides that she will smash the machine if she can, meaning the whole commercial and social organization of which she is part, and of which her uncle is content to become one of the leaders, Lawrence remarks of her: 'it was in these weeks that Ursula grew up'. In a later chapter he shows her, a schoolteacher, rebelling against the mechanistic spirit of systematic education which she finds herself involved in, and rejecting it as destructive; and in doing so he claims a direct affinity with the Dickens of 'Hard Times', who had also linked the workings of a society based on competitive acquisition with the murder of the innocents in the schoolroom.

Central to both Dickens and Lawrence is a distrust of the aridity of the commercial priority. In Gerald Crich of 'Women in Love' (1920) Lawrence gives us an idealist seizing on industrial management as an escape from his frustration of soul, transforming his energy into will, and living for and in his manipulation of material substance and the men under him, who in his sight are indistinguishable from the brute elements they work with. Dickens is again to our point in estimating what Lawrence means by this delineation; and Matthew Arnold, critical of the external priorities of philistine middle-class England, and, behind both, Carlyle and Coleridge attacking the over-valuation of utility as a measurement of wise conduct; and Blake on the sterile ego. The whole humane tradition of the nineteenth century demands to be brought in to amplify the significance, for example, of Lawrence's description of Gerald Crich recognizing the ugly landscape as newly sanctified in his ownership, and the red-mouthed miners surrounding his blocked car as his possessions rather than employees, slaves to his will, so much mere stock to be used up in the carrying out of his purposes and not conceded a life centre in their own selves. But his coal waggons, he feels for (chapter 17):

> He saw them as he entered London in the train, he saw them at Dover. So far his power ramified. He looked at Beldover, at Selby, at Whatmore, at Methley Bank, the great colliery villages which depended entirely on his mines. They were hideous and sordid, during his childhood they had been sores in his consciousness. And now he saw them with pride. Four raw new towns, and many ugly industrial hamlets were crowded under his dependance. He saw the stream of miners flowing along the causeways from the mines at the end of the afternoon, thousands of blackened, slightly distorted human beings with red mouths, all moving subjugate to his will. He pushed slowly in his motor-car through the little market-top on Friday nights in Beldover, through a solid mass of human beings that were making their purchases and doing their weekly spending. They were all subordinate to him. They were ugly and uncouth, but they were his instruments. He was the God of the machine. They made way for his motor-car automatically, slowly. (1920)

Gerald Crich is a more developed portrayal of what Tom Brangwen represents; and a third instance of the type is Sir Clifford in 'Lady Chatterley's Lover' (1928), original in that Lawrence uses him to exemplify the psycho-moral cost of the power and material worship here illustrated: that is, a collapse of the resources of the personality. This is a side of the industrial magnate not seen in Brangwen or Crich, but obviously their true condition beneath the brashness and power, according to Lawrence. He describes how Clifford gives up writing fiction when he assumes an interest in industrial management, having no further use for it; the imaginative side of his mind is to be let die. At a later stage he gives up looking after his own body, allows himself to be washed and shaved by another, and turns into 'almost a *creature*, with a hard efficient shell of an exterior and a pulpy interior, one of the amazing crabs and lobsters of the modern industrial and financial world, invertebrates of the crustacean order, with shells of steel, like machines, and inner bodies of soft pulp' (chapter 10). Further, Clifford has a representative function as the embodiment of the whole order of the industrial ruling class in England; and, paralleling our recognition of his growing imbalance, is Connie's observation of the external over-development and spiritual malnutrition of England herself. There has grown up within forty years, she concedes, a nightmarish increase in possessiveness and antipathy among the labouring population, driven further than ever from nature in that time, so that the Squire of Shipley feels himself being pushed out by the workers housed on his own estate and realizes that his day is over. Lawrence's insights cannot be separately followed through here, for lack of sufficient space to fill them broadly out, but they inform his essays and poetry as well as his novels, and all of them press the same point: that industrial capitalism threatens human life, by stifling men's knowledge of themselves and directing their endeavour towards false goals. Individual flashes of this steady perception come through when he recommends socialism to build on what is fundamental in human character, not externalize; advises men to search for the true sources, not the false material weapons of the power of life; and explains that historically sex-hatred and money-love are linked and that economic bondage is the overriding problem of modern society, dullness of life the next.(7) Despite an apprehension just before his death that the English social order was approaching some kind of wholesale liberalization, a glimpse of things to come uncannily exact in its predictions,(8) a kind of apocalyptic fatalism is Lawrence's predominant temper of mind, and the mood fills his letters as well as his poems and novels, especially those written during the last decade of his life.

Lawrence can claim to be the central voice of his generation because his themes - commercialism, lovelessness, cultural breakdown - are those of his age, and because he is the writer who offers the most sustained discussion of them. Thus it makes sense to consider other writers like Shaw, Conrad and Wells in relation to him, and aim at an overall impression of the age in that way, rather than by compiling a succession of separate studies of each one in turn. Lawrence, it may be said, provides a kind of deeply felt substantiation of the theories of capitalist menace which Shaw and Wells argue repeatedly for, but do not convincingly fill out in their own writings; and Conrad supplements Lawrence's English picture by a world coverage of the same phenomenon. Other writers can be fitted in around and within this observation. Arnold Bennett, for example, while offering no new ideas of his own of any importance, fills in plenty of extra evidence for Lawrence's analysis of commercial menace in his various carefully observed instances of the new techniques of industrial society, of provincial commerce, of changing fashion, and of fresh housing patterns and habits of intercourse, as the Victorian becomes the modern world. As 'The Lost Girl' (1920) shows, Lawrence himself is not by any means unobservant of this accumulation and change-over in material existence, but Bennett makes the subject of the developing outer world especially his. So we get cheap pottery manufacture described for us in 'Anna of the Five Towns' (1902); the ousting of the genteel order of trade by mass production and mass selling in 'The Old Wives' Tale' (1908); a run-down printing enterprise in 'Clayhanger' (1910); speculative house building for the artisan class in 'Hilda Lessways' (1916) and also in 'These Twain' (1916), and even a minor consumerist boom in the latter story; wholesale concerns replacing small shops in the Clerkenwell manufacturing district of London in 'Riceyman Steps' (1923); the operating problems of a commercial theatre in 'The Regent' (1913); and the inter-mixture of government propaganda and commercial advertising in 'Lord Raingo' (1926). The list is a selection, but shows how Bennett adds to Lawrence while, analytically, not moving outside the range of Lawrence's statement of the issue. In this he is like Joyce, if we limit Joyce to the commercial theme, for what runs through a collection of stories like 'Dubliners' (1914) is the author's recognition of the spiritual emptiness and the absence of hope in the lives of the Dublin commercial classes: Mrs. Mooney and her self-ruined husband in 'The Boarding House', Mr. Farrington in 'Counterparts', Mr Duffy the retired bank cashier in 'A Painful Case', Mr Henchy, Mr Lyons, Mr O'Connor and Mr Crofton in 'Ivy Day in the Committee Room', Mr Kernan in 'Grace' are sharp studies in futility and disappointment. They are all men of business; the hopelessness and the role seem to go together. The presentation of Dublin in 'Ulysses' (1922) differs in spirit because Bloom is there, and the force of his personality radiates through the otherwise identical city with a positive and healing effect. Bloom is an advertisement canvasser with an undistinguished mind, but a caring tenderness for other people, and a heart open to life, about which he is insistently curious; so an affirmation seeps into the portrayal. Joyce, it is to be added, probes knowingly like this into the psychology and social condition of commercial but not of industrial men and women, who do not figure in Dublin life.

An interesting addition to the literary discussion of capitalism in Lawrence's England is Galsworthy's Forsyte stories, interesting because, as Lawrence was one of the first to spot, the material appears to slip out of the writer's control halfway through and end up saying something different from what had been promised at the beginning. Soames Forsyte is the character to concentrate on, not at first a merchant, though the original Forsyte money has been made in the fine tea trade, but a solicitor, yet representative of the essential business man in his basic attitudes, for which, at first, he is satirized by Galsworthy as a stuffy materialist. By the time of the second trilogy Soames has been transformed into a company director making a stand for traditional English financial methods against slippery foreign ones, and he resigns his directorship on a point of honour rather than endorse dubious business deals. That is, Soames is acting heroically. By the final trilogy, 'The End of the Chapter' (1934), Soames is dead, and so is Galsworthy's satire, and so is the story's interest. What Galsworthy has been lastingly inspired by is not what he has started out with, the satirist's moral scorn, but something more elegiac and sentimental, his witnessing of the passing away of the order of the commercially dominant upper class of the England of the nineteenth century.

Such too is the fundamental emotion in E. M. Forster, the difference being that Forster recognizes this truth about his writing. In Forster's English novels the trade-based, power conscious upper-middle class is delineated as historically at the end of its period of dominance at home, and, if we add 'A Passage to India' (1924), not only at home but in the world at large also. Forster's awareness of the decadence of this commercial style is what matters; it links him with Lawrence and with Eliot. When he writes, he brings out his sense of an ending in the failure of nerve or of self-assertion of his finer characters. Rickie Elliott in 'The Longest Journey' (1907) wants to write, but, trapped by his culture, ends by teaching in a second-rate public school; both culture and school are products of the nineteenth-century commercial class. In 'Howard's End' (1910) Wilcox capitalism, a crass brand, is opposed to Schlegel capitalism, redeemed from worldliness by its German idealistic strain. The two are distinguished by the fact that the Schlegels can see the narrowness and the flimsy base of their class's outlook, and perhaps its shortness of duration, but the Wilcoxes cannot and will not. Forster thickens the narrative with precise details of the material and social redevelopment which threatens this order in England at the turn of the century. For example, a fury of property speculation is going on in and around London, which brings the Wilcoxes to a new block of luxury flats opposite the Schlegels, ejects the Schlegels from Wickham Place when their lease runs out, in another part of town transforms streets of villas into blocks of flats of extreme cheapness (this is where Leonard Bast lives), and at Howard's End itself, one hour from Kings Cross, has made out of the old coaching town of Hilton a dormitory suburb for the expanding city. The Wilcoxes may still be in charge, but not for long. Of Forster's other novels 'Maurice' (written 1914, published 1971) tries to portray in Maurice Hall a Wilcox type with charm and willingness in his make-up, but, presumably because such a mixture appears to the novelist especially hard to realize, his business side is hardly delineated at all. Virginia Woolf's sketches of commercial men, Willoughby in 'The Voyage Out' (1917), for example, and Louis in 'The Waves' (1931), tell us nothing that we do not already know, nor does her frank admission in 'A Room Of One's Own' (1928) that every writer needs economic security to produce his best work explore the implications behind such a statement of principle in the unfree lives of the producing multitude;(9) a recognition of just such pressures, though they remain outside his range, is what makes Forster considerable and sympathetic. A better contrast still may be supplied by Beatrice Webb, whose 'My Apprenticeship' (1926) is rich in its documentation of the inter-relationship between commercial and social-moral existence in the late nineteenth century, in the dependence of fine values on satisfactory trade returns, in the purchasable nature of social eminence and acceptance; rich, that is, in the insights of George Eliot.

Lawrence and the other writers of his generation describe over-commercialized and cumbrous England as a land drained and wasted of its vital energy and lost to its purpose in life. They lament, in Lawrence's words, 'so much beauty and pathos of old things passing away' and 'the great past, crumbling down'; they look forward to the 'winter and the darkness of winter' of our era, spring and summer having passed away and the 'great wave of civilization, 2000 years, which is now collapsing',(10) seeming to be irretrievably lost beyond the control of the strongest. In other words, the diagnosis is of heart failure. Our mind moves naturally from this despair to the vision of doomsday held out in the poetry of Eliot, Yeats and Pound, and afterwards in the politically angrier verse of the poets of the 1930s. Yet it is to be stressed that there is nothing merely symbolic in the doomsday theme. The invocation of apocalyptic judgment passed once and for all on a lost civilization follows naturally on from, and illuminates, the novelists' documentation: they are describing what they see around them, not some figment or analogy of social and economic functions, of a society given over in its tendency to material accumulation, to sharpening economic strife, to the assumption without question that happiness can be quantified and that it can be bought, to class antagonism, to the construction of ever-expanding centres of population breaking down the relations of men, yet packing them physically more densely together. Yeats, it may be simply said, except that his thought is not simple in its operation, rejects the values of the modern urban commercial world out of hand for a passionate historical and aristocratic mode of his own apprehending; poetically this means largely ignoring the present subject, or considering it only to dismiss it contemptuously.(11)

All these concerns form a central theme in the poetry of Eliot and Pound. But although Eliot accepts, like Lawrence, the responsibility of defining his civilization, and embraces the industrial-financial urban theme, he embraces it as part of a larger subject of which we do not have to try to include everything in the present discussion; indeed, we cannot do so. Separating the capitalist argument from its wider complex of associations, we find that Eliot picks out for emphasis the dreary rush hour of modern working life, a bizarre practice duly considered, the desolate industrial urban landscape, the monotony of standardized existence, the loneliness of the individual's plight in his home in the modern city, and the city's fragmentation of the relations of men and physical squalor. In other words, he lays an emphasis much like that of Lawrence on the spiritual deadness of men's social experience in the commercialized modern age. The poems in which these revelations are made include 'Prufrock' (1917), 'Portrait of a Lady' (1917), 'Preludes' (1917) and others; but chiefly they are explored in 'The Waste Land' (1922), which characterizes as the human embodiment of capitalist civilization, variously heard in the different speakers in those poems, the disoriented rootless modern consciousness. For such a soulless tenant, the twentieth-century city is a fit habitation, it is implied; and when Eliot, for example in section iii of 'The Waste Land', lists the material detritus of a working day in the money-making metropolis, he projects the physical filth as a symbol of the spiritual blight which has fallen upon the city's population ('The Fire Sermon'):

> The river bears no empty bottles, sandwich papers,
> Silk handkerchiefs, cardboard boxes, cigarette ends
> Or other testimony of summer nights. The nymphs are
> departed.
> And their friends, the loitering heirs of City directors;
> Departed, have left no addresses.
> By the waters of Leman I sat down and wept.
>
> (1922)

Perhaps it is an artificial exercise, the working risk of critical studies such as the present one, to try to isolate the commercial theme alone from the rest of such poetry, when it simply forms part of the larger discussion, and slides naturally, in 'Coriolan' (unfinished) and elsewhere, into the political and social theme and more widely into the question of modern culture in general. Eliot's emphasis in part ii of 'Coriolan', for example, on the dehumanizing nature of modern government in which committee administration, system and protocol muffle the preciousness of life, and in part i on a massive military display without a hero, in which the watching crowds recognize no one with whom they can identify, conveys the (to us) familiar totalitarian sense of things in the twentieth century. Capitalism is intimately tied in with such a dwarfing of man in our time, and in Eliot's, and by the same logical process, namely a reliance on physical strength and a valuing of the material over the spiritual sources of life. Such is the uniting vision of Eliot's writings, essays as well as poems, a vision judging competition, acquisitiveness and material greed as the main obstacles to social and religious harmony. To summarize its burden even so starkly as this, is to acknowledge the affinity Eliot's social thought shares with that of Lawrence, and with Conrad's and that of the other novelists and poets of the nineteenth and early twentieth centuries, since all remind us time and time again that man himself becomes mechanistic in a mechanical culture, endangering the continuance of his own identity and his ability to recognize a continuing reason for living. In 'The Rock' (1934), more narrowly, perhaps less successfully, Eliot depicts a group of unemployed workmen complaining of the society which can find no meaningful place for them, and lamenting their futile energy; and a little later on summarizes Britain's so-called great epoch, the capitalist-imperialist age, in ambiguous wording, calling it the product of God recognized and God forgotten, in other words a historical enterprise only capable of being undertaken when God's place had been 'fixed', and the saints and martyrs settled 'in a kind of Whipsnade' (chorus 2). It is one more statement of this opposition which lies behind all Eliot's writings on the subject: spiritual need ignored for the satisfaction of material hunger, God cast out by Mammon, the commercial pressure allowed to override and dominate all alternative modes of value. Eliot's poetry, it will be seen, looked at from our present standpoint, is strikingly close to the novels, essays and poems of D. H. Lawrence.

In Eliot the capitalist theme is brought into notice by relation, because it is to do with what is being discussed, but in Pound's writing capitalism is a subject present centrally and of itself. It even pushes to the side of the poetic argument other themes, like art, beauty and love. In other critical studies these have tended to receive more extended treatment than 'USURA', which Pound is thought a little bit eccentric for always discussing; they are thought to matter more to poetry and to the poet, perhaps. Yet it is the other way round really. Capitalism is the true subject of the 'Cantos' (1964); and probably no poet in English has ever attempted so extensive an analysis in verse of the nature and history of the capitalist phase of human development. Pound's term is not capitalism but usury, it is true, but he means the same thing: private profit extracted by men whose business is money-making from the common wealth of the community, hence all forms of paper credit, interest-charging and financial speculation, and by logical extension the historically built up machinery of manipulative capitalism in its full traditional establishment. The audacity of such a rejection of given social forms almost takes one's breath away. But Pound does not flinch. All these paper activities are condemned as forms of battening on actual wealth, for which, and for its authentic making, Pound has marked respect, and making unearned profit out of it, as forms of fraud. 'Hugh Selwyn Mauberley' (1920) 'with its age-old usury, market place *to kalon*, decline of standards, payments to Mr Nixon, and Mauberley an aesthetic or "sensitive" man unaware of what was going on'(12) is a verse expression of the Social Credit theory, which Pound, coming upon it in the writings of C. H. Douglas, received like an illumination of the obscurities of economic theory, and erected into the corner principle of his social thought; modifying it later, but not softening its capitalist antipathy. This is a technical discussion which we cannot enter, but the Social Credit theory stresses the difference between real credit and financial credit, the one a belief in what the community can produce, and hence a meaningful term, the other mere paper riches, and a harmful fiction; and one easily follows Pound's thought when he allows this distinction between real and unreal wealth to become a contrast between nature and artifice. After he has done with the theory, and after it has enabled him to relate and simplify his own ideas into a coherent scheme of thought, Pound is able to present us with an explanation of history in which the money interest is opposed to life. Monopoly capitalists are stigmatized as historical agents provocateurs who incite wars on purpose 'in order to create debts, in order to create scarcity, so that they can extort the interest on those debts, so that they can raise the price of money', and in their usuriousness 'completely indifferent to the human victim, to the accumulated treasure of civilization, to the cultural heritage'. (13)

Such is the thought behind Pound's 'Cantos'. The poem is digressive but single, a gigantic aperçu interpreting all European and American history as evidence of the money men's attack on life, and presenting the culture of China, non-industrial, rhythmic, natural, as an alternative way of life to the mode of savage competitive individualism. The discussion of usury, that is Pound's attack on the spirit and practice of western capitalism, really does dominate the poem. It appears in Canto xii's narration of the Honest Sailor's story before the prim, whining bankers; in xv's characterization of money, political power and economic theorizing as so much shit; in xxxviii's and xl's description of the mystification of bank business and the build-up of the arms industry; in xlii's review of the approved Bank of Siena; in xlv's analysis of 'USURA'; in xlvi's summary of the usury era, five centuries of misdirection of talent and waste of life. Contrastingly, lii takes us from the Sienese Bank to a symbolic recapitulation of the progress of the seasons; and liii, liv, lv and lxi present Chinese culture as a superior economic organization to that worked out and naturalized in the life of the west. This is like a refreshing middle section to the poem, after which Pound returns to the attack: lxv retails America's initiation into the commercial life; the Pisan Cantos lxxiv to lxxxiii criticise moneyed intervention between state and people; lxxvii relates usury to sodomy; lxxviii summarizes again the whole argument of the poem. Pound's connection with earlier English literature is vital. His kinship with the aesthetic radicals of the nineteenth century, especially the Pre-Raphaelites, is obvious, for instance in his contention that the line of art 'thickens' after the Renaissance,(14) and, as the summary just offered shows, his eager airing of economic and political issues in poetry is an older feature of English verse come back again, the poetry of public moral discussion of the ages of Dryden and Pope.

The poets of the 1930s inherit from Eliot and Lawrence the doomsday sense already described and give it a sharper political expression, losing in the process some profundity of thought but apparently willing to trade that for immediate impact. The slump and militarism of the 1930s harden their inherited disquiet into a specific persuasion that the capitalist phase of human life is played out; and this, it will be seen, is an attitude of mind ready made to divert the generalized vision and mystical apprehensions of the older writers into express political propaganda. Again we find ourselves being led by the ramifications of the economic issue in present times into a discussion of politics, which has to be kept to the side of our attention and prevented from taking over, yet cannot be kept out. Stephen Spender describes a case in point. John Cornford, he writes, read 'The Waste Land' 'not as a religious allegory...but as an anatomy of capitalist society in decay; it shaped his style, but more important, it was a preface to his politics.'(15)

In Auden the carry-over from Eliot of a generalized sense of the futility of modern social existence turns his own poetic symbolism specific and semi-literal, substituting in place of the waste land of desert and rock, for example, a smashed landscape of half-vanished roads, broken railways, locked power stations, fallen pylons, rotted factories and abandoned pit workings; an image, in short, of the England of declining capitalist enterprise. This is from the poem which begins, 'Get there if you can and see the land you once were proud to own', lyric xxii of 'Poems' (1930). Auden's diagnosis is more limited than Eliot's too. Eliot's drying up of religious experience, the loss of a sense of the meaning of life in the human race, becomes in Auden a definable social and historical failure of judgment, as in the implications of the succinct line, 'They gave the prizes to the ruined boys' from the same poem, but a little earlier, which singles out the competitive ethic of recent English culture as, not a symptom among others, but the founding cause of the historical error now exacting its price from humanity. It is, of course, a frequent Auden theme. Writing a witty 'Letter to Lord Byron' (1937) on the changes in English life and feeling since the first age of Romantic poetry, Auden stresses the inequality of her economic and social development, 'glittering' in the home counties, but, on 'the old historic battlefield' of the industrial north, slatternly and gaunt and with 'the scars of struggle' as yet unhealed (part ii). His epigram that the democratic advance since Jane Austen's day has simply meant a widening of the tolerance for new modes of stealing carries more meaning than at first appears.

His theatre sketches, which can hardly be called plays, give fabular dramatic expression to these assessments of terminal economic struggle and class struggle, English impotence, and modern lovelessness, and it seems unfair to condemn them as simplifying matters when they avowedly work in a cartoon mode.(16) For example, 'The Dance of Death' (1933) sketches the decline of capitalist England, summarizes the Marxist interpretation of history, and ends with the appearance on stage of Karl Marx; clearly this is to be read as a vivid dramatization, not an idea explored. 'The Dog Beneath the Skin' (1935), written with Christopher Isherwood, is a sort of line drawing of Hitlerite Europe with the type states Ostnia and Westland run by racketeers and bullies and the financier Grabstein a ruling presence. Grabstein is 'President of the

X.Y.Z.', 'Chairman of the Pan-Asiatic', 'practically owns South America' and 'the biggest crook in Europe' (act II, scene ii). In comic or horrific comic-opera fashion, after admitting that he has forged a report on the diamond mines on Tuesday Island, staged a fake attempt on the life of the Prince of the Hellespont so as to corner the rubber market, and murdered the would-be assassins of the Bishop of Pluvium, Grabstein sings about his disappointment and loneliness in a world in which everyone hates him. We do not have to search far to find a model for this kind of writing. Brecht's 'The Threepenny Opera' had been produced seven years earlier in 1928. 'The Ascent of F.6' (1937), another collaboration with Isherwood, dramatizes European economic imperialism and the contraction of British power abroad. Again the sinister, brutal 1930s mood is conveyed, a shift in sensibility which is general in the literature of the time, and can equally be noticed in the political adjustments of the spy thriller, as Desmond Maxwell has reminded us;(17) and it comes through in Auden and Isherwood in the timid complaints of Mr and Mrs A, and in the frightened intransigence of Stagmantle's words to Lady Isabel: 'We've got fifty millions invested in the country and we don't intend to budge - not if we have to shoot every nigger from one end of the land to the other' (act I, scene ii). A casualty of such stark capitalist depiction, it might be thought, is the notion that animosity between the classes may have blurred. But caricature may still remain subtle in its exaggerations, and so it is in Auden. Obviously in the years of the depression extreme antagonism would be the striking feature of their relation, but no less obviously, since capitalism managed to survive, an accommodation of interests of sorts between the opposed classes, or some holding back on either side, must have staved off the final violence. This accommodation was in part what Keynes in 1926 called the 'tendency of big enterprise to socialize itself',(18) that is to act counter to its primary driving impulse of gain hunger, and what Tawney had in mind when he argued in 1921 that company legislation since 1844 had transformed English industry out of recognition since the days of Cobden and Bright, so that their original concept of competitive individualism had become 'remote from the realities of the modern economic world'.(19) What the economists saw, the poets saw; but they thought they saw further. Auden admits this socialization or humanization of commerce in his cartoon drama, but views it with distrust nevertheless, as a development fraught with a threat to the working man's soul while it caters for his physical needs. Valerian in 'On the Frontier' (1938), head of the Westland Steel Trust, provides for his labouring employees a cafeteria, a housing scheme, a leisure park, a comprehensive store, a school with up-to-date teaching methods, a car each, a bank, and a funeral parlour. By the time the list has been run through we recognize the services offered to, or rather surrounding, the worker as modes of imprisoning rather than caring for him; and indeed, in Valerian's death at the end, fascist methods of action are shown arising in ordinary men tormented beyond endurance by the forces of big business. Valerian's murder carries within it the hints both of a just execution and a descent from social civilization into anarchy.

In this coverage of the economic issue in the 1930s Auden and Isherwood speak with an accent shared by most of their English contemporaries. Stephen Spender's poetry in parts repeats the same socially critical and anti-capitalist line of thought, for instance in 'The Port' and 'Moving through the silent crowd', though with less colouring and pressure, and Spender also argues in 'Forward from Liberalism' (1937) for a committed socialist line on literature and social change with a singleness which embarrassed him in later life.(20) The poems of Louis MacNeice and C. Day Lewis show solid agreement with this left-wing morality; one cannot claim that they anywhere explore capitalism, as opposed to being rhetorical about it. Auden's judgments may be taken as suggestive, if not inclusive, of theirs.

Marxist criticism at its most forceful is seen in the writings of Christopher Caudwell, the pen name of Christopher St John Sprigg, whose fiction and poetry, however, function at a considerably slacker pressure.(21) How interesting this commitment of the intelligence can be in what it makes possible in the way of specific insights may be seen in Caudwell's absorbing literary critical essays 'Illusion and Reality' (1937) and 'Studies in a Dying Culture' (1938). The first book named relates the growth of poetic style in English from Shakespeare onwards to the material development of English capitalism, and identifies the dynamic Elizabethan lyric, the rational Augustan verse epistle and the Romantic outburst of new forms as the expressions in literature of an age of primitive accumulation and of mercantile containment and of the industrial revolution, respectively.(22) This is very rewarding, and surely right, if less effective when it comes to the tricky business of explaining the nature of the literature of Caudwell's own times by the same criterion, since he sees that as heralding the immediate collapse of the social order; which did not happen, unless we judge the Second World War to have supplied the place of Armageddon. But Caudwell was not alone in that error of calculation, of course. 'Studies in a Dying Culture' (1938), enlarging on the last point, the imminence of cultural collapse, isolates as major instances in literature of the disintegration of the capitalist world, first Shaw, who is criticized for his 'instinctive bourgeois belief in the primacy of lonely thought'; and then in addition D. H. Lawrence, who appeals 'to the consciousness of men to abandon consciousness'; T. E. Lawrence, who is judged to have infected Arab culture with the very commercialism he fled; and lastly Wells, who writes in the pathetic belief, Caudwell declares, that 'by forsaking art, science and action for propaganda' he can hope to change the world.(23) These remain masterly critical analyses, and it is only Caudwell's millenarianism which now looks historically curious.

A cynical tributary feeding into the apocalyptic stream of thought in the 1930s is that provided by Aldous Huxley, who dallies with the subject of the immorality of modern advertising in 'Antic Hay'

(1923) and 'Those Barren Leaves' (1925), then, in 'Point Counter Point' (1928), sounds the familiar apocalyptic note when Rampion announces that the modern social arrangement will end in ruin unless men train themselves to be mindless workers during eight hours of each day, and human beings the rest (chapter 23); this is to anticipate the judgment of a totalitarian economic and cultural order, the imaginary extension of what seems the present condition of things, in 'Brave New World' (1932). Huxley later concedes the exaggeration of this estimate of the vulnerability of life in the 1930s and notes how much greater men's assimilative power has been of economic threat, and pressure, than was expected at that tense period in history.(24)

The significant novelists of the 1930s add splinters of recognition to this world picture, which holds to its conformation until the Second World War changed the world picture, and particularly the English social and economic scene, in a large way. Continuing, like this, to stress the downward sense of things as the literature of the first third of the century gives way to that of the second, continuing to look for the major articulations of what people thought was happening, is to concentrate by necessity on major and on comprehensive writers, and leave perhaps too little discussion room for interesting minor works like Walter Greenwood's 'Love on the Dole' (1933), a study of the mentality of deprivation, and Henry Green's 'Living' (1929) and 'Back' (1946), which bring out the constrainings of energy in a society whose members are organized under an industrial system, and pass so large a proportion of their lives in factory and office.

Joyce Cary's is a wider range; indeed his writing period takes us right out of the 1930s to within sight of our own time; and he persistently raises the question of where and how English society is allowing itself to be led by economic and other pressures in a rapidly changing world. He directs our gaze to the yielding of Victorian society to the modern age, but his mid-century stance, and Irishness, and African experience, all guarantee him from just repeating what is to be found in Galsworthy or Bennett. They are awarenesses which sharpen his response to the extremely rapid pace of economic development in the whole period, for instance in Ireland, where such a phenomenon is more noticeable, and of its unstable colonial aspect, and alert him to its fundamental insecurity of achievement; and all this is what his novels tell us. In 'An American Visitor' (1933) with its portrayal of Nigerian tin flotations, in 'Castle Corner' (1938) with its more extended discussion of the same theme, in 'A House of Children' (1941), in 'Mister Johnson' (1939), in 'A Fearful Joy' (1949), all novels which are set back in time to the imperial half-century, he explores the inter-penetration and inter-existence of Africa and Europe so as to bring out the 'subterranean disturbance in the foundations of society', as he calls it in 'A Fearful Joy' (chapter 28), produced by African and South African gold on its importation into Europe. But in 'A Fearful Joy' itself this colonial milking is just the first stage of what Cary is interested in. The novel proceeds onwards.

Its account of Gollan's automobile and components firm, munitions industry, ironfield and shipyard and coal combine, and, in the succeeding generation, of the profiteer Bonser's chain of dance centres and roadhouses springing from a boom of an independent making in a new society, and with its own style, sweeps us from late-Victorian to mid-twentieth-century England with an emphasis on the successive economic upheavals of an age now unpredictable in its released energies and running into new experience beyond its assimilative capacity.

Evelyn Waugh's explicit analysis is of a civilization that has lost its nerve, a doomed economic and moral order. Most of the supporting argumentation for this view comes through in the non-fictional writings not reprinted by the author because of their political nature,(25) but, in the novels, at the international level, Waugh keeps a noticing eye on the transformations thrown out by emerging world states locked in a receiving and rejecting economic struggle with developed capitalist countries, still dominant, but shaken in their hold; and, domestically, on the contortions of the economy and social arrangement of English life itself. 'Black Mischief' (1932) shows us savage and chaotic Azania papered over with economic modernity, hence easy prey for the adventurer Basil Seal, and 'Scoop' (1938) on similar ground exposes the vulgar western mass publishing business and its cynical staff and values, free of concern for truth. John Beaver's mother modernizes old London houses into single flats in 'A Handful of Dust' (1934) and succeeds, because, having recognized her era, she has adapted her commodity to what it thinks it needs, fragmented living arrangements, and chosen to make a profit out of its rootless selfish character; meanwhile her son remains jobless in the slump and Tony Last in his Victorian mansion finds life and livelihood crumbling to pieces in his fingers. Basil Seal reappears in 'Put Out More Flags' (1942) and declares his wish to be 'one of those people one heard about in 1919, the hard-faced men who did well out of the war' (chapter 1, section 6). He is an individual characteristically self-advancing as before, while not advancing very fast or far,(26) until his not very convincing self-sacrifice at the story's close. 'The Loved One' (1948) magnifies the thoroughness of the commercialization of the American way of life and death. Guy Crouchback in 'Men at Arms' (1952) has been a capitalist farmer in Kenya, Waugh explains to us, where he 'nearly made it pay'. The phrase offers a key to the meaning of all that we have read: in Waugh's fiction the elect are above or bad at money-making. One might in fact wholeheartedly agree with Edmund Wilson's view that Waugh 'has come to see English life as a conflict between, on the one hand, the qualities of the English upper classes, whether arrogant, bold and outrageous or stubborn, unassuming and eccentric, and, on the other, the qualities of the climbers, the careerists and the commercial millionaires who dominate contemporary society',(27) if its emphasis on a living conflict were once softened; for by the 1950s and 1960s Waugh sees civilization as lost and on the run.

At the opposite end of the political scale from Evelyn Waugh, both Graham Greene in his 1930s writings and to some extent those of the 1940s, and George Orwell in his entire literary output, convey an identical basic sense of the ending of an era; both add a political accent to the Lawrentian vision. In Greene's 'Stamboul Train' (1932) Myatt travels to eastern Europe to buy out Stein, a rival currants dealer, whose take-over will guarantee him a commercial monopoly, and also to look into shady commissions; and with the novel's trading issue Greene mingles industrial espionage, racialism and political intrigue to convey the international ramifications of capitalism and its sordid nature, and the ominous world atmosphere of the 1930s in all its generalized menace. Capitalism to the match girls in 'It's a Battlefield' (1934) offers a choice between death and disfigurement, unless, as seems likely to the Assistant Commissioner brooding over his sombre world, capitalism and the social order themselves collapse first under communism and the pressure of the times. Sir Marcus, head of Midland Steel in 'A Gun for Sale' (1936), a skeletal novel almost disdaining its legitimate form, like Auden's plays, has contrived the assassination of the Minister for War and gained half a million pounds by it in increased trade; a portrayal of purely evil commerce. But in Sir Marcus, too old and feeble a man to have any real passions and more or less kept alive by his valet, if we are allowed to press the symbolism, which perhaps we are not, superannuated capitalism is seen on its last legs. The Lawrentian echo, especially in the resemblance between Sir Marcus and Sir Clifford Chatterley, seems relevant here. When D in 'The Confidential Agent' (1939) arrives in England to negotiate a coal contract, the contrast seems intended to be drawn between secure England and unstable foreign parts. But it proves to be not so simple as that, of course. Touring the depressed areas of the Midlands a little later on, he notes from their closed pits, shortage of capital, and general unemployment that England needs foreign wars to sell her coal and her products, and maintain her economic status. When Austrian military orderlies steal penicillin in 'The Third Man' (1950) and sell it privately to local doctors, Greene represents their deals as relatively harmless; when criminals organize the practice as a racket and run it 'like a totalitarian party' (chapter 10) it turns sinister; when they dilute the penicillin with sand or water, spreading it further but rendering it ineffective, that is when they refine the proceeding into an industry, he terms it hellishly destructive, and so condemns it as it becomes more businesslike, criticizing the cruel and ruthless nature of its marketeering spirit, not its illegality. Otherwise, in Greene's postwar writing, the portrayal of the commercial theme loses its sharp edge,(28) as it does too in the later work of so many writers of the 1930s.

Orwell, however, found the temper of the 1930s decisive in his formation of a world view. When he declares a beggar in 'Down and Out in Paris and London' (1933) to be a business man 'getting his living, like other businessmen, in the way that comes to hand' (chapter 31), and adds that he is one more honest than most, he is announcing the theme which holds together all his writings about a commercial society, which is to say nearly all his writings whatever; and to judge from the despairing 'Animal Farm' (1945) and 'Nineteen Eighty Four' (1949), Orwell is kept from the condition of cynicism during the 1930s only by his diminishing hope that the system may be near its fall. 'A Clergyman's Daughter' (1935) portrays the squeezing towards destitution of the desperately respectable in a period of contracting wealth; 'Keep the Aspidistra Flying' (1936) the commercial mill's crushing of moral resistance out of all those who find themselves involved in it, adherents and foes alike; and 'The Road to Wigan Pier' (1937) the cynical treatment meted out to those on the bottom of the economic pile, reduced to the lowest subsistence possible consistent with their still being strong enough and numerous enough to keep on producing the community's wealth, but sweetened away from violence by cheap palliatives.(29) Most effective and original among Orwell's novels is the underrated 'Coming Up for Air' (1939). Here George Bowling, insurance salesman of several years' standing, and thus a man definitely in the know when it comes to the truth of capitalism, exposes the fraud of fashionable suburban housing offered to the socially ambitous working man by building societies, which are, in fact, trading on his snobbery and economic insufficiency and which exploit him at every separate stage of the transaction. A major alteration in the condition of the ordinary working people of the English nation since the nineteenth century is Orwell's subject here, their transformation from propertyless renters into proprietors, and one of Bowling's complaints has to do with the swindle of respectability which goes with the Ellesmere Road development and turns its inhabitants into 'Tories, yes-men, and bumsuckers' (chapter 2). Orwell's writing during the 1930s hovers between doubt and hope for the future, giving way in the following decade to unhesitating pessimism. When war is declared he remarks that what is happening, 'war or no war, is the break-up of laissez-faire capitalism and of the liberal-Christian culture'.(30) In another essay, similarly motivated, he calls Hitler 'the leader of a tremendous counter-attack of the capitalist class' (ii, 402). His reason why, if capitalism is disappearing, socialism is apparently not replacing it, directs us to James Burnham's theory of a new centralized society dominated by 'business executives, technicians, bureaucrats and soldiers' (iv, 192), an idea present in Belloc, Wells and Tawney.(31) Orwell, though he notes that every prediction Burnham has so far made has been falsified by events, says he considers this theory 'extremely plausible'; and Burnham's influence on the thinking behind 'Nineteen Eighty Four' is obvious and does not require spelling out. A detail to note, though, in this last novel, is that Winston Smith finds cause for hope in the junk shop among the proles; and George Bowling's ambition in 'Coming Up for Air' had been to run a small grocery establishment of his own. Such a resurgence of sympathy towards the unexciting world of the small town shopkeeper would have been unthinkable in Wells, or in Wells's writing lifetime. These are straws in the wind.

It does not concern a study of literature to pause for any length of time on why, in the event, capitalist civilization failed to extinguish itself after the 1930s. It is enough to note that in fact in post-war Britain the elements of society were shaken up into an entirely new relation in the decade between 1940 and 1950, and that the period thus marks a profound break with the past whose revolutionary nature may not be fully realized even yet. Unlike most historical changes of direction, it was a reconstitution of society specifically planned for in the Beveridge Report of 1942, the outcome of a century and a half of experience of and opposition to capitalism in its natural state,(32) but, nevertheless, it was a change which was unforeseeable in its wider and particularly its mental impact. This soon shows through in imaginative writing; particularly, a new attitude to work is revealed as the result of the new Keynesian commitment to the state guarantee of full employment. This was an innovation in labour experience which removed at a stroke a centuries-old fear from the working and non-working population, and necessarily therefore changed the British worker's attitude to his job. Thus when it came out in 1949 Orwell's 'Nineteen Eighty Four', it may be suggested now, though perhaps it did not seem obvious then, was a novel seriously out of key with the tendency of its time, the expression of a 1930s assessment of the world filled out by details taken from the austere 1940s, but failing to take into account the social effect of the establishment of a welfare economy. Signs of this effect were soon amply there. Writing only two years after Orwell, Wyndham Lewis in 'Rotting Hill' (1951) represents a decayed Britain massively rebuilding, but sloppily, and reeling from the indiscipline of the now uppish workers. Lewis's summary of the latters' labouring day is portentous: it marks the appearance in print of the villain of conservative thought in our time, the work-shy British workman (pp. 103-4):

> At 8 a.m. the workmen were supposed to arrive and start work, and the staircase painters were subject to the same timetable. In practice our workmen arrived not at 8, but 8.30. By a quarter to nine usually noises would be heard: the day's work had begun. At 10 they left in a body for tea. They returned at 10.30. At 12 o'clock they knocked off for dinner. At 1 o'clock they returned. This was the longest spell, namely two hours, passed of course in talk and in work mixed and alternating: in visits and counter-visits between rotworkers in different apartments, or flat-workers and painters, or outside friends working across the road or round the corner, or plumbers at a loose end or marking time between two assignments of burst pipes or stuck plugs. At 3 they left for tea. At 3.30 they returned. At 4.30 they began tidying up and preparing to leave. At 5 o'clock they left. The day's work was over.
>
> After a few weeks we grew tired of their joy. (1951)

Lewis sees demoralization in these slack working habits but their reason, if true, might be looked for, one would think, in race tiredness; two centuries of subjugation and endurance, and final comparative safety, had gone to make the routine possible. But all he registers is the outrage to propriety. Elsewhere in the same collection of essays he laments the recent widespread increase, as he sees it, in shoddy work and mushroom firms and factories, puts down the 1949 money crisis to the fact that the workers 'would - not - work' (p. 226), and in short sees England as suffering from a 'crisis of stupidity'. Stripped of their moral colouring, which may owe something to his politically nonconformist stance, Lewis's observations here certainly point to some of the predominant features of the new age. A new working-class and provincial consciousness, a new consumerism, libertinism and libertarianism, and, parallel with these forms of worldiness in the depiction of the younger generation, a reaction against them, especially among old unsatisfied socialists, and a yearning for the austere morality of the past: these provide some of the major themes in the literature of the 1950s and 1960s. Cast as a generation clash, they reappear innumerably in the period's novels and its plays.

Perhaps to look for a central sensibility in so conflicting and undistanced an age is unrealistic. But some of the shifting emphases of life in our time are registered in the work of Kingsley Amis and Philip Larkin, whose writing lives have spanned the whole post-war period, but do not reach back into the 1930s, and who, while no apologists for capitalism, show from the first a freedom from inherited antipathy or capitalist guilt. It is indeed a sign of the new consciousness in literature that writers so obviously concerned with the question of the morality of conduct should prefer exploring the nature of the life of their day to theorizing about its economic justifiability. Larkin's poem 'Toads' (1955) and its successor 'Toads Revisited' (1964) express the ambiguous attitude to work, both grateful and resisting, fostered by the welfare society. 'The Whitsun Weddings' (1964) and 'Here' (1964) reflect accurately the vulgar life and aspirations of working-class people in the industrial north of England, newly affluent, depressingly trivial and materialistic in their tastes, visited by deeper yearnings they cannot articulate, strangely impressive in a dogged way. When Larkin goes a little more abrasively into the economic aspect of modern life, in 'Homage to a Government' (1969), he regrets the diminished idealism of post-imperial, penny-counting Britain. In 'Going, Going' (1974) he criticizes a frenzied and cynical materialism which alters the outer establishment of English life with a pace too rapid to be contained; what is perceived and described here, in fact, is an epidemic of acquisitive greed among all classes of men and all sections of the community which now refuses to be restrained, Larkin tells us ('The Whitsun Weddings', 22-3), by any consideration, not even the imminent likelihood of a polluted planet:

The crowd
Is young in the M1 cafe;
Their kids are screaming for more ---
More houses, more parking allowed,
More caravan sites, more pay.
On the Business Page, a score

Of spectacled grins approve
Some takeover bid that entails
Five per cent profit (and ten
Per cent more in the estuaries):

(1974)

What makes Larkin so nostalgic for Edwardian England, perhaps, is his sense here expressed that this contamination of life is all happening very fast, though to the Edwardians their era appeared no less critical in its leanings. In other poems too, such as 'Livings' (1974), 'Poetry of Departures' (1955), 'Church Going' (1955), and 'High Windows' (1974) Larkin probes into the uncertainties of value and purpose in a society materially confident, because newly well-to-do, but on the whole superficial in its achievement. Even the irony is two-edged: half self-directed, half outward. None of Larkin's criticism amounts to a destruction of his relationship with his society, which appears integral, and this is something new in poetry; but it is a feature of modern literature in general, compared to what was written in the pre-war period.

One senses no anti-capitalism in Kingsley Amis's first novel 'Lucky Jim' (1954), nor especially any pro-capitalism either. Gore-Urquhart, the rich businessman, appeals because he can offer Dixon a job in London, which Dixon wants, and because in a world of hypocrites he is found to be a rare truth-teller; another is Bill Atkinson, the insurance salesman Dixon lodges with. But Amis sees no need to go into the question of the sources of Gore-Urquhart's wealth, which is not an issue, or to promote any connection, ironic or otherwise, between Atkinson's integrity and his profession; and the effect of his contrast between Gore-Urquhart and Professor Welch is to habilitate commercial activity as a way of life and to recommend it over nerveless hypocrisy.(33) 'Lucky Jim's' moral emphasis falls on the excellence of frank conduct, a deeper principle than condemning or approving a man according to whether he is engaged in money-making pursuits or not, and one which cuts through expected assumptions about the villainy of businessmen with some impatience. In the rest of Amis's novels too the business of commerce yields as a theme to the business of life, and we learn to look through the novels' commercial representation, which in any case tends to be sketchy, to their exploration of private and social experience which forms the true subject. In 'Take a Girl Like You' (1960) Julian Ormerod is charming, Dick Thompson odious, and it makes no difference to this assessment that the two of them conspire in some unspecified business deal;

they are charming or odious anyway. So we get no details of the enterprise, which sounds shady. Vassilikos the Greek tycoon in 'I Want It Now' (1968) has made his money out of the exportation of 'machine-made antiquities' (chapter 2); this ought to make him villainous, but, apart from being mean like all rich people, he is approachable and morally preferred to Lady Baldock. Her source of wealth, perhaps less fraudulent, is not gone into; it is not what Amis appears to want us to judge her character by. In order to free Maurice Allington for the sex and ghost adventures which fill 'The Green Man' (1969), and not become hampered in his concentration on them by Allington's pub and restaurant business, Amis writes in a trainee assistant for him called David Palmer and lets Palmer shoulder the burden of the commercial side; thus a commercial enterprise is adequately but mutedly conveyed. There is no need to labour the point; an identical non-commercial priority governs the portrayals of business and commercial men in all of Amis's other novels, such as Tobias Anvil in 'The Alteration' (1976), dealer in some unemphasized merchandise, the estate agent Furneaux in 'The Riverside Villas Murder' (1973), Keith McKelvie in 'Ending Up' (1974), a successful advertising executive, and Geoffrey Mabbott in 'Jake's Thing' (1978), employed in some evidently senior but unspecified capacity in a firm of chutney merchants. Looking over these snapshots of the commercial types in post-war England, or of ordinary persons in their economic role, which is probably nearer the truth, one notes how Amis's lack of rage against the capitalist order, which is not a defence of it, but a refusal to let himself be diverted into theorizing about it or prejudging it, enables him to explore the material condition of life and the moral relation between social classes and between men abstracted from imposed categories; that is, to give full expression to his preference for experience over theories of experience as the stuff of literature, a preference obvious, it might be suggested, in every page he writes.

Plainly this is a private emphasis, yet, in a sense, post-war writers more generally show a comparable shift in psychology even when their explicit meanings oppose or differ from Amis's. This suggests that, like Dryden's, who also stood opposed to some of the predominant tendencies of his age, Amis's may be seen as in its way a representative sensibility; and that the condition of life itself has had a part to play in the general accommodation to capitalism and the general draining away of guilt and hostility towards it in people's attitudes; in a word, in the abolition of a century and a half's obsession. What exactly is it though, it may be asked, that has changed in post-war England, and how does the literary depiction reflect it? What has faded is the insecurity, the fear of being out of a job; faded, not vanished; so in literature resentment fades too against a world dominated by capitalist influence. With it fades the anxiety that to be engaged in commerce is to become subject to some kind of moral suspicion, and at the same time a growing concession acknowledges the rebuilding of the provinces, the provision of new jobs and new life patterns deriving from higher rates of pay and guaranteed employment, and the redirection of attention towards glamorous London, a thorough reappraisal of Eliot's metropolis of the waste land, which are all signs of the economic upswing of the 1950s and 1960s. Jimmy Porter keeps a sweet stall in George Osborne's play 'Look Back in Anger' (1957); it is a detail; but a detail significant of the times. Archie Rice in 'The Entertainer' (1957), whose nude shows do not pay, and who is always one step behind with his money-making schemes, is pitiable because his worldly efforts have all failed, and not because he makes them. In Keith Waterhouse's novel 'Billy Liar' (1959) Fisher's ambition is to be a script writer under contract to the comedian Danny Boon, and this is a novel which pointedly emphasizes the small town of Stradhoughton caught half-way between its sombre old character and its gleaming new one, representative in its self-renewing agony of all industrial centres in the north of England, indeed in all England, at that turning point in recent history.(34)

More of this documentation of a new economic phase is found in Stan Barstow's 'Ask Me Tomorrow' (1967) and David Storey's 'Flight into Camden' (1960). In the latter's 'This Sporting Life' (1960) Arthur Machin enjoys financial and social success as a rugby footballer, mixing with industrialists, area managers, soccer stars and the local member of Parliament; one generation earlier Machin would have been condemned to obscurity in some dead-end job, if lucky enough to have one. 'Radcliffe' (1963) by the same writer tells of John Radcliffe's opting out of competitive commerce in a high position as textiles manufacturer-manager, then the similarly aimless pattern of life of his son Leonard, who drifts from job to job until settling with a firm of tent contractors. What Storey intends by this, perhaps, as we read in a note to 'The Contractor', a play drawn from the substance of the same novel, is the sinking away of the motive impulse of capitalism, now in its dying phase; yet it is difficult to see what he means by the phrase. Apart from the establishment of a mixed economy to some extent checking the operation of the profit drive, but hardly the appetite itself, capitalism in Britain seems as alive as ever. And in the literature a new interest in, a new acceptance of capitalist enterprise shows itself increasingly to have taken over from the old hatred. Vic Brown in Stan Barstow's 'A Kind of Loving' (1960) turns himself from draughtsman's apprentice into the manager of a gramophone record shop, and conveys the move as liberation of the spirit from the stifling of professional and factory disciplines. To compare it with George Eliot's 'The Mill on the Floss' (1860) is to recognize how thoroughly Barstow's novel lacks all George Eliot's criticisms of the commercial ideal; yet in 1960 social opinion is no longer the threat it was felt to be in George Eliot's world, and perhaps more important than what is discovered by Barstow's hero is his theme of the new chance in a comparatively affluent world for self-discovery and self-expression. The same supposition might help to explain Arthur Seaton's pleasure philosophy in Alan Sillitoe's 'Saturday Night and Sunday Morning' (1958), a principle which is reflective of a curious epoch, recently emerged from a generally devastating world war, ambiguously enjoying economic prosperity and social liberty, compared to the condition of things in the immediate past, while living under the threat of annihilation. Seaton upholds the pursuit of drink and sex, in other words of forgetfulness, and scouts the principle of saving as folly in such a world, in which jobs are easy to come by, wages high, work stultifying, and the future of the human race uncertain in the extreme. Here too is a statement in its way definitive of an era. In John Wain's 'Hurry On Down' (1953) Charles Lumley stands doggedly, or timidly,(35) outside the class structure, but not outside the structure of capitalist influence; he earns a living by free-lance window cleaning, then accepts the offer of a partnership from a pushy Manchester man, who calls himself a businessman, but is really a worker on the make, so as to make of his job a full-scale commercial operation. What is imaged here, if it can be said unheavily, and not so as to crush a small episode with significance, is a fresh acceptance of entrepreneurship, a new accommodation to commerce. Dougal Douglas in Muriel Spark's 'The Ballad of Peckham Rye' (1960) is a comic variant on the theme, and a more serious one is Morgan Rosser in Raymond Williams's novel 'Border Country' (1960). Williams recreates in Rosser's story more than a small episode. He makes of it a successful entrepreneur's life experience from just after the First to just after the Second World War. The story is condemning: Rosser's business interests detach him from vital contact with his mates; all his life's work vanishes, and all his care and expertise are thrown away after a take-over by an international firm of jam manufacturers: 'We're just a depot now, really,' he tells Matthew, 'labelling the pulp from abroad' (part 2, chapter 2). It is the familiar indictment. Yet a point well brought out is that capitalism too is basic, even natural, in its origins, a way man has of responding to his environment.(36) Williams's openness to the capitalist's viewpoint, given the story's primary meaning, seems imaginative, and of our time. Yet as Richard Portman illustrates in Doris Lessing's 'The Golden Notebook' (1962) a tough soulless tycoon, the older and more perfunctorily condemning attitude is also still alive. To suggest the new tendencies of recent literature is not to unwrite the numerous works which continue to appear and follow an older or a different mode of thought.

Along with this accommodation in our time to once dubious money-making is explored a new agony, the lost state of mind of those whose socialism has failed them. We might expect it; things did not and could not change completely overnight after the Labour election victory in 1945, or in a way to suit all opinions, though the electoral victory's completeness must have struck many supporters as ensuring their near approach to the promised land. Indeed, probably no historical redirection of national life has ever come up to expectation in the past, or will in the future. Hence into the literature of the 1950s and 1960s enter figures disappointed by the incomplete nature of the socialist reorganization they have watched being achieved around them, or disillusioned with the materialism and loss of faith of the generation succeeding theirs, as they term its unembarrassed and often wholehearted accommodation to materialism, worldly success, and capitalist modes of enterprise and thought. The two themes, of course, commercial acceptance and socialist embitteredness, run together, and form the same real theme: the drawing back of the economic priority in imaginative literature after the Second World War; not its disappearance, but its relegation to the side of life after an age of comparative and perhaps unnatural prominence. It is necessary to take detachedly the charge of apathy which issues from and characterizes some of these portrayals, since an apathetic generation, for example the new men in the early years of the Restoration as Milton might have viewed them, is one that feels keenly in new ways, and such a recognition of the advances being made into a decisively new historical course in English social experience is what some of these writers on failed socialism appear to wish to bring out to us.

Arnold Wesker's 'Their Very Own and Golden City' (1966), spanning the period from 1932 to 1990, laments the half success of British socialism to create a handsome popular life, and although obviously, since Andrew Cobham, on whom the action centres, is an architect not a merchant, the play's relation to the present theme is a tangential one at best, it does nevertheless bear a relation. By 1990 the Golden City is built, industry is its backbone, but where and what, Wesker asks, and offers no answer, is its heart? Similarly Wesker's trilogy on contemporary England - 'Chicken Soup With Barley' (1959), 'Roots' (1959) and 'I'm Talking About Jerusalem' (1960) - covers fragmentarily the period from the 1930s to the 1950s, and underlines the seeping away of radical spirit under the impact of increased social mobility, the clash of attitudes brought about by the succession and incongruousness of the generations, and the dissolving effects of material prosperity, and laments the watery idealism of an age, which, after so incomplete a social recônstruction of its elements, votes the Conservative Party back into power and the Labour Party out. Much is taken for granted about present-day politics in this last detail, it will be admitted, including the assumption that the two parties are any longer radically different by the time Wesker is writing. But in place of large ideals, Dave tells Ronnie, he has acquired some certainties: 'You wanted us to grow to be giants, didn't you? The mighty artist craftsman! Well, now the only things that seem to matter to me are the day-to-day problems of my wife, my kids and my work' (III, iii). The socialist Morris in Cecil Taylor's play 'Bread and Butter' (1966), also covering the period from the 1930s to the middle 1960s, owns a tailoring factory left to him by his parents, and agonizes over the Depression, the Spanish Civil War, and the war against Hitler, and the post-war confrontations with Russia in turn while all the time his socialist dream obstinately declines realization. Like Wesker's Dave, a furniture craftsman, Morris is in practice a capitalist and a socialist in theory, but a genuine one, and both Wesker and Taylor are attempting in their plays to capture the frustration, derived from endless small capitulations with the enemy, of left-wing theorists with a living to earn in the unresolved circumstance of our time.

Yet another dramatic trilogy on the theme is David Mercer's 'The Generations', which is made up of 'Where the Difference Begins' (1961), 'A Climate of Fear' (1962) and 'The Birth of a Private Man' (1963), and less theoretically, but not therefore less movingly, the same attitudes figure in a number of Arden's plays. Capitalism is usually dealt with at one remove in these works, which are really concerned with the question of why socialism has failed to establish itself as completely as it might have done, and with what accommodation is possible for convinced revolutionaries to an unfinished revolution, and it is necessary to keep the political argument to the side; yet obviously it forms an aspect of our theme. In the Mercer trilogy Richard and Edgar Crowther, middle-class sons of the engine driver Wilf Crowther, perceive the obsoleteness of their father's 1930s' world view in a period which has seen the slums come down and the rocket sites go up, and he, equally, perceives that they are as far off from his centre of feeling as a sputnik. There is an age difference between them, of course; but their age difference is a difference of outlook and has solidified itself into a difference of class, and is leading all involved in the relationship into a deeper antagonism still. In 'A Climate of Fear', the second play in the trilogy, Colin Waring attacks his father Leonard as a materialist and betrayer of his working-class origins, the third generation reaching back emotionally beyond the collaborating second generation, to the first generation of still pure socialists bred up in the class struggle of the 1930s. But in the end, in 'The Birth of a Private Man', the last of the three plays, we see Colin himself leaving protest behind, and going on the road, and he summarizes his disenchantment with public issues and the ideology of the left in a speech further exemplifying the frustration of old-style economic and political idealism in a stubbornly unidealistic world. The range of subject here has widened far beyond the once apparently simple opposition between capitalism and socialism, or anti-capitalism, we notice (scene v):

> I've marched. I've been on sit-downs. I've been arrested a dozen times and in prison twice. I've worked in the Labour Party and on the New Left till I couldn't stomach the one and the other disintegrated. I've hovered on the brink of joining the Communist Party - like a virgin waiting for the act of defloration - couldn't bring myself to do it. I've read and argued and talked...factories, dockyards...turned my home into a bloody office...refused to give my girl a child, which is what she wants more than me even. I've dropped my PhD. I live on handouts from the people who are 'sympathetic' to the movement...I'm poor, and tired, and rapidly turning nihilistic. You talk about history? All I want to do is crawl away and laugh. (1963)

The lines express fairly the experience of trying to be a young idealist in the materialistic 1960s. It was an experience of frustration; some went into social work, others to Africa, and neither choice turned out quite a pilgrimage or a crusade. John Arden's unwordy portraits of slippery local politicians and commercial dealers, the dramatic representation of the place and age and practice in business of John Poulson and his like, bring us sharply from theory down to earth. For example, his short funny play 'When is a Door Not a Door' (1958) dramatizes an industrial squabble, and also office and production staff rivalry, and without pushing the symbolism into heaviness, for it is a short sprightly piece, reflects for us the apathy already admitted to be afflicting Britain in the modern era. Butterthwaite in 'The Waters of Babylon' (1957) calls himself a Napoleon of local government, and boasts of his influence in affairs as preferable to possessing industrial-commercial power. His way to the top has been a classic path in recent times: from trade unionist to councillor to alderman to bureaucrat to uncrowned local king. This story of one kind of social influence achieved by the leaders of the lower classes may help to explain the continuance against expectation of the capitalist system, and the curtailed establishment of a socialist state in England; for, as Arden shows in this play, it leads its beneficiaries, or victims, into a politico-capitalism hard to avoid and initially, it may be, well intentioned, but doctrinally hostile and in the end corrupting. Margaret Drabble's 'The Ice Age' (1977) covers similar ground two decades later. 'Wet Fish' (1961) also underlines the socio-economic changes in post-war Britain: the lucrative commissions, such as those for modernizing Treddlehoyle's shop, planning a new office block for Amalgamated Corn Products and working out a design for a new city bus terminal, which redevelopment has brought into the hands of the architect Gilbert Garnish; and the collusion between Labour and Conservative interests on the local council. That is, Arden again portrays the mixing of orders and the decay of ideology which have appeared inseparable in Britain from the prosperity and welfare of the post-war world.

Trying to adjudicate between the sense of betrayal of the members of the leftover generation, and the worldly acceptance of those in the middle, and thirdly the frustrated idealism of the younger, in these portrayals, even if moral adjudication were possible among such alternative predicaments, is not to be the task of the present book. That has been, in this its closing chapter and pages, to note the sinking away of capitalist discussion in the imaginative literature of our time out of the forefront of attention, which these attitudes in their way all help to illustrate, and to note also its marked departure, in this respect, from the literature that went before it; the change of emphasis in the line from Eliot to Larkin, and from Lawrence to Amis. The recent history of the Labour movement and of modern society itself, to the archaic socialists in the writings of Wesker, Mercer and Taylor, seems a spoiling of the record, because they insist upon judging the present by some formulation of political morality which has made sense to themselves, which has been thrown up by the conditions of a preceding phase of life now perhaps less in evidence than they once were, and that, as literary portrayals, is their significance.

One last comprehensive example of the chief feature of the literary presentation of commerce since the Second World War, its movement towards neutrality or disengagement from passionate involvement on either side of the moral-economic argument, is Anthony Powell's 'A Dance to the Music of Time' (1951-75); not, of course, truly the last, but a work of literature worth ending on because of its sizeable nature, its completeness, and its coverage of the whole period. All the twelve novels which make up the complete work are post-war, but their story range is from the late 1920s to the late 1970s, so they give us one inclusive glance over nearly the whole of the period of the present chapter as seen from the point of view of our generation. Capitalist discussion, never a dominating theme, is, we find, nevertheless quite to the fore in the volumes which describe the 1920s and 1930s. Thus in 'A Question of Upbringing' (1951) Stringham joins Truscott in the Donners-Brebner firm, then in 'A Buyer's Market' (1952) Widmerpool follows him, at first as solicitor but by the time of 'The Acceptance World' (1955) operating as a bill broker and successfully manoeuvring Truscott out of his established place in the firm in order to make his own position in it more secure. This is competitive individualism of the old classic type. Widmerpool's stockbroker connections with Peter Templer are strengthened in 'At Lady Molly's' (1957), and in 'Casanova's Chinese Restaurant' (1960) he joins up again with Donner-Brebner after a separation, this time as an investments adviser. Sir Magnus Donners, the industrial financier who rules this extending world, impresses Jenkins in 'The Kindly Ones' (1962) by his 'immensely powerful stuffiness' (chapter 2), and lack of small talk on any subject, and at this stage of the story the discriminations are carefully drawn between Donners the boring tycoon, Widmerpool the pushy business man, and Bob Duport the rakish adventurer. Yet it is from this point that the capitalist theme recedes, never to resume its force in the story. Evidently Powell acknowledges it as predominantly an issue of the 1930s. Widmerpool, for example, had entered the war as a man of the city, but in the later novels he makes his mark as a politician and finally figures as a trendy dropout. Hints of post-war economic development are supplied for continuity, and because they still form part of life, as when Bob Duport gets himself fixed up in the oil industry, Bagshaw meditates an assault on the 'El Dorado of television' and Quiggin and Craggs keep Jenkins up to date with their publishing ventures, all in 'Books Do Furnish a Room' (1971, chapters 3, 5, 1). But these minor surfacings apart, capitalism is overlaid as a theme by literature, social change and counter-culture, and by the time we get to 'Hearing Secret Harmonies' (1975), the concluding novel of the series, the subject has travelled or lapsed far away from the centre of discussion. It is hard to see what significance attaches to Scorpio Murtlock's background in the antiques business, if any. In all this Powell suggests a receding of interest in the capitalist issue felt by other contemporary imaginative writers in English generally, and seems, if that is true, to reflect accurately enough a gravitational shift in the sensibility of British society at large during the last thirty years.

I write 'seems' deliberately. One is never certain of the significance of recent developments, and the second half of this last chapter, at least, has been written more than usually tentatively. It is possible that the central tendency of the literature of our generation may have been overlooked in this summary, or mistaken as something unimportant, while all the time it has been staring me in the face, while those things which have seemed to matter here and now may surprise the readers of the future by their slightness. All this I freely admit. For the same reason I make no attempt to assess the literature of the late 1970s; it is too close to us still, and cannot be assimilated except with time, and only then duly weighed. Equally I can see no justification for looking at the story here told as some kind of signpost or pointer or indication of the developments of the future, whether in literature or in commerce. The story of past literature may suggest to us, it is true, that both literary and economic developments will continue to move away from familiar explorations, and from familiar judgments, and will continue to do the unexpected; but we might have known that anyway. But it will not suggest any more decisive prediction, or does not to me at least, about the kind of art still to be written in late twentieth-century welfare-capitalist and now monetarist Britain. Will the economic theme recede further from the centre of preoccupation in imaginative literature? Will it return in strength? Will the quality of art change with these variations? If so, how? To these and similar questions, since no answers can be given, no answers can be sensibly attempted, for it is the function of art to elude the legislative critic and put into words what has never until that moment been articulately apprehended before; so that if I could describe future developments here, no writer would need to explore them later. The story is suspended then, still unfinished; awaiting completion; and we can only wait also to see and recognize in time what it is that events have been writing before our eyes in this passing moment.

NOTES

Chapter 1 The origins of capitalist portrayal: 1500-1650

1 In Raymond De Roover's 'Business, Banking, and Economic Thought' (Chicago and London, 1974) we may read an absorbing account of the scholastic attitude to trade and entrepreneurship from the eleventh to the fifteenth centuries which is designed to counter Weber's thesis that religious influence 'stifled the development of capitalism in the Middle Ages' (p. 345). Bankers, we read, though affected by the Church's ban on usury, operated on the exchange as a consequence of it instead of lending outright, but did not hold back from finance capitalism. A sympathetic critique of De Roover's position in relation to Marx, Sombart, Weber and their followers will be found in Julius Kirschner's essay in the same volume, which argues that De Roover demonstrates that the usury prohibition 'may have dampened economic growth' (p. 33) but did not hamper the development of capitalism itself. The bulk of De Roover's work constitutes a 'massive brief in defence of the continuity and of the conceptual precocity of the Schoolmen' (p. 35). This is very interesting. But a disagreement as to whether capitalism starts in the eleventh century or in the sixteenth century, as Marx judges, does not affect us particularly. In English literature nothing of much significance on the subject is to be found before 1500. For the present topic, this is as much as we need say about the banking capitalism of medieval Italy.

2 Starting points are Max Weber, 'The Protestant Ethic and the Spirit of Capitalism' (London, 1930); R. H. Tawney, 'Religion and the Rise of Capitalism' (London, 1926, repr. 1972 in Pelican Books); L. C. Knights, 'Drama and Society in The Age of Jonson' (London, 1937); Raymond Southall, 'Literature and the Rise of Capitalism' (London, 1973).

3 'Piers Plowman, The B Version' edited by George Kane and E. Talbot Donaldson (London, 1975), p. 286.

4 Sylvia L. Thrupp, 'The Merchant Class of Mediaeval London 1300-1500' (Chicago, 1948), p. 314.

5 Thomas More, 'Complete Works' (Yale, 1965) edited by E. Surtz, S. J. and J. H. Hexter, volume 4, p. 65.

6 See Peter Happe, 'Tudor Interludes' (Penguin, 1972), p. 14. Happe comments that the Vice figure 'develops gradually during the first half of the sixteenth century, and is not certainly identified by name until Avarice in "Respublica" (1553)'. He then goes on to say that gradually the villain becomes more cunning and his part more embellished, and the deception more ingenious; in other words as Avarice is more realized the plays get better. This is leading us directly up to Shylock.

7 All references to the interludes quoted in the text are to the fourth edition of Dodsley's 'Collection' edited by W. Carew Hazlitt (London, 1874). The passage quoted here is from I, pp. 30-1. All drama dates to 1700 are as given in A. Harbage, 'Annals of English Drama' (London, 1964).

8 'Respublica' (1553), attributed to Nicholas Udall, re-edited by W. W. Greg (London, 1952), Early English Text Society publication no. 226, p. 30.

9 R. R. Cawley, 'Unpathed Waters' (New York, 1967), p. 117. See the whole work for an account of the prevalence of the sense of adventure, to which mercantile endeavour is affinitively attached, at this period of literary history.

10 Raymond Southall finely demonstrates this aspect of Tudor and Elizabethan poetry in his 'Literature and the Rise of Capitalism', pp. 21-85. The point is taken up again at the end of the present chapter.

11 Dekker, 'Dramatic Works', edited by Fredson Bowers (Cambridge, 1970) I, 34.

12 Mowbray Velte, 'The Bourgeois Elements in the Dramas of Thomas Heywood' (Princeton, 1924), p. 139. Velte is speaking of 'The Fair Maid of the West'. This is the genre satirized in 'Eastward Hoe' (1605) by Chapman, Jonson and Marston, which nevertheless portrays a sympathetic city apprentice and later alderman in Golding, and in 'The Knight of the Burning Pestle' (1607) by Beaumont and Fletcher.

13 I cannot see what Alexander Leggatt means when he writes of the pearl scene that 'Gresham seems, at moments like this, to be a creature of a totally unreal world' (A. Leggatt, 'Citizen Comedy in the Age of Shakespeare' (University of Toronto, 1973, p. 23). The scene is an ideal representation of Gresham rising above material loss.

14 If 'a cat' is read as a corruption of the French 'achat', meaning a trading venture, as one version has it, the story makes a lot more sense. See the entry 'Whittington' in Paul Harvey, 'The Oxford Companion to English Literature' (1932).

15 Leggatt explains it succinctly. The material of civic legends may guarantee popularity with one section of the audience but is 'intractable material' for the dramatic writer interested in the exploration of character (op. cit., p. 15).

16 R. F. Jones, 'Ancients and Moderns' (St Louis, 1936; 2nd ed. 1961, repr. 1965), p. ix.

17 'Of Usury', in 'The Works of Francis Bacon' edited by J. Spedding, R. L. Ellis and D. D. Heath, vol. 6 (London, 1861), p. 474. Subsequent references to Bacon's writings in the text are to this edition.

18 Benjamin Nelson brings out in 'The Idea of Usury' (Princeton, 1949) how a slow but consistent relaxation of the early Church's ban on the taking of usury is the true account of the history of the subject. As a lead up to the present study it has some interest; what was once usury, and is now credit lending, is after all the oxygen of capitalism. Going backwards historically from Bacon's time, we may single out the main stages in the relaxation as represented by, nearest to Bacon's lifetime, Calvin (1509-64), who recommends that usury may be allowed when not opposed to equity or charity; Martin Bucer (1491-1551), who argues that usury is not in itself condemned in scripture; Zwingli (1484-1531), who says that private property implies the payment of interest charges and rents, and concludes that a society based on property cannot totally avoid usury; Luther (1483-1546), whose view is that consideration for the needy annuitant should prevent on its own any hasty outright condemnation of all taking of interest; and Thomas Aquinas (1224/5-74), who permits usury with foreigners so as to avoid a greater evil but considers it a transgression of the commandment to charity. These details are drawn from Mr Nelson's interesting book, which, however, seems to lose its way once it leaves the usury era and enters the period of capitalism. Edward Gibbon lists the usury rates set down by Justinian in the sixth century AD: from 4 per cent to 12 per cent ('Decline and Fall', IV, chapter 44). To Ambrose in the fourth century usury had been practisable only on one's enemies, and only then if one could claim against them a just right of war. J. A. Schumpeter notes that the life of classical Rome was commercially advanced and extremely busy, with usurers and money-changers common and numerous, but looked down upon professionally; and he remarks on Rome's complete failure to produce a single important economic thinker (J. A. Schumpeter, 'History of Economic Analysis', edited from manuscript by Elizabeth Boody Schumpeter, Oxford, 1954, p. 67). On fourth-century Athens, finally, see George M. Calhoun's 'The Business Life of Ancient Athens' (New York, 1926, reprinted 1968), which Schumpeter recommends, a lively argument that in Athens in the fourth century BC the businessman was an admired figure in society. Calhoun quotes evidence suggesting that the interest rate in ancient Athens on speculative mercantile enterprises was fixed at 22½ per cent, but could be raised to 30 per cent to cover extra risk. This puts the entire Christian controversy over twelve centuries in the shade.

19 'Works' 3, p. 164. A further list of achievements still waiting to be completed is appended to the original edition. It includes 'the prolongation of life', 'the restitution of youth in some degree' and 'the retardation of age'. Commercial enterprise receives only a modest glance in such a vision of things to come, the sort of attention paid to farming or coal mining at a cocktail party, perhaps.

20 'The married couples enter the lighted house and leave Antonio standing alone on the darkened stage, outside the Eden from which, not by the choice of others, but by his own nature, he is excluded' (W. H. Auden, Brothers and Others, in 'The Dyers Hand' London, 1963, pp. 233-4). This reading of the final scene strikes me as much too attractive to be wrong.

21 G. Bullough, 'Narrative and Dramatic Sources of Shakespeare' (London, 1957) I, p. 469.

22 Brian Gibbons, 'Jacobean City Comedy' (London, 1968), p. 21.

23 Partly the exaggeration comes from the individual nature of much of the satire. L. C. Knights explains why: 'The capitalist "system" was taking shape, and "impersonal" causes were already responsible for a good deal; but the individuals who were helping to form that system were, I think, more prominent, more obviously capable of exerting economic pressure, than their successors in the nineteenth century, who could claim, with at least a show of reason, that they were obeying the 'laws' of supply and demand and so on. Therefore attacks on the new order took the form of attacks on individuals (I am not referring merely to recognizable caricature); the diagnosis was moral rather than economic. Or to put it another way, the dramatic treatment of economic problems showed them as moral and individual problems - which in the last analysis they are' ('Drama and Society in the Age of Jonson', p. 176).

24 Thomas Middleton, 'Michaelmas Term' edited by Richard Levin (Regents Renaissance Drama Series, London, 1966, repr. 1967), p. xiv.

25 M. C. Bradbrook, 'The Growth and Structure of Elizabethan Comedy' (London, 1955, repr. 1973), p. 157.

26 For further discussion see A. B. Stonex, The Usurer in Elizabethan Drama, 'PMLA' xxxi (1916), pp. 190-210, which suffers, for us but not in itself, from being a bit limited in range; the usurer was only one representation of the money-maker. It is full of useful information. Stonex mentions 71 plays of the period in which usurers figure, 45 of them significantly. He shows how much is borrowed; yet the continued interest is most noteworthy.

27 Kathleen M. Lynch, 'The Social Mode of Restoration Comedy' (New York, 1926), p. 36.

28 For elaboration on this see Celeste Turner Wright, Some Conventions Regarding the Usurer in Elizabethan Literature, 'Studies in Philology', 31 (1934), pp. 176-97. The usurer here is revealed to be essentially a greedy old man with a big nose, spectacles and a loathsome cough, and to be half starved. Adherence to the limited traits seems to be remarkably consistent, but it is hard to see why.

29 For a sketch of the line of influence from Heywood and his kind to the literature of Dryden's period, see Tom H. Towers, The Lineage of Shadwell: An Approach to 'MacFlecknoe', 'SEL', 3 (1963), pp. 323-34. David M. Bergerson, 'English Civic Pageantry 1558-1642' (London, 1971) gives a thorough description of the whole genre, but does not offer to be critical.

30 Middleton wrote up to around ten or a dozen pageants and entertainments of the civic kind, Dekker somewhat fewer, and even John Webster wrote at least one, 'Monuments of Honour' (1624).

31 Harold Perkin even traces the origins of the Industrial Revolution in their springs ultimately back to 'the geographical discoveries of the post-medieval period, which transposed Britain from the periphery to the cross-roads of the commercial world' ('The Origins of Modern English Society 1780-1880' London, 1969, p. 9). See also E. J. Hobsbawm, 'Industry and Empire' (Pelican, 1968, repr. 1978, pp. 51-2), who makes the same point.

32 W. R. Scott, 'The Constitution and Finance of English, Scottish and Irish Joint-Stock Companies to 1720' (Cambridge, 1912, iii, p. 462). The information in the text is drawn from this work.

33 I am thinking of the unfixed yearning to keep on the move somewhere, anywhere of the speaker in 'Ulysses'. A useful corrective to the idea that sixteenth-century merchant adventurers were like this is supplied in R. F. Jones's account of Thomas James studying tides, recording latitudes, and so forth, in his search for the Northwest Passage during Elizabeth's reign (op. cit., pp. 71-2).

34 R. J. Fisher, The Development of London as a Centre of Conspicuous Consumption in the Sixteenth and Seventeenth Centuries, 'Transactions of the Royal Historical Society', 4th series, 30 (1948), p. 42. The whole essay is full of information directly relevant to the literature of the period.

35 See Raymond Southall's book 'Literature and the Rise of Capitalism' (op. cit.). Southall quotes the Spenser sonnet, and makes the points concerning it and sixteenth-century poetry in general which I have summarized, but with a patience and detail of expository analysis which must be read to be appreciated.

Chapter 2 Commerce approved: 1650-1700

1 Kathleen M. Lynch, 'The Social Mode of Restoration Comedy' (New York, 1926), pp. 216-7. Congreve, we are told, is the excelling master of this drama but one of his achievements is 'to reveal clearly how inexpressive such comedy must be of the realities of character, how profound must be its silences concerning human passions, how restrained and stereotyped must remain its rule of life' (p. 217).

2 'Granville's Shylock is a petty villain of an exaggeratedly melodramatic type, a most unconvincing rascal exposed to ridicule. He is a stock-jobbing Jew who has overreached himself and is properly punished' (J. Harold Wilson, Granville's 'Stock-Jobbing Jew', 'Philological Quarterly', 13, January 1934, p. 12).

3 However, it is interesting to note that when in James Howard's 'The English Monsieur' (1663) a contrast is drawn between English merchants and French merchants, Wellbred tells Comely that the latter 'are but of the lower rank of *English* Pedlars' ('Augustan Reprint Society Publication Reprint', 182-3 (1977), p. 1). The play is one which could hardly be less interested in serious commerce, and the line is throwaway; but why should English merchants be less despised than others when theoretically all trade is beneath notice? Because they were felt in real life not to be so contemptible as the dramatic tradition made them out to be, and because patriotism demanded they be accorded some respect. The fortress is in the process of being undermined with its defences fully manned.

4 'The Complete Works of William Wycherley' edited by Montague Summers (London, 1924) II, p. 107. Juvenal's third satire is the relevant classical source.

5 'If I go into the City, there I find a Company of Fellows selling of their Souls for Two-pence in the Shilling Profit', declares Stanford in 'The Sullen Lovers' (1668) (Thomas Shadwell, 'The Dramatic Works', 4 vols, London, 1720, I, 16). Stanford is a feebler Manly, an approved character. Theodosia in 'The Humourists' (1670) gibes at the citizen's life (I, 154), and is likewise described by Shadwell as 'a Witty, Airy young Lady, of a great Fortune'. In 'Epsom-Wells' (1672) Clodpate, himself a fool, ridicules and traduces the citizens Bisket and Fribble and their impertinent, ill-bred lecherous city wives; as the names suggest, they are ridiculous. More examples could be adduced but here are enough to suggest what matters to us: Shadwell, though he seems to think wit is the same as abuse, follows the fashion in scoffing at the merchant's world.

6 It can be found in Defoe's 'The Compleat English Gentleman' (1729, published 1890). But compare with the Shadwell extract Henry Peacham's gentlemanly syllabus of 1634: History, Cosmography, Poetry, Music, Antiquities, Art, Heraldry and Armory, physical exercise, Travel, War and Fishing (Henry Peacham, 'The Compleat Gentleman', 1634). In Shadwell is seen the half-modernization of this chivalric programme, its redirection towards the details of practical business. When Defoe writes the modernization is complete and the syllabus has turned into a manifesto.

7 Unless Gonsalvo counts in Dryden's 'The Rival Ladies' (1664), a young man just arrived from the Indies on his entry into the play. But Gonsalvo is not a merchant.

8 'In Trade, from its most innocent form to the abomination of the African commerce, nominally abolished after a hard-fought battle of twenty years, no distinction is or can be acknowledged between Things, and Persons. If the latter are part of the concern, they come under the denomination of the former' (S. T. Coleridge, 'A Lay Sermon' (1817)), in 'Collected Works' edited by R. J. White, London, 1972, pp. 219-20).

9 R. B. Sheridan's 'Pizarro' (1799) is a case in point. There was a spate of Pizarro plays around 1799, mostly translations of Kotzebue, and they all enforce the case against commercial imperialism. Thus a review of the times comments that Sheridan drew on his knowledge of East India Company adventurers for his portrait of the invading Spaniards, and that he 'exposes to just indignation and abhorrence the savage cruelty of the Europeans, inflamed with the lust of gold', etc. ('Dramatic Works' edited by Cecil Price, Oxford, 1973, II, p. 630).

10 'Milton, indeed, in spite of his early enthusiasm for Bacon, in spite of his visit to Galileo, in spite of his political radicalism, belonged firmly to the pre-scientific age, when philosophy was still a part of theology. And this was a matter not of the date when he was born but of his temperament and convictions' (E. M. W. Tillyard, 'Studies in Milton', London, 1951, pp. 138-9). The parallels to the 'Comus' passage are cited along with many more in 'The Poems of John Milton' edited by John Carey and Alastair Fowler (London, 1968), pp. 211-12.

11 'The Works of John Milton', edited by F. A. Patterson et al. (New York, 1937) xiii, 9; xiii, 17; xiii, 19-21; xiii, 55-7; xiii, 69; xiii, 317. In these letters 'commerce' means diplomatic interchange primarily. Other letters of the period press for unrestricted English trade to the West Indies and other Spanish dominions (xiii, 515, 521, 527, 529).

12 George Chapman's 'De Guiana' (1596) may be referred to as a contrast, in which we receive a clear impression of the earlier outlook which Denham's is now superseding. Chapman recommends exploitation and discovery in Guiana as both honourable and lucrative at the same time, a combination so far unknown:

> Sit till you see a woonder, Virtue rich;
> Till Honour having gold, rob gold of honour,
> Till as men hate desert that getteth nought
> They loathe all getting that deserves not aught;
> And use you gold-made men as dregges of men.

Denham and his contemporaries are beginning to look on gold-made men as respectable. By the early eighteenth century in Addison, Thomson and Defoe to be a commercial man is to be a patriot. Such is the revolution in taste. See the whole poem by Chapman in 'The Poems of George Chapman' edited by P. B. Bartlett (New York and London, 1941). The extract here is from p. 355.

13 'The Complete Works of A. Cowley', edited by A. B. Grosart (New York, 1967) i, p. 168.

14 By King Charles restoring trade, Waller means not that he will put it back on an earlier footing, undoing the commercial policy of the interregnum, but that he will authorize and legitimate it. Trade will be restored as the monarchy has been restored. There was no question of Charles II repudiating the Navigation Laws of 1651, which on the contrary were re-enacted in a new and improved form and supplied the basis for English commercial supremacy in time to come. The quotation is from Edmund Waller, 'Poems', ed. G. Thorn Drury, 2 vols. (Routledge, 1893), vol. ii, p. 44. All quotations from Waller in the text refer to this edition.

15 Leander's argument is that beautiful and precious things are more beautiful, more valuable, if used than if left neglected in their primary state ('Complete Plays and Poems' edited by E. D. Pendry and J. C. Maxwell, London

and New York, 1976, pp. 405-7). Obviously this is close to the present idea. But to add to a thing's value is to concede it some value in the unused condition. For Waller, the point of things is that man should use them. He is turning one of Marlowe's ways of looking into a programme. And note how egocentric the idea is becoming in the process. The Renaissance spirit of wonder acknowledges the otherness and the intrinsic excellence, independent of man's relation to it, of the external world.

16 John Evelyn, 'The Diary' edited by E. S. de Beer (Oxford, 1955) iii, 163; iii, 194; iii, 304; iii, 373-4; iii, 602; iv. 305-6.

17 John Evelyn, 'Navigation and Commerce, their Original and Progress' (1674), p. 2.

18 Sir William Temple, 'An Essay upon the Ancient and Modern Learning', in 'Works' (Edinburgh, 1754) ii, pp. 14-181.

19 'The Diary of Samuel Pepys' edited by R. C. Latham and W. Matthews (London, 1970) i, p. 269.

20 Pepys, op. cit: iv, 10-22; iv, 124-5; iv, 151; iv, 212; iv, 398; iv, 408; iv, 412; vi, 63; vii, 36; ix, 179.

21 Thomas Sprat, 'History of the Royal Society' (1667), p. 64.

22 R. H. Tawney, 'Religion and the Rise of Capitalism' (Penguin edition, 1964), p. 258. And see Tawney's earlier description of Locke's picture of society: 'not a community of classes with varying functions, united to each other by mutual obligations arising from their relation to a common end. It is a joint-stock company rather than an organism, and the liabilities of its shareholders are strictly limited' (p. 189).

23 See L. A. Harper, 'The English Navigation Laws' (New York, 1939), pp. 10-11.

24 Marvell's letters to the Hull Corporation, which he represented in Parliament, show his as a mind fully abreast of economic matters, and of their primacy of significance in the national life.

25 The question is fully explored in Earl Miner's essay, Dryden and the Issue of Progress, 'Philological Quarterly', vol. 40 (January 1961), pp. 122-9. Miner sees Dryden as a 'proponent' but not a 'supporter' of scientific optimism, and argues that for him the goal is rather 'union with God' than 'a rationalistic New Jerusalem through experimental science' (p. 128). As generally in the seventeenth-century discussion, commerce can be subsumed into the concept of science for our purposes in the present study; so Miner's distinction applies to Dryden on commerce as well as on science.

26 In the best book on Dryden known to me William Myers explains the meaning of Dryden's satires against city men and values as that Dryden 'saw things in terms of possession, not exchange', whereas to such as Slingsby Bethel, the Shimei of 'Absalom and Achitophel' (1681), 'property was precisely the right to sell, alienate, and destroy at will, a species, in effect, of arbitrary power' (W. Myers, 'Dryden', London, 1973, p. 87). Bethel's 'The Interest of the Princes and States of Europe' (4th edition, 1694) bears this out. He declares that England is geographically destined for trade, hence it is her 'true and chief intrinsick Interest' to put every effort into commercial expansion at the cost of other objectives. Against such pragmatic materialism Dryden pits his strength in 'The Hind and the Panther' (1687) and 'Religio Laici' (1682). On the question of the interest of states and individuals see A. O. Hirschman's informative book 'The Passions and the Interests. Political Arguments for Capitalism', (Princeton, 1976).

27 There is a selection in 'Poems on Affairs of State' edited by William J. Cameron (New Haven and London) vol. 5, pp. 486-523.

Chapter 3 The merchant as hero: 1700-1750

1 I have gone into Defoe's commercial journalism in Defoe and the Romance of Trade, 'The Durham University Journal' (June 1978), N.S. vol. 39, no. 2 pp. 141-7. Some of the following discussion is drawn from that essay.

2 Perhaps Defoe's breadth of idea is seen most clearly when he is set beside Charles King and King's associates on 'The British Merchant; or, Commerce Preserv'd' (1713-14); for instance, on the matter of French trade. Defoe,

in favour of it, stresses the ramified advantages to the shipping industries and all related industries, to psychology, and to social well-being, a sort of advantageousness, he says, beneficial beyond casting up. 'I shall *cast it up* for him with a great deal of ease,' replies King; the advantage amounts to less than half a million; all the vivid conception dies. This nagging mercantilist literalism is what Jacob Viner has in mind when he remarks in his 'Studies in the Theory of International Trade' (New York, 1937) that the level of economic discussion on Utrecht was low. But 'low' is hardly the right word for Defoe's passionate apprehensions.

3 The leading idea of Adam Smith's 'The Wealth of Nations' (1776) was to be that every individual's wish to better his lot combines with the same wish in every other individual to build up a harmonious economic and social community. Hence the importance of free trade; no kind of spanner must be thrown in the works. To Smith this appears an economically demonstrable truth about the relations of men. But we would call it an article of faith.

4 See Maximilian Novak, 'Economics and the Fiction of Daniel Defoe' (Berkeley and Los Angeles, 1962) for a detailed exposition of Defoe's economic thought.

5 'Atlas Maritimus & Commercialis' (1728), p. 253

6 From 'A New Voyage Round the World' (1724); in Bohn's edition of Defoe (London, 1856), this is to be found in vol. 6, p. 360.

7 'Review', ix, 108. By this time Defoe's 'Review' was almost solely given over to matters of trade, as he had always wanted it to be.

8 From 'A General History of Trade', Section III (September 1713), pp. 34-5. Defoe was to repeat this reflection fifteen years later in 'Atlas Maritimus & Commercialis' (1728), where he calls the herring shoals 'among the Infinites of finite Nature' and 'more numerous than the Stars of Heaven' (p. 9). Even so, he adds, they are no more than 'the Swarm to the Hive...thrust out from the yet more numerous Inhabitants which remain behind'. The observation of one of nature's commonest objects is alone sufficient, in other words, to defeat the merely calculating powers of the mind.

9 R. R. Cawley, 'Unpathed Waters' (New York, 1967), p. 143.

10 'The Literary Works of Matthew Prior', edited by H. Bunker Wright and Monroe K. Spears (Oxford, 1959), i, 179.

11 Of Ward Pope writes: 'To sum of the *worth* of this gentleman, at the several aera's of his life, At his standing in the Pillory he was *worth above two hundred thousand pounds*; at his commitment to Prison, he was *worth one hundred and fifty thousand*; but has been since so far diminished in his reputation, as to be thought a *worse man* by *fifty or sixty thousand*' ('Poetical Works', ed. A. W. Ward, London, 1930, p. 245). The character given of Chartres's money-making schemes is less ironic but no less hostile.

12 'The Poetical Works of Thomas Parnell', edited by G. A. Aitken (London, 1894), p. 142.

13 Richard Steele, 'The Englishman', edited by Rae Blanchard (Oxford, 1955), p. 320; p. 21; p. 17.

14 Steele, op. cit., p. 407

15 'The Spectator', no. 69 (19 May 1711), edited by Donald F. Bond (Oxford, 1965) i, pp. 295-6. Defoe took offence at Addison's willingness to disparage the natural produce of England and replied to it with some heat in a subsequent number of the 'Review' (viii, 122-4). The two essays are worth reading side by side for what they tell us about their writers. Defoe knows the subject, and says so. Addison's concern is to make a fine point. Naturally, Addison took no notice of Defoe's rebuke.

16 Ambrose Philips reflects on the river Thames's role as port and market of the world in his 'Epistle to the Honourable James Craggs' (1717, lines 43-62), and so does Edward Young on Britain's commercial predominance in the first 150 lines of his 'Epistle to Lord Lansdowne' (1713). Similar utterances are to be found in the poetry of Shenstone, Dyer, Thomson and others. A summarizing account of this interesting and in its day highly popular genre of verse will be found in C. A. Moore, Whig Panegyric Verse, 1700-1760 ('PMLA', vol. 41, 1926, pp. 370-401). But Moore's thesis that the poets educated public taste, for instance against slavery, has a forcing appearance.

The facts do not really fit it. Besides, the praise of commerce is a larger phenomenon during this period than just Whiggery.

17 John Gay, 'Poetry and Prose', edited by Vinton A. Dearing with the assistance of Charles E. Beckwith (Oxford, 1974), ii, 407.

18 Richard Savage, 'Poetical Works', edited by Clarence Tracy (Cambridge, 1962), pp. 221-2.

19 Jonathan Swift, 'A Short View of the State of Ireland' (1727-8), in 'Works', edited by Herbert Davis (Oxford, 1939, repr. 1965) xii, 8.

20 Swift, ibid., xii, 12. See also xii, 55; xii, 66; xii, 77; xii, 132; xii, 173-4. In these and many similar reflections Swift inveighs against absentee landlords draining the needed resources from a poor country, but behind the specific complaint is a larger distrust of economic colonialism and the money world.

21 Edward Young, 'Poetical Works', with an introduction by the Rev. John Mitford (London, 1896) ii, 357.

22 The drama can match such sycophancy towards the prevailing fashion, however. In 'The Beaux Merchant' (1714), in which Harpalus draws attention to the 'Lustre and Glory' which Britain has 'arriv'd to, by the Skill and Industry of the Merchant' (p. 2), long expository undramatic speeches exalt the favoured view of life and the world. Act III even includes a dramatization of a merchants' discussion, the whole being organized like a meeting, with chairman, formal speeches, seconded motions, and all the rest of the paraphernalia.

23 How true this observation is, Marx was to show a century or more later. But Thomson means it benignly.

24 'The Complete Works of Henry Fielding' (Frank Cass, London, 1967) xv, 202.

25 Fielding, ibid., i, p. 129.

26 The careers of all prominent London merchants of the mid-eighteenth century 'show a trend from commercial pursuits proper to those of pure finance, as the great credit expansion of the eighteenth century, the last stage of the mobilization of commercial capital, opened new ways before them' (L. S. Sutherland, 'A London Merchant 1695-1774', Oxford, 1933, p. 15). Sutherland refers also to L. B. Namier, Brice Fisher, MP: A mid-Eighteenth Century Merchant and his Connections ('Economic History Review', xlii, 514ff.). An interesting case history of such a merchant's 'tentative' progress along the road from shopkeeper to banker is T. S. Willan's 'An Eighteenth-Century Shopkeeper, Abraham Dent of Kirkby Stephen' (Manchester University Press, 1970). Dent does not quite succeed in achieving the 'metamorphosis', Willan tells us.

27 Thomas Gray, 'The Complete Poems', edited by H. W. Starr and J. R. Hendrickson (Oxford, 1966), p. 246.

28 John Dyer, 'Poems' (Scolar Press, London, 1971), p. 164.

29 'The Works of the British Poets', with Prefaces, biographical and critical, by Robert Anderson, M.D. (London, 1795), x, 781.

30 Op. cit., ix, 809.

31 David Hume, 'Essays Moral, Political and Literary' (Oxford, 1963), pp. 169, 275.

32 The four reasons why Rome fell, in Gibbon's judgment, were the injuries of nature, the hostile attacks of the barbarians and the Christians, the use and abuse of materials, that is the dismantling of buildings and of the fabric and stuff of daily life, and the domestic quarrels of the Romans themselves ('Decline and Fall', edited by J. B. Bury, London, 1900, vii, pp. 305-16). Gibbon's silence on the commerce-luxury-corruption concurrence of ideas is so noticeable that one half-looks for a meaning in it; but perhaps he just thought the syndrome intellectually unimpressive.

33 Smith, 'The Wealth of Nations', book 1, chapter 4. Smith's argument is that commercial and manufacturing towns afford 'great and ready' markets for the surrounding countryside; that the commercial temper is in its nature bold and speculative, thus improving; and that commercial enterprise introduces 'order and good government' and secures the liberty and security of the individual.

34 Christopher Hill explains the workings of the property and power nexus in the novel in his essay Clarissa Harlowe and her Times, 'Essays in Criticism', 5 (October 1955), pp. 315-40. The Harlowe uncles, 'one enriched by the discovery of minerals on his property', the other by his years in the East Indian trade, 'intended not to marry' (p. 316) specifically in order to increase the stock of family wealth. This would then be all concentrated on James Harlowe, Clarissa's brother, and enable him to aim at a peerage. Clarissa's inheritance from her grandfather threatens the success of this plan because it is subject to no family entail. A marriage with Solmes would keep the properties all together, but not a marriage to Lovelace.

Chapter 4 Disillusionment: 1750-1790

1 Caleb D'Anvers [= Nicholas Amhurst], 'The Craftsman' (1731 ed., 14 vols) i, p. 67.

2 Late sixteenth-century 'industrial' is formed from the Latin industria, but 'industrial' in the nineteenth century apparently comes by adaptation from the modern French industriel (OED, 'industrial'). A curious fact is that the word seems not to occur in either sense in English between the late sixteenth and the late eighteenth centuries. This is exactly the period of the present discussion. There must be a connection here, but I cannot suggest it.

3 The plan is to buy £500s' worth of jewels, pawn them, redeem them, re-pawn them, then extort money from the pawnbroker for charging an illegal rate of interest; in other words to exploit to a further stage the laws against commercial over-exploitation of the needy. The scheme falls through because the agent absconds to France with the stake money.

4 See J. H. Plumb, 'The Commercialization of Leisure in Eighteenth-Century England', University of Reading, 1973 (The Stenton Lecture, 1972). Plumb gives a summary of developments in commercial publishing, music publishing, and children's literature, among many other leisure activities.

5 Smollett explains the continued increase of commercial activity in Britain in the year 1760 in spite of 'manifold and grievous' impositions as due to the inner law of economic growth, which, he adds, would continue to its height then ebb again 'untill it is shrunk within the narrow bounds of its original channel' (History of England', p. 293). David Hume, writing to Lord Kames in March 1758, remarks that commerce, once begun, increases and increases until its efforts 'at last come to a *ne plus ultra*, and check themselves by begetting disadvantages, which at first retard and at last finally stop their progress' ('Letters of David Hume', edited by J. Y. T. Greig, Oxford, 1932, i, p. 271). This law of economic self-regulation Hume sees as a necessary and benign feature. Without it, he says, 'commerce, if not dissipated by violent conquests, would go on perpetually increasing, and one spot of the globe would engross the art and industry of the whole'. When Hume was writing this, commerce was in the act of breaking through his ne plus ultra.

6 See Louis L. Martz, 'The Later Career of Tobias Smollett' (Archon Books, 1967), pp. 104ff. for an account of how in 'Humphry Clinker' the novelist revivifies material first presented as economic geography in 'The Present State'.

7 Oliver Goldsmith, 'The Bee', no. 5, in 'Collected Works', edited by Arthur Friedman (Oxford, 1966) i, p. 442.

8 Not just England, though; what Goldsmith discerns is the same commercial spirit prevailing throughout the whole of Europe, and threatening to become the mode of thought of future humanity, as it has done ('The Citizen of the World', 1762, letter v).

9 Adam Smith, 'The Wealth of Nations' (1776), book 2, chapter 2.

10 In Churchill's 'The Ghost' (1763), to take just one example, trade is depicted as no more and no less than 'to be cheated and to cheat' (Charles Churchill, 'Poetical Works', edited by Douglas Grant, Oxford, 1956, p. 119). This is the voice of John Oldham come back again.

11 Horace Walpole, 'Correspondence with Sir Horace Mann', edited by W. S. Lewis et al. (London, 1967) vii, p. 400.

12 J. M. Holzman, 'The Nabobs in England' (New York, 1926), p. 15.

13 The anonymous author of 'The Saddle put on the Right Horse' (1783) judges of the Commons enquiry into the Company's affairs in 1772 that 'No Englishmen, nor any other men, have any thing to answer for at the throne of God' (p. 36). More relevant may be his point that the character of a nabob 'is incomplete, without having studied the vices of the age in London' (p. 59).

14 Johnson declined to prepare for the press papers relating to the trials, in India, of Joseph Fowke and Nuncomar, for conspiracy, on the grounds that he lived 'in a reciprocation of civilities' with Fowke's chief opponent, Warren Hastings ('Boswell's Johnson', edited by G. B. Hill, revised and enlarged by L. F. Powell, Oxford, 1934, iii, p. 471).

15 Smith, 'The Wealth of Nations' (1776), Everyman edition (London, 1910, reprinted 1970), i, p. 436.

16 William Bolts describes in the preface to his 'Considerations on India Affairs' (1772-5) how 'from a society of mere traders, confined by charter to the employment of six ships and six pinnaces yearly, the Company are become sovereigns of extensive, rich and populous kingdoms, with a standing army of above sixty thousand men at their command' (p. vi). He refers to 'The True Alarm' (1770) as recommending the separation of mercantile from sovereign powers; and yet earlier instances are cited in L. S. Sutherland, 'The East India Company in Eighteenth Century Politics' (Oxford, 1952, reprinted 1962), p. 137. Bolts even presses the analogy between India's relation to Britain and the decaying Roman Empire's outlying provinces, and it is impossible not to recall, reading his enforcement of the parallel, that when his work appeared Gibbon was actually engaged in writing 'Decline and Fall'.

17 'The transport of its plunder is the only traffic of the country', he says at one stage (Edmund Burke, 'Works', London, 1826, iv, p. 88). Near the end of his analysis of the Company's recent history, Burke offers that 'if it can be proved that they have acted wisely, prudently, and frugally, as merchants, I shall pass by the whole mass of their enormities as statesmen' (p. 94). But he finds 'not one trace of commercial principle in their mercantile dealing' (p. 97). There is a certain rhetorical rather than scientific feel to Burke's allusions to merchant honour here.

18 'The Tartar invasion was mischievous; but it is our protection that destroys India' (Burke, 'Works', London, 1826, iv, 39).

19 'I have known merchants with the sentiments and the abilities of great statesmen; and I have seen persons in the rank of statesmen, with the conceptions and characters of pedlars' (Edmund Burke, 'Works', World Classics edition, 1906, iii, p. 62).

20 R. B. Sheridan, 'Speeches' (5 vols, London, 1816) i, pp. 288-9.

21 George Colman, 'The Man of Business' (1774), p. 5.

22 'The Works of Samuel Foote' (London, 1830) iii, pp. 213-14.

23 For example, 'The Hastiniad' (1785), a mock heroic in praise of Warren Hastings and his wife; James Cobb's 'Love in the East' (1788), which reflects the current suspicion of Indian adventurers, but, being a comic opera, not analytically; William Cowper's 'The Task' (1785), in particular lines 729-38 of the first book; Charles Churchill's 'The Farewell' (1764), lines 439-56, in which the poet attacks nabobs and those who hunt them down together, but declares of satire that 'She cannot starve, if there was only CLIVE' (line 490); and the same writer's 'The Candidate' (1764), lines 447-56, which condemn nabobs for corrupting English elections.

24 'The Company had become the employer, as well as the landlord, of its new subjects. But this meant that the great evils of absentee sovereignty and absentee landlordism were increased by a third complication, and it was the abuse of power, anarchically and irresponsibly wielded, in the private interests, by the officials and traders, by the *banyans* and *gomastas*, who were the middlemen of this threefold absenteeism, that stirred the eloquent denunciation of Burke' (George Unwin, Indian Factories, in 'Studies in Economic History', edited by R. H. Tawney, London 1927, p. 364).

25 William Cowper, 'The Task' (1785) iv, 659-60.

26 Ibid., iv, 676-83.

Chapter 5 The response to industrialism: 1790-1830

1 William Blake, 'Complete Writings', edited by Geoffrey Keynes (Oxford, 1966), p. 19.

2 William Blake, 'Vala, or the Four Zoas', edited by H. MargoulIouth (Oxford, 1956), vii (b), p. 50.

3 Blake, 'Complete Writings', pp. 593-4.

4 S. T. Coleridge, 'The Collected Works', vol. 1, edited by Lewis Patton and Peter Mann (London and Princeton, 1971), pp. 223-4.

5 The contrast offered in 'Michael' (1800) is rural and urban rather than commercial and pastoral, yet Richard Bateman and his master both stand for honourable mercantile practice. The city is dissolute as a city, not as a capitalist centre. The woman's lover in 'Guilt and Sorrow' (1793-4) journeys to a distant town 'to ply a gainful trade' (Wordsworth, 'Poetical Works', edited by E. de Selincourt, Oxford, 1940, p. 109), but does not necessarily turn merchant. We might also call to mind Leonard in 'The Brothers' (1800), who returns home after a seafaring life 'with some small wealth/Acquired by traffic 'mid the Indian isles' (op. cit., ii, 2-3); and the shepherd's kinsman in 'Michael' (1800), unnamed but described as 'a prosperous man,/ Thriving in trade' (op. cit., ii, 88). It will be recalled that Coleridge objected to the figure of the Pedlar in 'The Excursion' (1814) as too mean a figure, and that De Quincey went out of his way to defend him on account of his wandering role, necessary to the poet's purpose. But even De Quincey sees no special relevance in his commercial character.

6 For instance, we might note the affinity between Wordsworth's poem 'To the Utilitarians' (1833, first published 1885) and Dickens's novel 'Hard Times' (1854). The two works are remarkably close in both spirit and language. The poem is (iv, 388):

> Avaunt this oeconomic rage!
> What would it bring? - an iron age,
> When Fact with heartless search explored
> Shall be Imagination's Lord,
> And sway with absolute control,
> The god-like Functions of the Soul.
> Not *thus* can Knowledge elevate
> Our Nature from her fallen state,
> With sober Reason Faith unites
> To vindicate the ideal rights
> Of Human-kind --- the true agreeing
> Of object with internal seeing,
> Of effort with the end of Being.
>
> (1833)

The poem is not a good one, but lines 3-6 and 11-13 rescue it from triteness, and could almost stand as a summary of the burden of Dickens's novel-to-be.

7 E. Halévy describes the appearance at the period of the Industrial Revolution of 'a new class - the captains of industry', who, belonging to no corporation, bound by no rules, did not simply make it their business to supply demand but tried their best to force production and aimed to conquer and create markets on a world-wide scale (E. Halévy, 'A History of the English People in the Nineteenth Century', 1913, translated by E. I. Watkin and D. A. Barker, London, 1949, p. 258.)

8 Robert Southey, 'Letters from England', edited by Jack Simmons (London, 1951), p. 51.

9 William Cobbett, 'Rural Rides', Everyman edition (London, 1966), ii, p. 50.

10 Thomas De Quincey, 'Collected Writings', edited by David Masson (London, 1897), vol. 9. The dialogues, of which there are a total of six, although De Quincey introduces them as four, appeared first in 'The London Magazine' for 1824.

11 'Malthus on Population' in De Quincey, op. cit. vol. 9, p. 18.

12 William Hazlitt, 'The Spirit of the Age' (1825; Scolar Press, 1971), p. 17.

13 Hazlitt, 'Mr Malthus' in 'The Spirit of the Age'.

14 Hazlitt, op. cit., 269-70.
15 William Hazlitt, 'Complete Works', edited by P. P. Howe (London and Toronto, 1933) xix, p. 281.
16 Byron, 'Poems' (London 1963, Everyman edition) i, p. 509.
17 Byron, 'Song for the Luddites' (December 1816), in 'Poetical Works' (Oxford, 1970), p. 101.
18 Byron, 'Life, Letters, and Journals' (1838), p. 480.
19 P. B. Shelley, 'Complete Poetical Works', edited by Thomas Hutchinson (London, 1934), p. 768.
20 E. Halévy, 'A History of the English People in the Nineteenth Century', i, p. 338.
21 John Keats, 'Isabella, or the Pot of Basil' (1818), stanzas xiv, xv in 'The Poems of John Keats', edited by Miriam Allott (London, 1970), pp. 333-4.
22 This is noted by Miriam Allott in the Longman 'Keats' (London, 1970), p. 333.
23 'The Works of Charles and Mary Lamb', edited by R. V. Lucas (London, 1903), i, p. 132.
24 Not that they are her preferred material. There is a useful brief discussion of mercantile figures in Jane Austen's novels in Barbara Hardy's little study, 'A Reading of Jane Austen' (London, 1975), p. 106.
25 See Kingsley Amis's 1957 essay in 'What Became of Jane Austen? and Other Questions' (London, 1970).
26 Such was the Company's flexible attitude to its items of treasure according to Karl Marx, who quotes John Stuart Mill: 'Silver ornaments are brought out and coined when there is a high rate of interest, and go back again when the rate of interest falls' ('Capital', translated by Ben Fowkes, Penguin edition, 1976, i, p. 232, footnote). There seems no reason why Scott should not know of this.
27 John MacQueen's persuasive essay John Galt and the Analysis of Social History ('Scott Bicentenary Essays', edited by Alan Bell, Edinburgh and London, 1973, pp. 332-42) is worth reading in connection with this point.
28 See Laurence Poston III, The Commercial Motif in the Waverley Novels, 'ELH', vol. 42, no. 1 (Spring 1957), pp. 62-87 for a descriptive view of the topic, with some emphasis on the contrast between honour and credit in 'The Fortunes of Nigel'.
29 For example, we find industrial experience turning up in all sorts of unexpected places. Louis XI in 'Quentin Durward' describes printing as 'this new-fashioned art of multiplying manuscripts by the intervention of machinery' (chapter 13), which is a curious way to talk of a book, though not of a manufactured article, or garment; that 'machinery' should 'intervene' is the nineteenth-century note. De Hagenbach in 'Anne of Geierstein' calls the gold and silver mines of the far east insignificant compared with the 'caves of treasure' possessed by the 'brutish Islanders' of England (chapter 13). It takes us just a moment or two to realize that he means coal. Doctor Lundin informs Roland Graeme in 'The Abbot' that civil war and the plague both come to 'phlebotomize' the population, and prevent it from starving 'for want of food' (chapter 26), anticipating Malthus by four centuries. Buckingham in 'Peveril of the Peak' calls his servant Jerningham no more subtle and ingenious than an old woman spinning flax by the ounce, whereas he himself, he boasts, 'must be in the midst of the most varied and counteracting machinery, regulating checks and counter-checks, balancing weights, proving springs and wheels, directing and controlling a hundred combined powers' (chapter 38). Of course, this is a list by no means exhaustive, and Scott knows what he is doing; in the preface to 'The Betrothed' he remarks that his Waverley novels have so established themselves as a genre that the time has perhaps come to see whether it may not be possible to begin producing their routine parts by steam.
30 To the catalogue of approved men of commerce, such as Flammock, Gow, Heriot, Jarvie and Geddes, almost automatically is to be opposed another catalogue of the approved men of chivalry: Ivanhoe, Durward, Sir Kenneth, Rob Roy, Tressilian. Which type is more approved? It is impossible to say.

How then is one to place Scott confidently with one group and not with the other? When we add to the reckoning the numerous villainous mercantile types, including Middlemas, Yellowley, Vere, Ashton, and so on, and also the trouble-making kings, aristocrats, and neutrals, it becomes plain that Scott's treatment of men of commerce, as of all other men, varies as his perspective in each separate story varies, that he avoids iron types. I am aware that Yellowley is perhaps not best described as a villain; but every reader can add more to each list.

Chapter 6 From industrialism to big business: 1830–1900

1 The apology as a whole is too long to quote here, but the gist of the message is to be found in stanzas 3 and 4:

> The heavy trouble, the bewildering care
> That weighs us down who live and earn our bread,
> These idle verses have no power to bear;
> So let me sing of names remembered,
> Because they, living not, can ne'er be dead,
> Or long time take their memory quite away
> From us poor singers of an empty day.
>
> Dreamer of dreams, born out of my due time,
> Why should I strive to set the crooked straight?
> Let it suffice me that my murmuring rhyme
> Beats with light wing against the ivory gate,
> Telling a tale not too importunate
> To those who in the sleepy region stay,
> Lulled by the singer of an empty day.
>
> (1868–70)

2 Stephen Spender, 'Forward From Liberalism' (London, 1937), p. 32. Why Romanticism today is a failed position, Spender goes on to say, is because events have bypassed it and 'the world against which the romantics protested has come into being' (pp. 35–6); hence instead of a protest it has become an evasion. Which modern poets is Spender thinking of? Yeats, presumably; but it is not easy to think of others.

3 Wordsworth's lines on factory labour in 'The Excursion' (1814), discussed in the previous chapter, supply Mrs Trollope's essential insight, the novelist spreading them out, so to speak, and enlarging them in a melodramatic but sometimes effective revelation of little-known conditions of work. She brings in Wordsworth by name more than once. No importance attaches to the representation of Sir Matthew Dowling, the industrialist, a sentimental villain.

4 Thomas Carlyle, 'Collected Works' (London, 1869), x, p. 352.

5 J. A. Froude, 'Short Studies on Great Subjects' (London, 1890, repr. 1898), p. 198, where Froude speaks of Lancashire with its 'hundred thousand chimneys, the church spires of the commercial creed', flattening Carlyle's effect.

6 'The difference between Marx and Dickens was that Marx knew that he was a revolutionist whilst Dickens had not the faintest suspicion of that part of his calling' (G. B. Shaw, from the Foreword to 'Great Expectations' published in 1937; quoted in 'Charles Dickens', edited by Stephen Wall, Penguin Critical Anthologies, London, 1970, p. 288).

7 Trying to compile a full account of bankruptcy in Victorian fiction would mean listing every other novel of the age, so the task would be pointless. Bankruptcy, it can be simply said, is an omnipresent calamity in the whole creative writing of the age, as central to the poem 'Maud' (1855), for instance, as to 'Dombey and Son', and is portrayed as horrendous to think about, devastating to endure. This exaggeration itself tells us that it was a reversal feared rather than experienced; for if the event had been as common as all that it would have lost much of its terror. We are dealing here

with the haunting of the age of the self-made man. Parallels might be suggested with the image of imprisonment in eighteenth-century fiction and poetry, and of sexual inadequacy in the literature of our own time, cases too, both of them, in which an anxiety characteristic of the culture of the times is being voiced.

8 Here is Cobden quoted by David Thomson in 'England in the Nineteenth Century' (Pelican, London, 1950, repr. 1951, p. 32), who gives no date for the passage: 'Commerce is the grand passion, which, like a beneficent medical discovery, will serve to inoculate with the healthy and saving taste for civilization all the nations of the world', etc. etc. This can be compared with Addison or Steele in chapter 3 above. Theoretically Cobden has not moved on for 150 years.

9 Chester in 'Barnaby Rudge' (1841) is another instance. But he is no merchant. An unusual contrast with the aloof icy Dombey is provided by R. S. Surtees's merchant Mr Jorrocks, who is also old-fashioned but warm-hearted and usually to be found shovelling currants with a wooden spade when wanted, wearing his brown paper cap, in his dingy, out-of-date but attractive warehouse. Jorrocks is always ready for anything, especially a day in the saddle or a night's drinking. It is curious to think of him and Dombey as contemporaries and perhaps business acquaintances.

10 Dickens calls it heresy to look on him as 'anything less than all the British Merchants since the days of Whittington rolled into one, and gilded three feet deep all over' (book 2, chapter 12). The first and seventh of Carlyle's 'Latter-Day Pamphlets' (1850), those on 'The Present Time' and on 'Hudson's Statue', especially the latter, seem to be the direct influence here.

11 Examples of commercial growth include Flintwinch and Mrs Clennam's conspiracy, Doyce and Clennam's partnership, Pancks, Rugg and Chivery's 'Moleing partnership', Mrs Plornish's grocery shop, Plornish's building business, and Cavelletto's investments.

12 In Canto I of the poem Claude writes back to Eustace of some middle-class English people whom he has met in Italy, with a sketch of their manners:

> Middle-class people these, bankers very likely, not wholly
> Pure of the taint of the shop; will at table d'hôte and restaurant
> Have their shilling's worth, their penny's pennyworth even:
> Neither man's aristocracy this, nor God's God knoweth!
> Yet they are fairly descended, they give you to know, well connected;
> Doubtless somewhere in some neighbourhood have, and are careful to keep, some
> Threadbare-genteel relations, who in their turn are enchanted
> Grandly among country people to introduce at assemblies
> To the unpennied cadets our cousins with excellent fortunes.
> Neither man's aristocracy this, nor God's God knoweth!
>
> (1862)

A reason for the more sinewy nature of this poetry, compared with most Victorian verse, may be that Clough is describing some of the actual people of the age for a change.

13 See Raymond Williams, 'Culture and Society 1780-1950' (London, 1958), which gives excellent summaries, analyses, and comparing judgments.

14 Sidonia's father makes a fortune by means of military contracts during the Peninsula War, moves to England and risks everything successfully on the Waterloo loan, then establishes relatives in the world's principal capitals so that he can through them control the destiny of mankind by controlling its money. He dies suddenly, leaving his empire to his son, Coningsby's Virgil of real life; the portrait of the father is a new slant on the moneylender of Byron's poem.

15 Margaret sighs whimsically over her misconceived old tirades against commercial men when her 'preux chevalier' of a brother marries into a Spanish mercantile family; it is one of those numerous places when Mrs Gaskell reduces the distance between her character's personality and her own.

Another representation of the entrepreneurial hero in her work is Openshaw in 'The Manchester Marriage' (1858), but after this short story, and really after 'North and South', she lets slip the commercial theme. Old-fashioned smuggling appears in 'Sylvia's Lovers' (1863), but nothing at all in 'Wives and Daughters' (1864-6).

16 As Harold Perkin notes, Smiles draws most of his examples from the eighteenth and early nineteenth centuries, not from his own time. Perkin remarks on the matter: 'Even that optimist betrays a feeling that the heroic age is past' (Harold Perkin, 'The Origins of Modern English Society, 1780-1880', London, 1969, p. 425). Still, Smiles completely endorses his own age, and suffuses his narrative with the Carlylean terminology of affirmation but not of criticism.

17 'This same Scottish sycophant and fine talker, Macaulay, says: "We hear today only of retrogression and see only progress." What eyes, and above all, what ears!' (Karl Marx, 'Capital', Penguin edition, London, 1976, i, p. 385). Marx adds that Macaulay 'falsified English history in the interest of the Whigs and the bourgeoisie' (pp. 384-5).

18 Thomas Buckle, 'History of Civilization' (1857-61) i, chapter 2.

19 All the sailors in a Greek merchant vessel, Kinglake says, contribute to the cost of the venture and choose the captain. Then they choose an opposition captain so as to keep him in order. Such personal freedom is compared not unfavourably with that of their ancient forefathers. 'They do not act under the word of the great Capitalist - a power more withering than despotism itself to the enterprises of humble venturers' (Alexander Kinglake, 'Eothen', 1844, chapter 6).

20 For example, in the lines 'Suggested by Reading an Article in a Newspaper' (1852) and in the poem 'The Third of February, 1852' (1852), both of which resemble and were written at the same time as 'Maud'.

21 'All his speculations had of late gone wrong with the luckless old gentleman. Ventures had failed; merchants had broken; funds had risen when he had calculated they would fall. What need to particularize?' (chapter 18).

22 Henry James provides a contrast in 'The Princess Casamassima' (1886).

23 'There is no wealth but life. Life, including all its powers of love, of joy, and of admiration. That country is the richest which nourishes the greatest number of noble and happy human beings' ('Unto This Last', section iv, 'Ad Valorem'). 'Unto this last' is a title taken from the parable of generous over-payment.

24 John Ruskin, 'Praeterita' (1885-9; repr. London, 1949), pp. 7, 119, 267.

25 See Suzanne Howe, 'Novels of Empire' (New York, 1949), p. 82.

26 Walter Bagehot, 'Lombard Street, A Description of the Money Market' (London, 1873), p. 272.

27 J. A. Froude, England and Her Colonies, 'Fraser's Magazine', January 1870; also reprinted in 'Short Studies on Great Subjects' (pp. 348ff.). Froude returns to the subject in his little allegory, 'The Merchant and His Wife', in which the merchant informs his wife that she is free to go from him; she sees he lacks affection; when she elopes he has the asininity to be surprised. The wife is the colonial territory, the merchant the home country in this engagingly simple lesson in international relations.

28 'In brief, the game was still free and the State was still the referee, but the rules, which had been few and applied only to proven dirty players, were tightened up, increased in number and applied universally' (Harold Perkin, op. cit., p. 439). See the whole discussion.

29 The story's setting is a west of England country district 'not so full of life, indeed, nor so widely spoken of as some of its manufacturing leviathan brethren in the north' (chapter 1), and with towns which function as no more than seed, grocery and ribbon depots. As Hardy was to show adequately, and as George Eliot was already showing, to choose a non-industrial setting need not preclude capitalist discussion of some sort, if the interest is there. But Trollope is disclaiming any intention of dealing with the topic.

30 'I went beyond the iniquities of the great speculator who robs everybody, and made an onslaught also on other vices' ('An Autobiography' by Anthony

Trollope, 1883, Worlds Classics edition, 1923, repr. 1928, chapter 20), including girls wishing for marriage, young men wishing to avoid it, puffing authors, and so on. Trollope adds that 'the accusations are exaggerated' (loc. cit.). There is a case for seeing Trollope's meaning here, and in the novel, as Juvenalian, and putting down its exaggerations to the satiric mode he adopts. But is not a claim or admission made by the author himself.

31 'Thus the great banker stood, a colossus of wealth and stability to his age, though ready to crumble at a touch; and indeed self-doomed, for bankruptcy was now his game' (chapter 8).

32 Adrian Poole, 'Gissing in Context' (London, 1975), p. 18.

33 'You have Archimedes, Newcomen, Watt, Telford, Stephenson, those are your father's direct ancestors. Have you forgotten them? Have you forgotten your father and the railways he made over half Europe, and his great energy and skill and all connected with him as if he had never lived?' (book 1, chapter 14).

34 Stigmatizing Dutch finance as the degrading principle of English politics from the time of William III onwards, Disraeli summarizes the money man's progression over the centuries from Turkey merchant to West India planter to nabob to loanmonger to manufacturer (chapter 3). He adds that he is describing not an alternating but an accumulating money power, a remarkable insight.

35 Raymond Williams, 'The English Novel from Dickens to Lawrence' (London, 1970, repr. 1973), pp. 114-15. The whole Hardy chapter expands this observation.

36 How unshocking the revelations of Dickens, Disraeli, Elizabeth Gaskell and Kingsley really are may be seen from the kind of information found in Engels and Marx, which the novelists might have included had they wished, taking it from the same factory inspectors' reports, but chose not to assimilate into their fiction: such as rotting geese and pigs and adulterated food sold off late in the day to those who could afford no better, ears nailed to the counter to train backward apprentices, and so on. No less mild are their conclusions, as William Aydelotte has pointed out: they repudiate rationalistic utilitarianism, fail to anticipate the potentialities of state social services, favour class distinctions, look to the past instead of the future. 'The practical proposals of these writers are amazingly tame in comparison with the vehemence of their social criticism' (William O. Aydelotte, The England of Marx and Mill as Reflected in Fiction, 'Journal of Economic History', viii, 1948, Supplement, pp. 42-58). As we see, even the social criticism is tame enough; such writers yield unsatisfactory results when approached as documenters, or as programmed reformers, since they are novelists concerned with imaginative truth before all else.

37 'The Poems of Arthur Hugh Clough' edited by A. L. P. Norrington (London, 1968), p. 61.

38 Chapter 2 of Raymond Williams's 'The Country and the City' (London, 1973) is illuminating on this literary nostalgia.

39 Mark Rutherford, 'The Autobiography' (London, 1881), p. 3.

40 'The Collected Works of William Morris' with introductions by his daughter May Morris (London, 1915) xxiii, p. 5.

41 'To those that have hearts to understand, this tale of the past is a parable of the days to come; of the change in store for us hidden in the breast of the Barbarism of civilization, the Proletariat' (p. 204).

Chapter 7 Waste Land to Welfare State: 1900-1980

1 J. M. Keynes is one of the few writers after 1918 bold enough to deny that the English way of life is about to break down: 'I do not perceive in England the slightest possibility of catastrophe or any serious likelihood of a general upheaval of society' ('The Economic Consequences of the Peace', London, 1919, repr. 1971, p. 168). But Keynes admits to feeling no such hope about Europe as a whole. He writes: 'Very few of us realize with conviction the intensely unusual, unstable, complicated, unreliable, temporary nature of the economic organization by which Western Europe has lived for

the last half century' (p. 1). Struggles over capitalism there, he goes on, are a 'matter of life and death, of starvation and existence, and of the fearful convulsions of a dying civilization' (p. 2). Being confident of English stability in the context of this surrounding collapse strikes me as a bit weird, like balancing a cup of tea in a sinking ship.

2 Shaw writes in 1930 in the preface to his novel 'An Unsocial Socialist' (wr. 1883) that the work was planned as 'the first chapter of a vast work depicting capitalist society in dissolution, with its downfall as the final grand catastrophe' (p. v). He adds that 'when I had finished my chapter I found I had emptied my sack and left myself no more to say for the moment, and had better defer completion until my education was considerably more advanced'. The confession is an epitaph.

3 'The decisions conducted in London have a far-reaching importance, and so the decision issued from the fog-veiled offices of the Borneo Company darkened for Almayer the brilliant sunshine of the Tropics, and added another drop of bitterness to the cup of his disenchantments' (chapter 3). Conrad draws out the moral at length, and it may be taken as a general truth in his fiction.

4 A good starting point would be, on the negative side, Michael Wilding's essay on The Politics of Nostromo in 'Essays in Criticism', xvi (October 1966) number 4, pp. 441-56; and, on the positive side, Arnold Kettle's essay in 'An Introduction to the English Novel' (London, 1953, repr. 1969), volume 2.

5 In his 'Experiment in Autobiography' (London, 1934) Wells makes a point of admitting that his works are haggard compromises. They are compromises he says such as everyone makes. But how does he know that everyone makes them?

6 'At any rate, you *must*, *must* read *Tono-Bungay*. It is the best novel Wells has written - it is the best novel I have read for - oh, how long?' etc. (D. H. Lawrence, 'The Collected Letters', edited by Harry T. Moore, London, 1962, repr. 1970, i, 51).

7 D. H. Lawrence, 'Phoenix, The Posthumous Papers of D. H. Lawrence', edited by Edward D. McDonald (London, 1936, repr. 1970), ii, 221; ii, 265; ii, 528; ii, 557; ii, 563.

8 'The whole money arrangement will undergo a change: what, I don't know. The whole industrial system will undergo a change. Work will be different and pay will be different. The owning of property will be different. Class will be different and human relations will be modified and perhaps simplified' ('Phoenix', ii, 566). The Welfare State set up less than twenty years after Lawrence wrote this had, and still has, many imperfections. But it has certainly transformed and largely humanized 'the whole industrial system' in men's ordinary experience of its workings and pay arrangements. Since Lawrence wrote, again, Britain has changed from a substantially renting to a substantially property-owning nation. Class? Perhaps this has changed least of all. But as prophecy this forecast, it will be acknowledged, relegates the combined similar efforts of Wells, Huxley and Orwell down into the second class.

9 One does not have to be a Marxist to allow that R. D. Charques has a point when he writes of the unpolitical novelist Walpole, whose sympathies, he judges, are 'restricted to materially rosy conditions of society, and the outlook on life which they beget', that 'he would appear to be on the side of existing authority' (R. D. Charques, 'Contemporary Literature and Social Revolution', London, 1933, pp. 37-8).

10 Lawrence, 'Letters', i, 378.

11 A constant opposition in Yeats is between spontaneous action and timid calculation, a pair of contraries always handled in a way hostile to the bourgeois style, and to the virtues of small advantage taking and self-restraint. All Yeats's poems on the subject place high spiritedness before profit, stressing this preference, and in a small number of poems such as 'September 1913' and 'At Galway Races' the theme comes in specifically. A full account of this side of Yeats's thinking will be found in C. K. Stead, 'The New Poetic' (London, 1964).

12 Hugh Kenner, 'The Pound Era' (London, 1972, repr. 1975), p. 408.
13 Quoted in Clark Emery, 'Ideas Into Action, A Study of Pound's Cantos' (Miami, 1958), p. 51; Emery has taken it from Pound's essay 'America, Roosevelt and the Causes of the Present War' (1944).
14 Pound explains what he means by this interesting claim in a letter to Carlo Izzo of 8 January 1938: ' "With Usura the line grows thick" -- means the *line* in painting and design. Quattrocento painters still in morally clean era when usury and buggery were on a par' ('The Letters of Ezra Pound', edited by D. D. Paige, London, 1951, 397). He adds: 'I can tell the bank-rate and component of tolerance for usury in any epoch by the quality of *line* in painting. Baroque, etc., era of usury becoming tolerated' (p. 397).
15 Stephen Spender, 'The Thirties and After' (London, 1978), p. 204. Spender points out the difference, but stresses the continuing affinity here remarked on: 'the two generations often agreed in their diagnoses: they came to opposite conclusions with regard to remedies' (loc. cit.).
16 As Richard Hoggart suggests in 'Auden, An Introductory Essay' (London, 1951), p. 85; although it is also Hoggart who complains that the plays are too simply conceived to be convincing.
17 Buchan and 'Sapper', both of them patriotically British, anti-Communist, and pro-Empire, are replaced by Greene and Ambler, and for the latter writers 'the world of financial cartels, political assassination and intrigue supplies the background and the narrative impulse' (D. E. S. Maxwell, 'Poets of the Thirties', London, 1969, p. 6). See the whole interesting discussion. James Bond is a reversion to type evidently.
18 J. M. Keynes, 'The End of Laissez-Faire' (London, 1926), p. 42.
19 R. H. Tawney, 'The Acquisitive Society' (London, 1921), chapter 5.
20 In 'The Thirties and After' Spender calls his own earlier adverse rigorously socialist judgment on D. H. Lawrence an example of wearing blinkers and a self-deception (p. 29).
21 Ian Venning in 'This My Hand' (1936) is a dishonest business man and murderer. The author is more interested in him in the latter capacity. Lord Carpenter of Affiliated Publications in 'Fatality in Fleet Street' (1933) enjoys power rivalling that of the Prime Minister and plans to use it to bring about war, but is killed in the first 30 pages. Iconia in 'Death of a Queen' (1935) is a Transylvanian oil-producing country dominated by British experts and British interests, and the plot framework for 'Death of an Airman' (n.d.) is provided by the international drugs traffic; but in both novels the author keeps the economic theme firmly in the background and does not forget that he is writing thrillers.
22 Christopher Caudwell, 'Illusion and Reality' (London, 1937), pp. 117-22. Caudwell's own summary of the five centuries of poetry that he deals with is tabulated with specific detail and great verve and confidence, and is well worth looking at, though it can only be dealt with in a summary fashion here.
23 Christopher Caudwell, 'Studies in a Dying Culture' (London, 1938), pp. 4, 59, 36, 84.
24 In 'Brave New World Revisited' (1959) Huxley describes the general amusement with which people have come to accept revelations of the 'blunt cynicism of the Motivation Analysts' (p. 74), which an earlier generation would have found outrageous.
25 It is in 'Labels, A Mediterranean Journal' (1930) that Waugh speaks of the 'collective inferiority complex of the whole West' (p. 110). In 'Remote People' (1931) he argues robustly that commercial and imperialistic struggle is historically inevitable, therefore natural, and in 'Robbery Under Law' (1939) condemns Mexico's expropriation of British oil holdings on the grounds that British activity in Mexico was unpiratical and benign. In the opening chapter of 'Waugh in Abyssinia' (1936) he stresses the contrast between Stanley and Livingstone, one commercialist, the other inspirational, in their advocacy of an African empire, and adds, though it is the fashion to 'exaggerate the criminality' of this imperial undertaking, 'many of the high qualities of European civilization' (pp. 5-6) appeared as a result of it. It will be seen

that Waugh differs from left-wing writers in his attitude to the collapsing west, but does not doubt its collapse.

26 Seal's jobs in the ten years since 'Black Mischief' have included composing leaders for the 'Daily Beast', attending Lord Monomark as his personal aide, travelling in champagne, writing film scripts, delivering the first in a projected series of broadcast talks, serving as press agent to a female contortionist, and acting as tourist guide. That is, he more than ever parodies the Victorian entrepreneurial type.

27 Edmund Wilson, 'Classics and Commercials' (London, 1951), p. 144; it was an essay on Waugh written in 1944, however.

28 Wormold in 'Our Man in Havana' (1958) is a comic vacuum cleaner salesman whose story raises few laughs. 'The Comedians' (1966) portrays stagnating Haiti, destitute of the confidence of the money world, desperate to modernize. In 'Travels With My Aunt' (1969) a retired bank manager discovers his true nature once the restraints of business have been lifted from him. This is a potentially big subject, but Greene only glances at it.

29 Whether he realizes it or not, Orwell's speculation in 'The Road to Wigan Pier' that 'fish-and-chips, art-silk stockings, tinned salmon, cut-price chocolate (five two ounce bars for sixpence), the movies, the radio, and the Football Pools have between them averted revolution' (chapter 5) confirms a fear voiced by William Morris over half a century previously about the likely gullibility of the working class in the clash with a capitalist minority always one jump ahead of it in the manoeuvrings of the class war; a fear surely confirmed and fully realized by our own time. Morris was talking about the deflection of revolutionary awareness in ordinary men and women away from political action and into sensationalism by Harmsworth's innovation of cheap newspapers carrying trivial news stories and nothing else.

30 'The Collected Essays, Journalism and Letters of George Orwell', edited by Sonia Orwell and Ian Angus, 4 volumes (London, 1968), Penguin edition 1970, i, p. 576.

31 R. H. Tawney singles out the emergence of the manager class as 'one of the most impressive economic developments of the last thirty years' ('The Acquisitive Society', London, 1921, p. 203). Belloc's 'The Servile State' (1931) predicts after capitalism a state in which the mass of men are enslaved, a few are free and rich, and things are kept ticking over by a middle band of administrators. Wells's story 'The Sleeper Awakes' is written under the influence of Belloc's reasoning.

32 Outlined in the report was the plan for 'a comprehensive "welfare state" based on national insurance, guaranteeing minimum well-being for all "from cradle to grave" ' (C. L. Mowat, History: Political and Diplomatic in 'The Twentieth Century Mind', edited by C. B. Cox and A. E. Dyson, Oxford, 1972, ii, 23). Some found the half-heartedness of the social reshaping disappointing, like Stephen Spender, who writes: 'Both Orwell and I expected something more spectacular than Atlee's England of the Beveridge Plan and the Welfare State which followed on the sweeping Labour victory of 1945. As a material and spiritual phenomenon, this was aptly summarized by the Festival of Britain on the South Bank of the Thames, with its look of cut-rate cheerfulness cast in concrete and beflagged' (Spender, 'The Thirties and After', p. 99).

33 In 'A Tribute to the Founder' ('A Look Round the Estate', 1967) Amis contrasts universities skinning vice with politeness and businessmen open about their greed, the judgment favouring the latter. This recalls Lawrence's poem 'Nottingham's New University' ('Pansies', 1929) of forty years earlier, a piece similar in subject but more hostile to businessmen.

34 The novel opens with a contrast between old and new elements of Market Street.

35 Wain tells us in his autobiography 'Sprightly Running' (1962) that 'Hurry on Down' is less a social documentary than an autobiographical novel; 'the mood at its centre was born that afternoon in 1935, as I scrambled to my feet, dazed, nursing my knee, and saw, on the one hand, the glowering

faces of the elementary school boys, and on the other the aloof backs of my schoolfellows - and wondered how, between the two of them, I was ever going to find a place to live' (p. 62). This is a salutary reminder to studies such as the present one not to read too much of the wrong thing into literature. Wain's 'The Smaller Sky' (1967) is a novel repeating exactly this theme from 'Hurry On Down'.

36 'What it is, at the start,' Rosser explains, 'is a man working for his family. Caught, see, and anxious, and knowing he's got to go on' (chapter 8, section 6). Harry's uncondemning refusal to join Rosser is a strong feature of the novel.

BIBLIOGRAPHY

No bibliography of primary sources is given since the whole of English literature, as I have been able to assimilate it, provides the basic material for the study and no purpose can be served for any reader to have it all listed in this place once again. Similarly I omit the basic historical and economic texts, which are to be taken for granted, and can be found catalogued and described in the obvious primers. All the following studies, though, I found extra suggestive in one way or another, even when I disagreed with them, and so I include them as indications of the ways in which my understanding of the subject was led on and formed from period to period. I cannot discriminate between each work and the next, since all had a critical influence on me, and I list them alphabetically.

Auden, W. H., Brothers and Others, 'The Dyer's Hand', London, 1963.
Aydelotte, W. O., The England of Marx and Mill as Reflected in Fiction, 'Journal of Economic History', viii (1948), Supplement, pp. 42ff.
Bell, H. J., Jr, 'The Deserted Village' and Goldsmith's Social Doctrines, 'PMLA' vol. 59 (1944), pp. 747ff.
Calhoun, G. M., 'The Business Life of Ancient Athens', New York, 1968.
Caudwell, C., 'Illusion and Reality', London, 1937.
Cawley, R. R., 'Unpathed Waters', New York, 1967.
Cobban, A., 'Edmund Burke and the Revolt against the Eighteenth Century', London, 1929.
Cox, C. B. and Dyson, A. E., eds, 'The Twentieth Century Mind', Oxford, 1972.
De Roover, R., 'Business, Banking, and Economic Thought', Chicago and London, 1974.
Dixon, P., 'The World of Pope's Satires', London, 1968.
Emery, Clark, 'Ideas Into Action, A Study of Pound's Cantos', Miami, 1958.
Fisher, R. J., The Development of London as a Centre of Conspicuous Consumption in the Sixteenth and Seventeenth Centuries, 'Transactions of the Royal Historical Society', fourth series, vol. 30 (1948), pp. 37ff.
Gibbons, B., 'Jacobean City Comedy', London, 1968.
Gide, C. and Rist, C., 'A History of Economic Doctrines', translated by R. Richards, London, 1967 (first published 1915).
Hardy, B., 'A Reading of Jane Austen', London, 1975.
Hill, C., Clarissa Harlowe and Her Times, 'Essays in Criticism', vol. v (October 1955), pp. 315ff.
Hirschman, A. O., 'The Passions and the Interests, Political Arguments for Capitalism', Princeton, 1976.
Holzman, J. M., 'The Nabobs in England', New York, 1926.
Howe, S., 'Novels of Empire', New York, 1949.
Kennedy, W. F., 'Humanist Versus Economist, The Economic Thought of Samuel Taylor Coleridge', Berkeley and Los Angeles, 1958.
Kenner, H., 'The Pound Era', London, 1972.
Keynes, J. M., 'The Economic Consequences of the Peace', London, 1919.
—— 'The End of Laissez-Faire', London, 1926.
Kilroy-Silk, R., 'Socialism since Marx', London, 1972.
Knights, L. C., 'Drama and Society in the Age of Jonson', London, 1937.
Laski, H., 'The Rise of European Liberalism', London, 1936.
Loftis, J., 'Comedy and Society from Congreve to Fielding', Stanford University Press, 1959.
—— 'The Politics of Drama in Augustan England', Oxford, 1963.
Lynch, K. M., 'The Social Mode of Restoration Comedy', New York, 1926.

Macpherson, C. B., The Social Origins of Hobbes's Political Thought, 'Hobbes Studies', ed. K. Brown, Oxford, 1965.
MacQueen, J., John Galt and the Analysis of Social History, 'Scott Bicentenary Essays', ed. A. Bell, Edinburgh and London, 1973.
Marshall, P.J., 'East Indian Fortunes', Oxford, 1976.
Maxwell, D. E. S., 'Poets of the Thirties', London, 1969.
Melada, I., 'The Captain of Industry in English Fiction 1821-1871', University of New Mexico, 1970.
Miner, E., Dryden and the Issue of Progress, 'Philological Quarterly', vol. 40 (January 1961), pp. 120ff.
Moore, C. A., Whig Panegyric Verse, 1700-1760, 'PMLA', vol. 41 (1926), pp. 370ff.
Myers, W., 'Dryden', London, 1973.
Nelson, B. N., 'The Idea of Usury', Princeton, 1949.
Novak, M., 'Economics and the Fiction of Daniel Defoe', Berkeley and Los Angeles, 1962.
Plumb, J. H., 'The Commercialization of Leisure in Eighteenth-Century England', University of Reading, 1973.
Poole, A., 'Gissing in Context', London, 1975.
Poston III, L., The Commercial Motif in the Waverley Novels, 'ELH', vol. 42 no. 1 (Spring 1975), pp. 62ff.
Sandison, A., 'The Wheel of Empire', London, 1967.
Sherburn, G., Fielding's Social Outlook, 'Philological Quarterly', vol. 35 (1956), pp. 1ff.
Southall, R., 'Literature and the Rise of Capitalism', London, 1973.
Stewart, M., 'Keynes and After', London, 1967.
Stonex, A. B., The Usurer in Elizabethan Drama, 'PMLA', vol. 31 (1916), pp. 190ff.
Sutherland, L. S., 'A London Merchant 1695-1774', Oxford, 1933.
—— 'The East India Company in Eighteenth Century Politics', Oxford, 1952.
Tawney, R. H., 'The Acquisitive Society', London, 1921.
—— 'Religion and the Rise of Capitalism', London, 1926.
Thrupp, S. L., 'The Merchant Class of Mediaeval London 1300-1500', Chicago, 1948.
Velte, M., 'The Bourgeois Elements in the Dramas of Thomas Heywood', Princeton, 1924.
Viner, J., 'Studies in the Theory of International Trade', New York, 1937.
Warner, W. J., 'The Wesleyan Movement in the Industrial Revolution', London, 1930.
Wilding, M., The Politics of 'Nostromo', 'Essays in Criticism', vol. 16 (October 1966) no. 4, pp. 441ff.
Williams, R., 'Culture and Society 1780-1950', London, 1958.
Wilson, F. P., 'The English Drama 1485-1585', Oxford, 1969.
Wright, C. T., Some Conventions Regarding the Usurer in Elizabethan Literature, 'Studies in Philology, 31', (1934), pp. 176ff.

INDEX